Dear Reader:

The book you are about to read is the latest bestseller from the St. Martin's True Crime Library, the imprint *The New York Times* calls "the leader in true crime!" Each month, we offer you a fascinating account of the latest, most sensational crime that has captured the national attention. St. Martin's is the publisher of bestselling true crime author and crime journalist Kieran Crowley, who explores the dark, deadly links between a prominent Manhattan surgeon and the disappearance of his wife fifteen years earlier in THE SURGEON'S WIFE. Suzy Spencer's BREAKING POINT guides readers through the tortuous twists and turns in the case of Andrea Yates, the Houston mother who drowned her five young children in the family's bathtub. In Edgar Award–nominated DARK DREAMS, legendary FBI profiler Roy Hazelwood and bestselling crime author Stephen G. Michaud shine light on the inner workings of America's most violent and depraved murderers. In the book you now hold, DARKER THAN NIGHT, veteran true crime author Tom Henderson investigates the disappearance of two hunters in Michigan, and the surprising developments that shone light on the case 18 years after the events unfolded.

St. Martin's True Crime Library gives you the stories behind the headlines. Our authors take you right to the scene of the crime and into the minds of the most notorious murderers to show you what really makes them tick. St. Martin's True Crime Library paperbacks are better than the most terrifying thriller, because it's all true! The next time you want a crackling good read, make sure it's got the St. Martin's True Crime Library logo on the spine—you'll be up all night!

Charles E. Spicer

Charles E. Spicer, Jr.
Executive Editor, St. Martin's True Crime Library

Titles by

TOM HENDERSON

Darker Than Night

Blood Justice

A Deadly Affair

Afraid of the Dark

Blood in the Snow

From the True Crime Library of St. Martin's Paperbacks

DARKER THAN NIGHT

TOM HENDERSON

St. Martin's Paperbacks

DARKER THAN NIGHT

ISBN: 0-312-93676-1
EAN: 9780312-93676-1

Printed in the United States of America

St. Martin's Paperbacks edition/October 2006

St. Martin's Paperbacks are published by St. Martin's Press, 175 Fifth Avenue, New York, NY 10010.

FOREWORD

None of this—the solving of a horrendous, long-unsolved crime or the writing of this book—could have happened without Bronco Lesneski. His given name is Robert, but most people—friends, colleagues, people he's arrested and put away—call him Bronco.

He's a triathlete, a longtime member of the Michigan State Police SWAT team, a relentless, passionate advocate for crime victims and their families and, despite a career fighting bad guys, still a gentle soul.

And incredibly helpful.

You never know how cops are going to take to reporters. Even if police are friendly enough at first greeting, you don't know how forthcoming they are going to be with reports, evidence and their all-important knowledge of events.

I was told by one of his superiors that Bronco was an open book who wore his emotions on his sleeves. He was, and is. More important to me, he *opened* the books, too. Right from the start, before he had official approval from the powers that be in the state police bureaucracy in Lansing, Bronco welcomed me into his small office at the East Tawas post in northeastern Michigan and shared his voluminous files, three thick loose-leaf binders made decipherable by an indexing system that would have done the Library of Congress proud.

I'll never forget buckling up in his car and racing at NASCAR speed across M-55, a major two-lane highway that bisects the northern Michigan woods, to intercept a trooper he needed to talk to. Or, moments later, Bronco asking if I minded if we detoured past his house so he could show me his new golden Lab puppy, whom he picked up and nuzzled and cooed and kissed, unabashedly, a few yards away from a shiny Harley and two big weight machines sharing space in a room in his house.

A SWAT team leader who could get a tear in his eye at the kissing lick of his 9-week-old puppy, he could play it as soft or as tough as was needed.

Once a young cat showed up on his doorstep. Bronco had never had a cat, didn't fancy himself a cat person. But there it was, looking up at him, glassy-eyed, ribs sticking out, flea-bitten. Bronco took it to the vet, told him to fix it up and he'd pay the bill, figure out later who to give it to. While sitting in the lobby reading a cat magazine, he read an article on the need to neuter your pets. So he told the vet to take care of that, too.

He got a friend to adopt the cat, but it didn't work out. The friend's old cat didn't get along with the new cat, so Bronco took it back. Now, he's a cat person, too.

Tough guy and a kid at heart.

The disappearance of two deer hunters from the Detroit area in the woods of northern Michigan in 1985 had a particular resonance in the state. "Up north" is where folks generally flee from the metropolitan Detroit area—on weekends in the summer to rent a motel room on a lake, or, if they're lucky, to stay in the family cottage; in winter for the downhill and cross-country skiing and snowmobiling; and, by the hundreds of thousands the last two weeks of November, for the annual deer hunt.

Detroit is the place you flee from, with its congested highways or fear of crime or just the job you barely tolerate. "Up north," as everyone calls it, is the sanctuary, where the worst thing that can happen to you is kids breaking into your cabin in the off-season, looking for booze or stealing a TV.

So when David Tyll and Brian Ognjan, two friends since childhood, left their families to go hunting a week into deer season in 1985 and were never seen or heard of again, it wasn't just another possible crime. It was *special*. It was *scary*.

There's a reason fairy tales and slasher movies often take place in the woods. Woods are primeval, even modern ones with their neatly planted rows of red pines. Even the ones we go to to get away from it all. They may be our sanctuary, but on some instinctual level, they're still the woods. The missing hunters reminded us of that. If we thought the woods were a haven, if we thought we could escape there, well, we were wrong.

The hunters went missing, and weeks that became months that became years of investigation and relentless searching yielded little more than newspaper headlines.

Were they fed up with the ennui of family routine and their jobs as a mechanic and a machinist? There was some evidence they had been. Had the two just decided to take up new lives somewhere?

Had they run afoul of the wrong people at the wrong time in the wrong place? There was evidence of that, too.

Only a few things were certain. They disappeared. Their Ford Bronco disappeared. Families were left shattered.

A series of state police investigators worked this case harder than you'd ever imagine. Worked it when it was fresh, of course, but kept working it as the years went by. Would drop it for a while when leads ran out or other cases demanded attention, then pick it back up. Worked it well after it would have been reasonable to declare it hopeless and stuff the files in a box in a closet.

When Bronco inherited the case, he also inherited an enormous work load and a beat that covered roughly 2,500 square miles, four sparsely populated counties filled with dense woods, swamps, rivers, creeks and lakes, and crossroads towns and villages. He also inherited two cardboard boxes filled with reports that, quite frankly, no one would have blamed him for sticking back in the closet.

There was no time and nearly no budget for working the old case, but it was there if he felt like it.

He felt like it. He made the time.

By the time he was done, he and his co-workers had looked into hundreds of tips—credible or not—from thirty Michigan counties, ten states and several provinces in Canada. They had matched the dental records of Tyll and Ognjan against all unidentified bodies in the U.S. in an eighteen-year period. State police dive teams had been in ponds, lakes, streams and several branches of the AuSable River. Aerial searches had been done in Newaygo, Ogemaw, Iosco, Oscoda, Alcona and Roscommon counties. There had been at least five searches by cadaver teams over the years in four counties. Interpol had looked for David Tyll's car around the world.

This is a story about the relentless search for justice. Bronco and his cohorts made Inspector Javert look like a slackard just biding his time till retirement.

PROLOGUE

If you followed Bronco Lesneski around in his off-duty hours and didn't know who he was that winter of 1998, you might have thought he was a Jehovah's Witness or maybe someone running for the school board. Dressed in a sport coat and tie, getting out of his car again and again to knock on the door of a house, introduce himself and ask if he could come in.

Leaving moments later. If you were good at reading faces, you might have seen just a hint that he'd gone in there hoping to accomplish something and hadn't. Back in the car, off to the next house down the road in the sparsely populated woods of northern Michigan, outside the small town of Mio, the only town in thousands of square miles big enough to have a stoplight.

He'd put in an hour or two knocking on doors, call it a night, head home to his wife.

And, schedule permitting, in a day or two, he'd be back out knocking on doors, introducing himself some more.

One morning, breaking up the routine, feeling like banging on doors in the daylight for a change, before he went into the office to work on his active cases, he pulled into another driveway, walked up to the door and knocked.

A woman opened the door and peered out. He introduced

himself, told her what it was about. "Are you Barb Klimmek?"

The woman flinched. No, it was stronger than a flinch. Her body jolted almost convulsively, as if she'd been hit with a Taser. She started shaking.

"You're going to get me killed," she said, pushing the door back in his face.

PART 1
MISSING

1
GONE HUNTING

Deer hunting is a Michigan phenomenon. A seasonal rite of passage for fathers and sons, mothers and daughters. An economic bonanza for business owners who both welcome the hunters' money and despise them for clogging the roads, filling the woods, making it impossible to go out and enjoy a meal or a drink for the last two weeks each November.

Some 800,000 hunters pour into the woods. Caravans of cars from the Midwest fill the interstates. They jam the freeway rest stops. Some own hunting cabins. Some camp in motor homes. Others fill the motels along the state and county roads. Many pitch tents and set up camp where their dads and grandfathers have been pitching tents and setting up camps for decades.

They fill the restaurants and the bars. It's even an economic boon for the farmers, who get to take some measure of revenge for all the corn and grain stolen from them by the marauding deer of summer and fall. Misshapen carrots that can't be sold in supermarkets are wrapped in big plastic bags and sold as deer bait, to be left in clearings or near blinds in hopes of drawing a whitetail close enough for a killing shot. Huge bags of bait are wedged in between pumps at every gas station, or stacked up out front on the grass next to the driveway. Inside the gas stations, many extra cases of beer are laid in for the siege, too, stacked high and narrowing the aisles.

Whitetails love man. They thrive on the edges of his civilization. They sneak into his fields to eat his corn if he's a farmer; if he's a suburbanite, they nibble buds of the lower branches of trees in the spring, trim his lawn in the summer and snag low-hanging or fallen fruit in the fall. In the northern Michigan woods, their population exploded at the end of the 19th century, when the hordes of lumbermen clear-cut tens of thousands of acres of giant white pine, which for a generation supplied the needs of homebuilders across the U.S.

As the pines fell to the ax and were hauled off, aspen saplings by the millions with their tender, juicy leaves, and seemingly endless acres of raspberry and blackberry thickets replaced them, an endless, nutrient-rich cornucopia. As the deer population grew, the new forest that grew with them was shaped by their appetite. Voracious feeders of low vegetation, the deer kept things trimmed on the ground as the new trees grew to form a canopy.

Other species couldn't compete and left or died. By the mid–20th century, the deer were the dominant animal. Where once a sighting of a whitetail was an adrenaline-jolting highlight of the day, something you told folks about later, they became as ubiquitous as squirrels. They spread throughout the state, finding the edges of suburbia to their taste, too.

Eventually there were so many whitetails that the hunters and the bureaucrats who ran the state's Department of Natural Resources stopped talking about them as if they were animals and began to refer to them as if they were rows of corn or soybeans. The kill during hunting season came to be called "the deer harvest."

There were millions of the things. Nearly a million hunters sitting in blinds or stalking through the woods hoping to kill one. In any given year, 300,000 would be successful. Just the rope needed to tie that many big animals to the roof of a car or an SUV was a cottage industry. Add in archery season, and the kill was 500,000 deer.

A bountiful harvest, indeed.

2

"WHAT TIME DID DAVE LEAVE?"

Brian Ognjan and David Tyll had grown up together, fast friends from the time Brian moved into the east-side Detroit neighborhood in fourth grade. They went to Gabriel Richard, a Catholic school, through ninth grade and then to a public school, Detroit's Osborn High, graduating in 1976. They'd taken their first drinks together, tried picking up their first girls together, had gone from being kids to teen-agers to men all the while best friends. In 1985, they were both 27.

Tyll was Irish. Ognjan was mostly Polish on his mom's side—Helen Jenusz was her maiden name—and Croatian on his dad George's side, with a little German mixed in.

David was a machinist living in an apartment in the generally upper-middle-class Detroit suburb of Troy. Brian was a mechanic in St. Clair Shores, another suburb just a few miles from where they'd grown up. Both were pretty straitlaced for 1985. They'd smoked a little weed in the 70s and might go out to the bar on weekends and have a couple of beers and shoot pool, but they worked hard, saved their money, paid their bills promptly and stayed out of trouble.

On November 22, 1985, they left for what was supposed to be a weekend of deer hunting at the Tyll family cabin near White Cloud, a small town on the western side of the state. David wasn't an avid deer hunter, had never shot one, in fact. It wasn't one of the highlights of his year, as it is for many hunters. Most years he went, but it wasn't a religion for him. Truth of it was, sitting in a deer blind was more of a good, quiet way to get over his hangover from the night before than it was a place of stealth from which to kill deer.

Brian wasn't much of a hunter, either, though he went every year, too, mostly to drink beer with the guys and play cards. His girlfriend, Janice Payne, would joke about him and David: "They seen a deer, they wouldn't shoot it, you know?" In fact, Brian wasn't a hunter at all. He might not admit it to the guys, but he told Janice he'd seen many a deer walking by over the years but had never even aimed at one, much less pulled a trigger. He just liked drinking with the guys at night and sitting out in the woods, at peace, during the day.

The two never even bought deer licenses. They'd mistakenly assumed that if they were hunting on private property, they didn't need them. In medieval England, the deer belonged to the king. In late 20th century Michigan, they belonged to the state. No matter where you hunted one, you were supposed to buy a license.

They had planned to go hunting the previous weekend, the opening weekend of the season, when most of the bucks are taken, but David decided to take his wife, Denise, to a party instead.

So now they were going for the second weekend. A grade school and high school buddy of theirs, Daniel Jacob, who stopped by Brian's most Saturday mornings to drink coffee and shoot the breeze, was supposed to go with them, but his mother got sick and he had to cancel. Another friend, Richard Musto, had talked of going, too, but a day or two earlier Brian had run into him at a car-repair shop and Musto said he was going to have to pass.

David's father, Art, and one of his brothers, Archie, were already at the cabin hunting. Before they'd left, Brian joked with Art that he was going to get his money back from him at poker this year. Forget any thought of the old man skinning him, again.

Another brother, Matt, and three of Matt's buddies, were leaving Friday afternoon, too. Matt was getting married in the spring and wanted his friends to join him as sort of a celebration of what might be his last hunting trip with the guys for a while, depending on how his wife took to him traipsing off each fall. Matt was eight years younger than Dave, but they were close, nonetheless. They'd even worked four years together for a landscaping company owned by one of David's old school buddies—David, the responsible one, the crew chief; Matt, the college kid in need of a summer job.

To say the Tylls came from a large family was to understate it. Catherine Tyll had thirteen kids, and when she was done having babies she went back to work full-time as a nurse.

She used to tell people that, of all her kids, David was the most level-headed.

If Brian had poker revenge to look forward to, David had the new rifle Denise had bought him for his birthday. This'll be the year I finally get a buck, he'd told her when he'd opened it.

Some thought David a bit henpecked, but, truth be told, that's how he liked it.

David's father-in-law owned the tool and die shop where he worked, Deland Manufacturing. The morning of the 22nd, David called his wife, told her that her father had given him the afternoon off so he could get ready for his trip and asked her out to lunch at a nearby McDonald's.

As deer-hunting trips go, it wouldn't last long. He wouldn't need much in the way of clothes. He had his Pittsburgh Steelers jacket and a green Army jacket. He was wearing blue jeans and a flannel shirt. He'd pack a sleeping bag to keep him warm in the drafty cabin at night and a small duffel bag with some socks and hunting gear. That was about it. They'd be back about 6 p.m. Sunday night so they could get a good night's sleep before going back to work on Monday.

Over lunch, David asked Denise if she wanted to go along. Nope. He'd cashed his paycheck on the way to meet her. He gave most of it to her, keeping 50 or 60 dollars for himself, enough for a long weekend.

David drove over to Brian's house. When he got there, about 2 p.m., Janice was pulling up in her car. She worked at the Post Office and had either worked an early shift or had the day off. Brian lived in a nice corner house on Jefferson, a main street that ran all the way from downtown Detroit to Selfridge Air Force Base in Mt. Clemens. He was proud of his house, proud that he owned it, proud of how he kept it. He was a self-described "neat freak" and everything was always in its place.

When they got there, Brian was sleeping, dead tired from all the overtime he'd been putting in for Michigan Bell. His shift was 4 p.m. to midnight, but he routinely worked overtime till 4 or 5 a.m. They got him up. About 3 p.m., David called Denise from Brian's house and asked her if she wanted to change her mind and go with them. No, she had plans to go shopping with her sister. It wasn't unusual for David to ask Denise along on excursions with Brian. The three of them had hung out a lot, until Brian started dating Janice four years earlier.

David asked her if she wanted him to call her later that night. The family cabin didn't have a telephone and it was a twenty-minute drive to the nearest pay phone in that pre-cellular era, so she told him not to bother.

David called his mother and talked to her a few minutes about Jimmy, his younger brother. Despite their ten-year age difference, they were close. Years earlier, Jimmy had been really short for his age and was picked on a lot. When Jimmy was 10, David told him, "Never mind, Jimmy. When you're seventeen, we'll have a boxing match and we'll see who can beat who."

Jimmy was 17, now, and David told Cathy he had a joke in mind for Thanksgiving. He was going to wear a sling and pretend he'd broken his arm and wouldn't be able to follow up on their plans to see who could take whom.

Then he asked her to put Jimmy on the line. He asked him if he wanted to go hunting with him and Brian, but Jimmy said he had to work over the weekend.

Brian wasn't sure he still wanted to go. If they did go, he

wasn't all that fired up about joining the big crowd already at the cabin. It was a little too crowded for both their tastes.

Both were worried it was going to be too much men being men, sitting around drinking beer between trooping through the woods, not shaving, not worrying if they showered or not, belching and farting when they felt like it. A little too much hale-and-hearty shit and dumb jokes.

David and Matt might be close, but close or not, hanging with Matt's friends in close quarters for the weekend didn't have either of them much excited.

Maybe they'd visit an old friend from high school, Dennis Gallop, who had moved up north to a small town—just a few cabins, really—named Luzerne a few miles east of Mio the previous February, to a place his parents owned. Jacob had been up there a couple of times and had drawn them a map so they could find him if they wanted to. He'd bragged to Brian that he was great with maps and the one he'd drawn would get them there, no problem. It'd have to, since Gallop didn't have a phone and they'd have no way to let him know they were coming or to ask for directions.

Or they could go to Brian's parents' cabin on Higgins Lake, a giant beautiful inland lake in central northern Michigan. His parents lived there in the spring, summer and fall, and down in Florida for the winter. They'd just left for Florida, as a matter of fact, so the hunters would have the place to themselves.

No, on second or third thought, they'd go to White Cloud, after all. Janice wrote Brian a check for $50 to go with the $40 he had to make sure he had enough spending money. She was that kind of girlfriend, one who'd write her boyfriend a check so he could head off for the weekend with the guys. Lately, tired of maintaining separate residences, ready for a change, they'd been talking of marriage. Brian was a saver. Had a bank account, stock accounts. If he didn't need it, he wasn't going to buy it. If he was short that weekend, it was probably because he'd put more than he should have in the bank. He was saving for a bigger, nicer house and salting away as much as he could.

Brian threw his gear together in minutes—his Marlin. .35-caliber, Model No. 336C, lever-action rifle, his sleeping bag, enough clothes for the weekend—and tossed it into David's six-cylinder, four-speed manual transmission Bronco, alongside David's clothes and his .12 gauge pump action Ithaca shotgun. He told Janice he'd see her late Sunday afternoon.

About 5 p.m., David called Matt and told him they were coming up, but it might not be till Saturday. Matt and his buddies were just getting ready to leave. Several hours later, having crossed the state on I-96, Matt and his friends dropped their gear off at the cabin, then headed out to a bar in White Cloud. They left David and Brian a note saying where they'd be if the two got in and wanted to join them Friday night.

They didn't. When Matt and the gang got back to the cabin, no sign of his brother or his friend.

They didn't show up Saturday, either.

Or Sunday. Matt and his father weren't worried. Obviously David and Brian had changed their minds. Matt knew they were thinking of going north, instead. He knew David was having second thoughts because of how many guys were going to be crammed in there. That devil, gonna go up north and do a little carousing on the side, eh? Let Denise think you're with the family?

Janice started to worry by nightfall, when Brian hadn't come home. That he hadn't called wasn't a surprise. It would have been a surprise if he had. He was too tight with a buck to ever spend one on a long-distance phone call. He was just always on time.

Tyll was punctual and responsible, too, the kind of guy who'd call his wife if he was going to be late. By 10 p.m. Denise was scared, almost panicked, really, worse than you might expect over a husband just a few hours late from a weekend out of town with the guys. Her husband wasn't home, as promised, and he hadn't called.

Denise called her father to make sure she hadn't misunderstood Dave. Maybe he had gotten Monday off, too, and was coming back Monday night, not Sunday. No, said her dad, he was due in first thing Monday morning.

She called her in-laws. Matt answered. He was back already.

"What time did Dave leave?" she asked.

"Oh, about the same time I did," he answered, but he was vague when she asked him what time that was. He couldn't, or wouldn't, give her the time.

That's odd, she thought.

At 1 a.m., freaking out now, she called the State Police to see if there had been any accidents or incidents they were aware of involving Brian or David.

Nothing.

She tried to sleep, but couldn't.

She went to work the next day, and just after arriving, her mother-in-law, Cathy, called. Matt had made a confession. Brian and David had never shown up. He'd been covering for his brother when she'd called the night before, figuring he must have decided at the last minute to go someplace else instead, in search of a good time. He didn't want to get David in trouble with her.

Archie and their dad were still at the cabin. The boys hadn't shown up on Monday, either.

Panicked, Denise called another of David's brothers, Larry, who was Brian's roommate. Brian hadn't come home, yet. He hadn't called over the weekend.

Denise told her boss she had to leave work, and drove over to the Troy Police Department to file a missing persons report. Janice called Brian's parents in Florida, and tried to file a report with the St. Clair Shores police, but because she wasn't a relative, they wouldn't take one.

At 2:30 p.m., she called the State Police post in Pontiac again, to ask if they knew about any accidents. They didn't.

Janice checked with her bank. Brian had cashed the check in St. Clair Shores on Friday. For nearly two decades, it was about all she'd find out about what happened after David and Brian left her.

3
SEARCHING

An anguished first week passed without word for the Tyll and Ognjan families. Over the long Thanksgiving weekend, Janice, Denise, Matt and Janice's Uncle Dick drove up to the Tyll family cabin. Maybe something explainable had happened. Maybe Brian and David had gone somewhere else first, then swung by the White Cloud cabin after everyone had left. Maybe something had happened to their car and they were stuck there with no phone. Maybe they'd find a note. Maybe, maybe, maybe.

There was no sign of the two at the cabin. No trace of them. They asked around. Checked in at the Cozybar, the Drift Inn, the Highway Bar. It was frustrating work. They'd show pictures and sometimes get a "No," other times a "Yeah, I think they might have been in." Nothing you could trust. No real sense that anyone had seen them. No proof they hadn't, either.

They stopped by the state police. They stopped by the local radio stations and the newspaper, which promised to help get the word out. They weren't real sure of the area, but people pointed them in one direction and then in another and they pretty much got it all covered.

They even hired a pilot. The plane was too small for all of them, so Matt got in and had him fly him around White

Cloud, and then over the Hardy Dam, not sure what they were looking for or what they'd be able to spot from the air, trying to peer through the water to see if they could see a submerged Bronco, then flying over a bar on the other side of the dam Matt had heard about—maybe they'd see something there.

The search gave them a sense of accomplishing something without accomplishing a damn thing, but it made the time pass by better than sitting at home staring at the wall, waiting for the phone to ring.

They came away confident the two had never shown up in White Cloud. David was 6 foot 2, and so thin that he looked even taller. Brian was much shorter. You would have noticed them if they'd been hanging out together, kind of a Mutt and Jeff. If they'd been in the area, someone would have been able to say, "Yeah, they were here. I know it. I saw them," instead of the vague "maybes" and "I think so"s they were getting. It would always irk Janice, though, that as soon as the TV crews started showing up and the cameras started rolling and the bright lights beamed on, everyone, it seemed, had a story to tell, a sighting to share.

They'd been everywhere. And nowhere.

Over the coming months, Denise kept checking David's credit-card statement when it came, hoping for new activity in some far-off place. That would at least be an explanation. But there was never anything new. She'd check his bank account. Same balance.

4

CHANGE OF PLANS

Tyll and Ognjan left St. Clair Shores, all right, but they didn't head west, they drove north, first on I-75 above Standish and then up US-33, deep into the woods of northeastern Michigan, their eventual destination a three-hour drive from where they were supposed to end up.

Today, the Walter Reuther Freeway runs due west out of St. Clair Shores and connects to I-75, which goes north, and to I-96, which goes west. In 1985, though, Ognjan and Tyll could have either gone west to I-75 on the surface street later made famous by Eminem, 8 Mile Road, or wanting to avoid all its red lights, looped miles out of their way, heading downtown on I-94 till they came either to I-75 or to US 10, which would connect them to I-96.

Either way, they could have begun their destination not sure where they were going, but at some point early on, they'd have had to decide: okay, north or west. Maybe it was a decision made at the spur of the moment, White Cloud or Mio, you decide, no you decide. Turn of the wheel at an exit ramp and fate's course is set. Friends would say later it would have been typical of Brian to suggest at the last second that they change their minds one last time and go north. The neatnik had an impulsive streak.

What caused them to choose this direction will never be

known. What is known is that White Cloud and the mob scene with the family and friends was out, Mio was in. They'd go north. Maybe get a motel room, maybe look up Dave Gallop, definitely sit in the woods, definitely find some bars, definitely, based on a reconstruction of what would become known of that weekend, flirt with some women.

Fate's course *was* set. A chain of events began with their decision to take a right turn or not, a long chain that took years to unsnarl.

5
SIGHTINGS

Larry Barker lived two miles northwest of Mio, at 820 Cherry Creek Road. Larry and his boys were hauling some firewood into the house when a dark Ford Bronco pulled into the driveway. Barker never did check the time, but it had been dark awhile, not too long, it was maybe 8 p.m. By the time he was asked about the Bronco and its contents, he couldn't be sure whether it had been Friday, November 22, or Saturday, the 23rd.

The Bronco just sat there, so Larry walked over to the driver's window. The driver rolled it down.

"Can I help you?"

There were two young guys in the car, one of them holding a map.

"Well, we're kind of confused."

Barker laughed. "You got it upside down," he said, and reached in and turned the map around, so north would be on the top.

"I got directions from the bar," one of them said. He was looking for a road, one with the odd name of Camp 10.

"It's the next paved road down."

Their end destination was a cabin off M-55, a major east–west road in northern Michigan. It wasn't going to be easy. Barker tried to talk them through it. After Camp 10, they'd hit M-72, another major east–west road north of 55. That'd take them to 18, which would take them south to Roscommon, then from there it was a short hop to 55.

They shot the breeze awhile, Larry, his two boys and the two guys in the car. They told the Barkers how happy they were to be up north. That they were up hunting. They weren't necessarily drunk, but you could smell from the time they rolled down their window they'd been drinking. Barker could see a cardboard twelve-pack container on the back seat. Couldn't see if it was empty. But nice-talking gentlemen, nonetheless, he thought.

It went on for twelve or fifteen minutes. Larry's wife came to the front door of the house to see what was going on. If it was some friend of hers, too, she needed to come on out and talk. It wasn't.

Finally, "thanks," and the guy with the map rolled up the window and the Bronco backed out of the driveway and headed back down Cherry Creek. If the Bronco went the right way, it would have run into Camp 10, which ran north–south, and they would have gone over the Camp 10 Bridge.

Years later, locals would hear rumors of a Bronco that had gone in there, not by accident, and supposedly was still there at the bottom.

If the Bronco went the wrong way, it would have run into Mapes Road, which ran parallel to Camp 10. They were about three miles apart. There were a few paved roads in the area, lots of dirt roads, trails and two-tracks. If the Bronco had gone toward Mapes by mistake, and they turned onto it, they could have driven by Linker's Lost Creek Lodge.

The Barkers didn't stare after their taillights long enough to see which way the Bronco turned.

The next time Barker saw them was maybe a month later. Their faces were on TV. They were missing. It was a big goddamned deal. A mystery.

"Man," he said to himself, "those guys was in my driveway." He told his wife, and she called the cops.

• • •

The owners of Walker's Bar and Bowling Alley in Mio, Paul
and Beverly Pasternak, who lived upstairs, saw the missing
hunters twice, once at night and again the next afternoon.
Beverly engaged them in some conversation both times.

Brenda, their daughter, who worked there, would be sure,
later, that it was the hunters who had come in. She remembered them specifically because they started playing pool
with a guy known as Coke, for the thickness of his glasses.

Some people let the bad eyesight fool them. But Coke
was a tough guy, unpredictable.

"Coke was the kind of guy you kept your eye on," said
Brenda. So she kept her eye on him, and on the hunters.
Nothing materialized.

David Welch lived in Mio. If you frequented Walker's,
you might have thought Welch lived there. He was an unem-
ployed construction worker who was there seven nights a
week most weeks.

Welch was eating in the restaurant section, 8:30, maybe
9. Later, he'd be pretty sure it was Saturday night, November
23, though it could have been Friday if you twisted his arm
about it. About 9:30, two young guys walked in. When he
was done eating, he walked over and sat down next to them
at the bar and introduced himself. And they told him their
names: David Tyll and Brian Ognjan.

They were up hunting, drove up in Dave's Bronco, they
said, staying over at Ma Deeter's place in Luzerne, eight
miles to the east, renting a room.

David did most of the talking. Was real easy to keep a
conversation going with him. Brian just sort of sat there.

Welch asked them why, if they were staying at Ma
Deeter's, a lodge and restaurant, they were drinking in
Mio. Why not just drink there where they wouldn't have to
worry about driving home?

"The law in Mio is pretty stiff on drinking and driving,"
he warned them. It was pretty common, small a town as it
was, with just a few places to drink and a fair number of
hard-drinking locals there, for the cops to just sit in wait

down the road and pull cars over on one pretext or another and see what kind of red eyeballs were looking back at them.

Looking for women, said Tyll. Made sense to Welch, to come to Mio. Weren't many women in Mio, but more than in Luzerne, though they might have found some action near there at Linker's. Had a band. Long as they were here, though, they ought to go to the Northwood if they wanted action. Northwood Gardens, about a mile and a half north, up the road. Walker's really wasn't the place for it.

They said they had a couple of buddies they went to school with they wouldn't mind hooking up with, one in South Branch, the other in Luzerne. They asked Welch if he knew either one of them. He didn't. They were more interested in the one in South Branch. Sure you haven't heard of him? Everyone knows him. Nope.

They told him they were supposed to be over in White Cloud, meet up with Dave's dad there.

"Why aren't you?"

"Who wants to go to a hunting camp where all they do is sit around and fart?" one of them responded.

At some point, out of the blue, Tyll said, "Wouldn't it be nice to up and disappear?"

He told Welch he'd like to just head off to the Bahamas for the winter.

"You'd have a better chance of disappearing if you go to Alaska," said Welch.

Maybe, Welch would think later, this wasn't no big mystery, after all. Maybe they hadn't come to a foul ending. Maybe it was all nothing more than a couple of bored city boys who'd run off, gone searching for adventure in Alaska or for women and a tan in the Bahamas.

The two told him they were going to be hunting by Hoy Road and County Road 489. They talked about Tyll's Bronco. They told Welch they'd bought a .45 revolver from a friend of theirs in Detroit before they left. Asked him if he wanted to go out and shoot it.

No, said Welch, wanting to play it safe. Maybe they were thinking of robbing him or something once they got him outside. Didn't seem likely, but you never know. They were from Detroit and Detroit had a fearsome reputation, even then.

They sat there drinking and bullshitting, the hunters drinking beer, Welch doing straight schnapps, taking turns buying each other rounds. Welch didn't drink his schnapps by the shot, he drank it by the glass.

Brian got up and said he was going to the Northwood, after all.

~

Ken Fox was working the bar at the Northwood about 10:30–11, when a young deer hunter came in, new face, hadn't seen him before.

He sat down at the bar and Fox got him a drink. He sat just a few seats down from the cash register. A few minutes later, two very good-looking women, age 25 or so, came in. Way better looking and way better dressed than the typical women at the Northwood in deer season. He'd never seen them before, would never see them again. They couldn't help but catch Fox's eye, and the deer hunter's, too.

They sat at the bar, maybe ten feet down from the hunter. They ordered drinks. The hunter caught Fox's eye and told him to put it on his tab. The hunter wrote a note on a piece of paper and handed it to Fox, asked him if he'd mind passing it on to them. It must have been some note. They read the note, put it down, got up and walked out. Never touched the drinks.

The hunter finished his drink, didn't rush it down, didn't nurse it, either, and left. What the hell was that all about? wondered Fox.

He'd remember it all, long after. Wasn't sure of the day, though, by the time they asked. Thought it was Friday.

~

David stayed with Welch. At one point, David got up to go to the bathroom and stumbled and Beverly told the barmaid to quit serving him. When he came out, Bev said to him, politely, letting him know she wasn't casting aspersions, "I think you've had enough."

Usually, you see deer hunters stumbling, trouble's the next thing you see. She expected some from him. But he was polite. Took it calmly. "Okay. Fine. But can I wait for my buddy?"

"Sure."

Tyll started drinking coffee. A little while later, Brian returned and he and Tyll walked out the back door into the night.

Pasternak would say later that it must have been about 10:30, no later than 11, when they left. She figured that had to be the time because they closed the kitchen about 9, 9:30, and after she was done in the kitchen, she came out and saw Tyll take his stumble.

Welch finished another schnapps and left fifteen minutes later. There was a black Bronco in the parking lot. Tyll's car, he figured. He walked over to check and see if it was running, that maybe they'd gotten in and fallen asleep. "I don't want them to set there and gas themselves to death," he thought.

It wasn't running and they weren't inside. They must have gotten lucky. Brian must have brought some of those women they were looking for back from the Northwood.

The next day, Beverly and Paul Pasternak opened up at noon. Soon after, in walked Brian and Tyll. They ordered a Coke and a Bud, something to get a little blood sugar back in their system, to go along with some hair of the dog.

"How's your head today?" asked Bev, in from the kitchen to grab something she needed.

"I think I had enough last night," said David, polite again. Bev thought they were very nice, very mannerly. Later, she'd be one of the few people claiming to be sure what had happened and when. They'd gotten drunk on Saturday, cured their hangovers on Sunday.

The next time Welch saw the hunters was some weeks later—hard to judge the passage of time when you're sitting at the bar in Walker's every night. But one night he walked in and there were their pictures, Tyll's and Ognjan's, up on the wall. They were missing, wanted by the police. The flyer asked anyone who had seen them to contact the authorities.

Bev Pasternak was only too happy to post the photos. The sheriff had walked in about two weeks after she'd last seen them sitting there drinking a Coke and a Bud.

He went to show her something and she said, "I can't talk to you right now, I'm busy."

He said, "Well, I wish you would."

And he showed her Brian and David's photos and told her they were missing.

Shocked her. And reminded her. David had left a heavy flannel shirt on the bar stool. She went and got it and gave it to the sheriff, and he gave her copies of their photos and she stuck them to the wall.

~

Michael Parent was hunting deer in an area known as Malty Hills near Rose City a few miles south of Mio when two men approached him in the woods. They had gotten turned around on the back roads and wanted directions to Mio.

Both had on hunter's orange. One had a beard. They mentioned they were driving a Bronco, and snow wasn't a concern if they had to take unplowed dirt roads.

~

David and Brian had struck Bev Pasternak as mannerly. They'd struck Cindy Socia as assholes.

The weekend of November 23–24, she was working at Linker's Lost Creek Lodge, where the lodging was upstairs over the one big room that served as restaurant and bar. It was big by north woods standards, and classy, too. Didn't have that old seen-too-much-weather-seen-too-much-shit look most joints had. Steve Linker and his wife had bought it a few months ago and were working hard at making a go of it. It was a hybrid kind of a place—a house band brought in the younger locals, the kind who'd slip out into the parking lot for a joint or into the bathroom for a toot of coke, but the food was good and people didn't think twice about coming in with their kids for a family dinner.

Years later, when it came time to promise to tell the truth, the whole truth, Cindy, like Bev Pasternak, was sure of her dates. They'd come in on Sunday, the 24th. No doubt about it. The time she was a little hazy about. It got dark so early up north in late November that it seemed like night most of the time. Later than 5 p.m., earlier than 8.

She remembered clearly, too, that it was a quiet night, not many people there, especially considering it was deer season, the action slow enough she noticed the headlights from their car as it turned off Mapes Road into the parking lot.

The guys came in—she'd never seen them before, took them for deer hunters—came in and ordered two Budweisers. One of them—she found out later his name was Brian—went to the bathroom. When he came back, the other, David, was about to pay.

"Don't take his money or I'm going to fucking smack you," said Brian. He might have been joking. She took it as an insult. She collected his money and his $2 tip and went to Linker and told him she didn't want to wait on them.

Linker had only owned the place a little more than a month and was eager to keep all the customers he could. He went over, sat down with them and had a quiet talk. They promised to behave, said they didn't mean anything by it, and he came back to Cindy and told her they were okay. By then, though, she'd traded duties with someone. She was bartending by then and didn't wait on them anymore.

~

Barb Klimmek wouldn't remember if it was Saturday or Sunday. A heavy drinker and self-styled party-hearty girl, she was out at one or another of the local bars most nights, but Sunday was usually the one night she could be found at home, just a mile or so up Mapes Road.

Her best bud, Ronnie Emery, had stopped by her house just after the early nightfall of the northern Michigan woods, all excited. He'd shot the first legal buck of his life and wanted to go out and celebrate. He'd shot all kinds of deer over the years, but this was the first one he'd shot while in possession of a license, which made it seem special. So, it could have been a Sunday was how she figured it later, if that was the day he shot his buck.

The rest of it was clear enough.

She and Ronnie were playing pool and drinking. She favored Bloody Marys or something called a Salty Dog, and favored them pretty much one after another.

Maybe half an hour after they got there, two deer hunters came in, strangers to her, though she hadn't, yet, started to hang out much at Linker's. At least she figured them for deer hunters, which got them off to a bad start in her mind. She didn't like hunters in general—Emery didn't count.

Just after they arrived, the short one grabbed her ass. "Keep your fucking hands to yourself," she said. Feisty, she didn't take shit from tourist deer hunters.

Five, six minutes later, she was leaning over the table getting ready for a shot, her rear end sticking out. She had, she didn't mind admitting, a pretty good rear in those days. The tall hunter slid past, rubbed his groin area into her butt, no way it was an accident, though it might have looked that way if you happened to be glancing over. She turned and told him where he could shove it, and went back to her shot.

Most guys would have been embarrassed or sulked off, but not these two. They put two quarters on the table, calling for next game. When the game was over, Ronnie and Barb left the table to them and went and sat down.

Barb was fuming. She kept giving the hunters the evil eye. And it got more and more evil with each drink. The hunters bantered occasionally with other women, traded a line or two with some guys, nothing too out of the ordinary, but they rubbed her the wrong way.

"Those guys need to get their asses kicked," she said to Ronnie.

• • •

Dick Smith wouldn't remember years later which night of the weekend it was, they all kind of blended together during deer season. He was a sheriff with the Oscoda County Sheriff's Department, not the sharpest tool in the drawer, truth be told, the kind of guy who, once or twice, might have let a minor wrongdoing slide if it meant not having to mess around making an arrest or doing paperwork near the end of a shift.

The way he'd recall it years later, as usual during deer season he was out with Paul Owens, a conservation officer with the state's Department of Natural Resources. Owens wrote out the citations for hunting violations, Smith did the other stuff.

It was about 2 a.m., definitely end-of-the-shift time. Smith was driving, and they were nearing the Camp 10 store when, driving east on M-72, a black Bronco pulled out in front of them. Smith couldn't tell for sure in the dark, but it looked like it had driven right out of the ditch just east of the store. Probably a drunk with four-wheel drive, this time of night.

Shit, thought Smith. It's cold out, it's two in the morning. "I didn't want to be bothered arresting a drunk driver," he'd tell a state police investigator years later. In coming weeks, he'd come to realize the possible significance of the Bronco he'd seen. Had it been the hunters'? Was Tyll driving it? Or was someone else at the wheel, someone with blood on his hands? Literal or figurative, it didn't matter.

6

TIMELINE

Eventually, a state police detective sergeant named Norman Maxwell would write a report with his interpretation and timeline of events for the deer hunters' weekend for November 22–24.

It would read:

FRIDAY

   Left St. Clair Shores (Ognjan) residence for Mio. Once in Mio they stopped at Walker's Bar-Restaurant where they were drinking. Ognjan left Tyll at Walker's and went to the Northwood Bar.

   At the Northwood Bar is where Ognjan requested Mr. Fox to give the note to the two girls. After the girls left, Ognjan finished drinking and returned to Walker's Bar where Tyll was at. Tyll had been cut off drinking at Walker's Bar due to being intoxicated. The pair left Walker's Bar with Tyll leaving behind his shirt.

   After leaving Walker's Bar, the pair proceeded out of town and stopped at the Barker residence where they obtained directions for Roscommon.

   Nothing further on Friday.

SATURDAY

Nothing until they showed up at Walker's Bar in mid-afternoon and ordered food. It is unknown their whereabouts until they showed up at Linker's Lost Lodge Bar in the evening.

Nothing further on Saturday.

SUNDAY

Unknown whereabouts until they returned to Linker's Bar in the evening, where they gave the barmaid/waitress (Cindy Socia) a rough time and spoke with Steve Linker.

After leaving Linker's Bar, the whereabouts are unknown.

7
POLICE REPORTS

If there's one constant about missing persons reports, it's that the families filling them out never think the police are taking them seriously enough. There's a reason for the cops to be more blasé than panicked loved ones—a vast preponderance of people who go missing come back on their own. They weren't missing. They were just gone, of their own volition, taking a left turn when expected to go right.

The Tylls and the Ognjans tried to inject a sense of urgency to the complacency they were sensing.

David was happily married. He had a good job working for his father-in-law. He had no history of personal or emotional problems. Not a bit of irresponsibility in his past, if you discount the usual stuff with underage drinking and chasing girls.

No reason for Brian, either. A nice girlfriend, one willing to finance his weekend hunting trips. Owned his own home at a relatively young age. Had a car, a boat, a bank account, worked a lot of overtime at a job he liked.

The local police took their reports, calmly. The St. Clair Shores police wouldn't let Janice file a report. Longtime girlfriend or not, the one most acquainted with his plans and the first to suspect something was wrong, her opinion meant nothing to the legal bureaucracy. Brian's parents had to come back from Florida to get the paperwork started.

The police promised they'd follow up. It was hardly cause for alarm, in their minds, that a couple of young deer hunters might be a day or two late coming back to the city.

But by the end of the following long Thanksgiving weekend it was clear something was wrong. Payne had told them Brian and David had talked of visiting their old friend, Dennis Gallop. They prevailed on an Oscoda County sheriff's deputy to drive by Gallop's place in Mio, but he hadn't seen or heard anything.

By December 4, Oscoda was working the case. One of their sergeants, Dick Smith, had hard news, or at least harder than they'd come up with so far. He'd seen their Bronco, or one just like it, anyway, in the parking lot of the Mio Saloon on Sunday, November 24.

The Oscoda deputies stopped by the Northwood and the Mio Saloon and other likely stops for a pair of young guys up for the weekend, nosing around, asking owners to spread the word, let them know if they heard anything.

The local TV stations were running reports, now, and Larry Barker called in to say he'd given the hunters, who were lost and likely drunk, directions when they stopped at his house on the 23rd or 24th.

By the 6th, Oscoda deputies had physically checked every motel, bar and restaurant in a wide area. A woman at the Loon Lake Resort said she'd seen them, but they hadn't stayed there. They'd been spotted in the Mio, at Linker's Lost Creek Lodge, at Walker's Bar and Bowling Alley. Bingo! They'd rented a room at Ma Deeter's.

By the 8th, they'd driven down all the obvious trails and two-tracks hunters in a car might have used while out hunting. Nothing. That day, deputy Michael Wesolowski wrote in his daily report:

> *There were a large amount of fresh snowmobile*
> *tracks and other four-wheel-drive tracks traveling*
> *the trail roads in the [county's] townships. If these*
> *subjects were deceased in this county, this officer or*

*a citizen should have spotted them. Officer feels
these subjects are not in this county.
   Open refer to Sgt. Richard E. Smith.*

Smith was his boss. It wouldn't come out for many years, but
there was an irony in how Wesolowski ended his report.
Eventually, state police *would* be referred to Smith. And
what they'd find out would shock them: Smith had been dispatched to Linker's Lost Creek Lodge because of a report of
a fight either brewing or in progress—something about a
couple of deer hunters and some locals. According to one
witness, he hadn't finished the run. He hated breaking up bar
fights. He'd allegedly pulled into the parking lot of the
Camp 10 store nearby to wait things out.

But he did see a Ford Bronco later that night, pulling out
of a ditch by the store, but he hadn't pulled it over, not wanting his shift to run over filling out paperwork on a drunk
driver.

Who knows how the hunters' fates might have differed
had he gone to the bar, or pulled over the Bronco?

~

Meanwhile stories were running in Detroit's two big-city
dailies, the *Free Press* and the *News*, which circulated
around the state. They were either picked up by the smaller
dailies and weeklies, or editors at those papers assigned their
own reporters to localize them. Detroit's 50,000-watt news
radio stations, WJR and WWJ, which had a wide geographi-
cal reach, carried frequent updates.

As the story grew, tips began coming in from all over.
Two deer hunters answering the description and Broncos of
the right year and color had been seen, seemingly all over
the state.

But it was clear from the work done by the Oscoda Sheriff's Department by mid-December that most of the sightings were in error. The hunters hadn't gone to White Cloud
or to the Upper Peninsula. Enough consistent and confirmed

sightings had come in that it was clear the two missing friends had, indeed, gone to Mio.

Janice Payne and Denise Tyll drove up to snoop around. They stopped in at the sheriff's department. They talked to the sheriff and his deputy. They visited Gallop. They couldn't call him ahead of time, he didn't have a phone. But they found him at home. He hadn't seen them in a year and a half. Brian and David hadn't left a note at his house saying they'd been by, either. He didn't think all those reports of sightings in and around Mio could be true. If they'd have come up, they'd have looked him up—wouldn't they?—and they hadn't.

They stopped in at Linker's, where they even spent a night. They showed everyone they met photos of Brian and David. Just more nothing. No one knew where they were. No one knew where they might have gone.

Posters went up everywhere, in all the bars and restaurants, at the Post Office, in all of the Glen's supermarkets throughout northern Michigan.

For months, Denise called the sheriff and the Mio area news people. Searching for news. Trying to make news. She kept on doing what she could, she kept trying to feel some hope, but after the first week, she knew in her heart David and Brian were dead. It was the only explanation that made sense. And it made no sense. How? Why? Where were their bodies?

Six months went by. The Troy police made periodic inquiries, as did the St. Clair Shores police. Oscoda deputies followed various leads to their dead ends. Nothing.

Oscoda County Sheriff Michael Larrison hung photos of Tyll and Ognjan on the walls of his ten-cop department to serve as inspiration and reminder. They would hang there for eighteen years.

8

GOOD IRISH GIRL

Cathy O'Reilly grew up on the east side of Detroit. Her father, Frank, was a machine operator. Frank and Mary O'Reilly were born in Canada and lived on a family farm near Montreal before moving to Detroit. Frank came in 1927, as did thousands of immigrants from Canada and Europe and thousands of migrants from the deep south who wanted to get in on the good life the auto boomtown offered. Mary joined him a year later.

Good Catholics, they had seven children, a boy and six girls. Cathy was the second youngest, a serious girl and good student who had just graduated from nursing school and passed her state boards to become a registered nurse when she met Arthur Tyll at a New Year's Eve party at her sister-in-law's in 1952.

Arthur was just back from Korea, wounded by shrapnel from what in a later war would be known by the oxymoron of all oxymorons, friendly fire. He told folks the Army should have given him a Purple Heart, but because he'd been shot by his own troops, they wouldn't. Didn't seem like a meaningful distinction to him.

If it wasn't love at first sight, it was pretty close to it. They were married on September 26, 1953.

Cathy was a nurse at Providence Hospital for a year, and

then they started having kids. Once they started, they didn't stop. Kevin was the oldest, followed in quick order by Steve, Kathleen, Brian, David, Larry, Denise, Shawn, Matthew (born on Cathy's birthday), Archie, Linda, Jim and Michael, thirteen kids in all. You could have been mistaken thinking it was fourteen, Brian Ognjan over as often as he was, pretty much inseparable from Dave.

The large family didn't stop Cathy from going back to work part-time at Holy Cross Hospital, working the occasional midnight shift in obstetrics and pediatrics.

Art worked three jobs, including one selling burlap to nurseries. Most firemen moonlighted, you'd be crazy not to, working just two twenty-four-hour shifts a week at the firehouse, all hell breaking loose when something was going on and playing cards and basically just hanging out when it wasn't, which was most of the time.

In 1976, when Michael was just a year old, Art took a disability retirement. He said working as a fireman aggravated his old foot injuries from Korea, when they'd been frostbitten and then hit by shrapnel. Three years later, Cathy resumed nursing full-time, in the psych unit at Holy Cross and moonlighting on weekends in the psych unit at St. John.

The Tyll family grew up on the northeast side of Detroit, near 7 Mile and Gratiot, the heart of a neighborhood called Copper Canyon, not for the metal but for all the police who lived there. The city no longer requires its cops and firemen to be residents of the city, but it did in those days, and over the years, it became a tradition that they all lived out near the northern edges of the city, as close to the suburbs as they could.

Eminem made 8 Mile Road, Detroit's northern city limit, famous. It separates the city from the suburbs and Wayne County, one of the poorest counties in the state, from Macomb and Oakland Counties. Oakland is one of the richest counties in the U.S., third- or fourth-ranked depending on which statistics you're using. It is a county filled with forests and lakes and palatial estates.

If all the city's cops and firemen couldn't quite get to the suburbs, they could at least live in a neighborhood just about as safe. You'd have to be a moron *and* a crook to try a B&E in that neighborhood, with its high concentration of police-issue sidearms.

Dave and Archie were the two best athletes in the family. Dave, skinny as he was, was a good baseball player in grade school. He enrolled at Austin High, a Catholic prep school known for its athletics, having produced among others Dave DeBusschere, a pitcher for the Chicago White Sox who later was player–manager for the Detroit Pistons and went on to a Hall-of-Fame career with the New York Knicks.

When Dave Tyll, all ninety-eight pounds of him as a freshman, announced to his mother that he was going to try out for football, she teased him: "Dave, I don't think the coach is going to be too excited about that."

But football practice interfered with his paper route and, always a good worker, he opted for commerce.

~

The Tylls knew David hadn't run off, that he wasn't away on some fling, that he and Brian hadn't gone up to Canada or out to Vegas or down to Florida or any other place. He'd gone hunting and he hadn't come back and something horrible had happened. It was a close family. He was a good husband who could be forgiven the occasional eye at a cute barmaid if he'd had too much too drink.

Born between two active, even rowdy brothers, Brian and Larry, David struck people as quiet and polite, behaving like the altar boy he was. "You could take him anywhere. He'd always behave," said his mother.

And he was endearingly sensitive. Once, in Little League, Dave was having an overpowering day. He'd had a bunch of strikeouts, striking one kid out so badly the kid's own teammates razzed the heck out of him. The next time the kid came up, Dave didn't try to strike him out. He grooved him the ball, trying to let him hit it instead of being the cause of further humiliation.

In seventh grade, one teacher wrote on an evaluation his mother would long remember: "Dave is a gentleman."

At 15 he was a Boy Scout, working for some honor or other, maybe a badge—his mother doesn't remember—and he fell just short. He was upset. There was a ceremony involved and all the mothers whose kids were honored got corsages. Dave was devastated. He didn't care for himself, he told his mother. "I wanted you to get the corsage."

At 19—you could legally drink in Michigan then at age 18—he met his future wife in a bar. He'd been toying with the idea of college, but meeting Denise put an end to that. He wanted to get married, get a good job and settle down. He did all three.

He was the kind of son who would come by his parents' house on the spur of the moment and cut their grass or trim their bushes, see what they were up to.

No, David didn't run off. Something bad had happened. Very bad. Those who knew him were convinced.

9

GOING WORLD-WIDE

On May 22, 1986, an inexplicably long time to the families, the Michigan State Police took over the case. Detective Sergeant Norman Maxwell was asked to get hold of the Troy and St. Clair Shores police, get copies of their files and see what he could come up with.

He was also told to check with various out-of-state police agencies as well as other police posts around the state.

Lt. August Blumline's St. Clair Shores report was brief, not much to show for the passage of time. Case number 85-30181, Brian George Ognjan, white male, born 1/16/58. He had two registered weapons, a .357-caliber revolver and a .22-caliber pistol. Both were found at his home at 31825 Jefferson in St. Clair Shores. He had gone missing on November 22, 1985.

Maxwell's own terse report made it clear what he thought of the St. Clair Shores police work. It wasn't what he said about their efforts, but what he noted about the Troy report:

> Det. [Phil] Steele of the Troy P.D. Crime Prevention Bureau was contacted and provided a lengthy report on their missing David Kenneth Tyll, 8/21/58. Det. Steele has kept up to date in his reports and they provide good information.

Maxwell checked to make sure both men were in the computerized Law Enforcement Intelligence Network (LEIN) system that was available to police nationwide. They were. Tyll, 6 foot 2, 180 pounds, brown hair, brown eyes. Ognjan, 5–8, 175, sandy brown hair, brown eyes.

Tyll's 1980 black Bronco was in there, too. Michigan plate 447HRZ, set to expire on August 21, 1986.

A LEIN check turned up nothing new by any U.S. or Canadian agency. The check didn't just look for activity by Tyll or Ognjan that had run afoul of the law, it showed if any of the local agencies had in fact been actively using the computer network to search for them.

The St. Joseph County Sheriff's Department had checked in several times, but that was about it. The other departments didn't seem to be following up. There was one hit from Oklahoma. Maxwell called out and was told that the Oklahoma State Bureau of Investigation had seen an earlier notice and wanted to cross-reference the descriptions against their own unidentified persons' file. Nothing matched.

The U.S. Marshal's office in Detroit had also been on LEIN. It turned out one of the marshals was a friend of the Tyll family and as a courtesy monitored the network periodically.

Maxwell contacted Interpol in Washington, D.C., and asked for help internationally. Agent Tim Horan called him back and told him that the case of the missing hunters had been assigned Interpol Case No. 860607283. It was officially, now, an international mystery. He would work Canada and Mexico, himself, looking for leads on the car or the men.

Maxwell called investigators with Blue Cross Blue Shield of Michigan to see if either man had used his insurance since November 22. Tyll was extraordinarily healthy, apparently. He hadn't used his card since getting some dental work in 1980. Tyll had last used his in July of 1985 for some outpatient care for a brief illness.

Detective Sergeant Richard Miller of the Newaygo State Police Post, near White Cloud, was contacted, too, and he had something exciting to report, some hope that the case might be closed sooner rather than later. A large metal object had been spotted by divers in the water near the Hardy Dam by the County Sheriff's Marine Patrol. They weren't able to get below eighty-five feet because of murky water that would clear as the rains of spring abated. The object looked to be at 120–150 feet and they were waiting for better weather and clearer water before they went back in. It wasn't certain what the object was, but it looked like it might be a car or truck.

What made it particularly interesting is that Tyll always took a shortcut near a boat livery by the dam, and the road went right near the water. If a car slid off the road there on a wintry night—and it had been snowy and blowing the weekend they disappeared—it could have gone into the water, right about where the object had been spotted.

All in all, a productive morning. Maybe this was nothing more mysterious than the two men going off the road in their Bronco into the freezing water behind the dam and drowning. Maybe he'd be able to change the last line on his next report, the one under the word "STATUS," where he'd typed in "Open."

10

THE WIFE STOPS TALKING

Maxwell worked the case as if it were brand-new. Over the next two months, he confirmed with U.S. Customs that the missing Bronco, to the best of their knowledge, had not crossed into Canada in the last year.

State police up north in West Branch were asked to reinterview Dennis Gallop in Luzerne, and do it with a lie detector if they thought he warranted it, and to check out his house and land for anything suspicious. They eventually did run a lie-detector test on Gallop and he passed it, claiming he hadn't seen the two and knew nothing about their whereabouts.

Maxwell was gung-ho, which was a change for the families. But gung-ho ticked a lot of them off, too. Catherine Tyll would talk years later of her first meeting with him, him barging into their house, full of attitude, saying, "I'm going to have everyone in this house take a lie-detector test." Like they were suspects. Like it was their fault David hadn't come back. He was just doing his job, of course, rattling cages, leaving nothing unturned.

Accompanied by Troy Officer Steele, he interviewed Denise Tyll at work in Troy. She told them that David was supposed to have gone hunting the opening weekend, on November 15, instead of the 22nd, but she'd had an office party that Saturday, and he'd decided to be the good husband and go with her to that, instead.

She confirmed the time-line she'd given earlier, of him and Brian leaving Friday afternoon, not coming back Sunday night, calling his family in a panic.

There was a little something that maybe raised one of Maxwell's eyebrows. Denise was already living with a new boyfriend, Roger Dudley, the brother of a good girlfriend. She'd met him a month or so after David went missing and moved in with him two months later.

She told Maxwell that she and David had been separated once before, for five months or so about three years earlier. She didn't think David had dated anyone, but she had dated around, had even started to get serious with someone. She even filed for divorce, but had decided to try to repair her marriage.

The repair had worked, she said. They had gotten along fine and she didn't want to divorce him, but she and Roger were talking about getting married next spring.

Another thing raised an eyebrow. On her own, without being asked, Denise said she hadn't checked out whether or not David or Brian were gay, that David never showed any signs, that Brian had never really dated much until he met Janice. Maxwell noted it in his report, underlined that Denise had "voluntarily advised" she hadn't asked him about whether or not he was gay.

She told him David had hung around three bars on 7 Mile Road, but had curtailed his bar time when he got arrested for operating a car under the influence while they were separated.

She and Dave had been to Idaho, once, and he'd liked it, but she didn't think it a likely destination for him and Brian. Besides, the Bronco wasn't up to any cross-country travel.

They interviewed her father, Dennis Wygocki, at Deland Manufacturing in Madison Heights, and he confirmed he'd given Tyll Friday off so he could get an early start, and that his daughter had called him Monday hoping against hope that he had given David Monday off, too.

Maxwell interviewed Arthur and Catherine Tyll. They

didn't appreciate one line of questioning, but he had to pursue it. Maybe Brian and David had a thing going with each other and just decided to run off?

They weren't the type, the Tylls insisted. They knew Brian was close to his parents, David was close to them, neither of them would cause them any alarm. And neither was the type to run off with another woman, either.

Janice Payne was cooperative, but didn't have much to add.

Steele and Maxwell met with a *Detroit Free Press* reporter, Eric Kinkopf, who interviewed them, told them he was going north to scout around and interview people and if he found out anything, he'd let them know.

A little while later, there was a disturbing development. On July 15, 1986, Maxwell wrote in a report that Steele had called him to tell him that Denise had been advised by her attorney not to answer any more questions. He noted that he and Steele were about to interview Brian's old girlfriend, Janice, and "will see if the same attitude applies to her."

What was up with that? Living with a new boyfriend, met him right after her husband went missing. Gets an attorney? Talks to him after their last interview and now says she won't talk to them anymore? If you're just the aggrieved wife, innocent of nothing more sinister than having your husband either disappear or run out on you, why in the world would you need an attorney? Why wouldn't you want to cooperate with the cops working the case?

11

CASE CLOSED

What followed next for Maxwell and the families can be summed up in two words: Nothing much.

The tip about the object hidden in the deep waters behind the Hardy Dam didn't pan out.

In late November, a year after the two hunters disappeared, an anonymous tip came in to the West Branch State Police Post about a black Bronco found in the woods in Comins township. Wrong Bronco.

On December 12, Brian Ognjan's parents gave Maxwell their new Florida address for the winter.

On December 18, Maxwell went back through the reports looking for something he might have missed. Nothing popped out.

On January 22, 1987, his boss asked him to check with the Troy police one more time, see if they'd heard anything. If not, mark the case "closed."

On January 23, Maxwell wrote a brief report. He'd talked to Steele and there was nothing new.

> Undersigned advised Det. Steele that this complaint was going to be closed at this time; however, it will be reopened at a later date if further leads develop. Steele advised that his police department

*was going to go ahead and close their complaint,
also, and will wait for further leads, if anything developed at a further date.*

*Complaint status: Closed at this time, to be re-
opened if further leads develop.*

12
CASE OPENED

On February 22, 1988, the case reopened in dramatic style. An elderly woman from the northeast Michigan town of Prudenville had been asking about the deer-hunter investigation, who was handling it, what she should do if she had information.

She was referred to Detective Sergeant Curtis Schram, who had recently inherited the closed case from Maxwell, getting promoted from trooper at the Romeo post to detective sergeant at the regional headquarters in Northville.

Genevieve Yaklin was an avid deer hunter, hadn't missed a season in more than thirty years. She told Schram that about 9:30 a.m. on November 23, 1985, she and her husband had headed into the woods off a road in Roscommon County. They'd seen a black Ford Bronco on the shoulder, but no one was with it. It was on Highway 55, on the north side of the road, near the drive-in theater that was closed for the season.

When they walked out of the woods about 5 p.m., the Bronco was still there. This time, there were two men at the front of the vehicle and a third man near the rear. She and her husband got a look at them, didn't think much of it, and kept on walking.

It wasn't until the spring of 1986 that she saw pictures of

a man who was wanted in the shooting and killing of a sheriff's deputy who had picked him up while hitchhiking. She couldn't remember his first name, but his last name was Hanna, and she recognized him as one of the guys at the Bronco.

The reason she was calling, though, was that right after she'd seen Hanna's picture, she'd seen missing photos of the two hunters. They were the same two she'd seen with Hanna.

Her description of them was almost photographic. She said she'd been able to keep them fresh in her mind because at the time, she thought the three of them together looked out of place, two of them dressed up like hunters, the other one not at all.

Hanna had long blonde hair. He was wearing a blue turtleneck sweater, fatigue pants and lace-up boots. No facial hair.

Of the other two, one was shorter, with a red shirt or jacket, a few days' worth of facial hair; the other was tall and slim, wearing an orange vest.

It got better. Her husband always slept with the window open. Early in the morning of the 24th, about 12:30 or maybe 1, they heard two shots from a high-powered rifle coming from Lake St. James. And this Hanna guy supposedly had a cabin on the lake.

Yaklin was sure Hanna had shot the hunters and that their bodies and the Bronco would be found somewhere near the lake.

Why hadn't she come forward before now? Schram wanted to know.

Since her husband's death the year before, it had pestered her more and more that she might know something about the missing deer hunters that could help in the search. Besides, she said, she wasn't just now coming forward. She'd gone to the Houghton State Police Post when she'd seen the missing posters the year before. She couldn't remember who she talked to, but he didn't seem to take her too seriously and she'd never heard back.

To Schram's surprise, and boosting his adrenaline, her

story checked out, a lot of it, anyway. There had been a guy named Hanna, first name of Joel. He'd shot an Otsego County deputy named Carl Darling Jr., and later had been shot and killed, himself, after trying to attack two cops in Georgia with a pitchfork.

It didn't all check out, though. Hanna lived on a lake, all right, but it was Lake George, and that was over near Harrison, not anywhere close to the Yaklins', and way out of hearing range of any gunshots. And two state police detectives at the Houghton post interviewed her in person. She didn't seem nearly so sure of herself with them as she had on the phone with Schram. Worse, she couldn't positively ID any of the three from photos.

Nonetheless, it was something. Movement of one kind or another, even if it was sideways.

On the last line of his report, where it said "Status," Schram typed in "Open pending further tips."

13
"HE BURIED THE BODIES"

On March 22, 1988, more movement. Another good tip.

Luella Trolz of the unlikely named Dodge City called the Houghton post to say that a Timothy Slade had told her he had participated in the burial of two bodies, murder victims of a friend of his.

Slade was supposed to be in Kentucky. Police ran a LEIN on him and found out he had an injunction against him involving spouse abuse out of Waterford Township, down near Detroit.

On March 29, Schram interviewed Slade's ex-wife, Judith Slade, who was living in Pontiac. They'd been married in January of 1987 and divorced ten months later. He wasn't in Kentucky, he was in a halfway house in Midland, Texas, in connection with drug charges, and was scheduled to be released in April.

He'd had a troubled past and used to live up north, in or near the town of Gladwin, but she'd never heard talk of any murders or burials.

In April, Slade called Schram from his halfway house and said he had an alibi for the time the hunters had gone missing. He was living with a previous wife, then, and working for a tobacco company in Springfield, Kentucky. Kentucky police checked out his story and reported back to

Schram that Slade had worked at the tobacco company, all right, but only for a month, from November 21 to December 30, 1984. He'd split up with his wife in January, left the area and hadn't been seen since.

It was time to reinterview Luella. She said she had lived in the Harrison area of northeastern Michigan for fifteen or twenty years and often hired locals to help with chores around the home. She'd hired a guy named Ron and his wife for several jobs back in 1985–86. Slade did some work for Trolz, too, and one day came over all beat up. She asked him what happened. He was upset and they spent the next several hours talking about Ron and his activities.

She offered to drive him to the police or to the hospital to get his head wounds fixed. Slade told her he was more interested in revenge—he was going to do to Ron what he'd done to the two hunters. And that was beat him to death. Trolz was aghast.

Don't worry, said Slade. "I didn't kill them but I did help him bury them."

She started asking questions a mile a minute.

"I knew I shouldn't have told you," he said. "I'll be killed if Ron finds out about this."

She kept prodding and he kept talking. He said there had been a fight between Ron's gang of buddies and these two young hunters, who were buried on property belonging to Ron and his family.

Had it been the hunters? Schram asked. Trolz didn't know. Slade hadn't mentioned whether they were hunters or not. He hadn't mentioned anything about a Ford Bronco.

On May 1, Schram talked to Trolz's son, Gary. His mother was of sound mind, he said. Not the kind to make up something like that. And she'd told the same story to him two years earlier.

On May 4, Schram met with Slade, who was out of the halfway house and back in the state, down in Pontiac. They talked in Schram's police car, outside Slade's house. He told the detective that he had in fact, worked at Trolz's house. Ron had beat the pee out of him with a lead pipe. As for the bodies, he didn't know what that was about, maybe she was confused.

Confused? Schram wondered. About what, and how?

Well, Slade allowed, he had told her some true-enough stories about Ron, that he had shot a phone out of someone's hand once, that he poached deer and used to bury the hides. Maybe that's what she was getting confused about.

On May 10, in front of her son, Schram put Trolz through a grilling. Her story held up. The details never changed. She might not be telling the truth, but she certainly thought it was the truth.

Three days later, Slade took a polygraph test administered by the state police. He admitted he had told Trolz about helping Ron bury bodies. The machine said he was telling the truth. Slade said he was just making the whole thing up. The machine said that was the truth, too.

Dead end.

14

ANOTHER TRIP NORTH

In November of 1988, Detective Sergeant Norman Maxwell, the original investigating officer for the State Police, was working out of the Ypsilanti post, in the southeast corner of the state. On November 2, he was briefly back on the case, as part of a three-day trip to the Mio area with Chris Hansen, an investigative reporter for Detroit's NBC affiliate, WDIV–Channel 4, who later would distinguish himself as a national correspondent.

They started the trip by meeting with the Ognjans at their summer place in Roscommon. Then they huddled up with Oscoda County Sheriff Donald Smith and his undersheriff, Michael Larrison, to review county efforts on the case and to get tips and directions for various bars and other areas where Tyll and Ognjan had reportedly been seen. Two of the spots were bridges—the Chase Bridge, where a Bronco had been spotted, and the Camp 10 Bridge, where, rumors continued to claim, the Bronco had gone into the water.

Larrison told them he'd dragged the river behind the Camp 10 Bridge with negative results. But the river was sixty feet deep in spots and locals swore there were several vehicles down there, so you never knew.

In quick order, Maxwell and Hansen interviewed the Barkers, whose driveway the Bronco had pulled into in search of directions; Ken Fox of the Northwood; Paul and Beverly Pasternak at Walker's Bar and Bowling Alley; Steve Linker of Linker's Lost Creek Lodge; and Cindy Socia, who'd taken their orders for Bud and sicced her boss on them when Brian made a crack about kicking her ass.

Socia, who by then was working over at Hank's Bar in Algier, had something interesting for them to mull over. She had once worked with Dennis Gallop at a small manufacturing plant, maybe for three months. He was a weird kind of guy, she said, a loner, very quiet, kept to himself. She hadn't heard directly, but it was rumored that Gallop had told several people at the time that some guys from Detroit he knew were up, and he wished they'd leave.

WDIV's budget allowed for the hiring of a helicopter, which took Hansen, Maxwell and Smith on an extended search by air. They flew over all the spots where the Bronco had been rumored to be, including the southeast corner of Crawford County, the southwest corner of Oscoda County, the northeast corner of Roscommon County and the northwest corner of Ogemaw County. They flew southwest to Newaygo, too, and looked over the Hardy Dam and the Tyll family cabin. They were aloft four hours. They saw nothing.

In his report on November 7, Maxwell urged that the river behind Camp 10 Bridge be searched as soon as possible, cold water or no, by Michigan State Police divers. WDIV would be airing a special on the case and Hansen's trip and was going to establish a tip line, asking people to call either the Troy police, the St. Clair Shores police or the Michigan State Police Post in Northville.

A tip line by its very nature is an offer of hope to the families of the missing.

But the end of Maxwell's report of the trip showed he, for one, held out little hope:

> It is the opinion of the undersigned detective that all information leads one to believe that the two missing persons are still within the Mio/Luzerne/Roscommon area and have met with foul play.

It is a possibility that the vehicle is hidden out (barn, buried, etc.) or that a local has repainted it. It is unknown by undersigned how one would go about a search of a state forest area with so many miles of rough terrain in an attempt to locate the victims and/or the vehicle or both. Sheriff Smith from Oscoda County advised that the two missing are definitely still up in that area and met with foul play.

But it was officially Curtis Schram's investigation, now, and on the update he filed on November 9, he wrote, "This complaint is being reopened." If nothing else, he had a dive team to arrange for.

Hansen's TV show ran on November 9. The first week, three tips came in to the state police, none to Troy or St. Clair Shores. None of them amounted to anything. The second week, seven more tips came in and all were cleared without much effort.

The weekend of November 19, the State Police dive team went into the deep, cold waters behind the Camp 10 Bridge. Nothing.

15

THE BIG BREAK?

On December 8, 1988, eighteen police officers from a wide variety of jurisdictions gathered at the Flint Township Fire Hall for a meeting on the case. There had been dramatic movement. How dramatic, who knew? There had been other big moments in the case that had gone nowhere.

But just the size of this gathering and the jurisdictions involved were proof that Schram held hopes that this could be the real deal.

Other attendees included Howard Isham of the St. Clair Shores police; Phil Steele from Troy; Doug Halleck and Wes Hubers from the West Branch State Police Post; Garly Sheply from the East Tawas State Police Post; Jay Dorenbecker from the Flint State Police Post; Richard Anderson of the Washtenaw County auto theft unit in Ann Arbor; Maxwell; and Mark Porta of the Monroe Police Department.

Anderson began the meeting. He had an informant who claimed that he had overheard, in a bar in Wixom, a conversation that a certain J. R. Duvall had killed the two hunters and buried them in the woods. The bar was O'Shea's Tavern and the occasion was a birthday party. Duvall said he'd gotten into a fight in a bar, taken the hunters outside and shot them.

It was Anderson's guess that the Bronco had ended up in the possession of a South Lyon resident, north of Ann Arbor.

He'd been conducting a surveillance of the house in October and saw the Bronco, which had been converted into a short-bed pickup. It had the wrong plate on it, but you'd expect that it would.

The South Lyon guy had gotten the Bronco from a well-known "re-tag" guy up in the northern Michigan village of Kalkaska, who specialized in changing vehicle identification numbers or switching plates. The re-tag guy was in turn a good friend of J.R. Duvall.

Maxwell had done background checks on both J.R. and his brother, Coco. They were considered extremely violent. J.R., born on November 11, 1950, as Raymond Wilbur Duvall Jr., was living in South Branch. Coco was born February 26, 1952, as Donald Dean Duvall, and was living with J.R.

Others spoke in turn. Sheply knew the Duvalls personally and confirmed their violent natures. Halleck had been asked by Maxwell on November 29 to check out the Duvalls. He then got their mug shots from the Iosco County Sheriff's Department and showed them around the Mio area bars where the hunters had been seen. Some of the witnesses who'd seen the hunters thought they recognized the Duvalls, others did not.

The meeting had a certain feel to it, of traction at last.

PART 2
THE DUVALLS

16

TOUGH GUYS

J.R. and Coco Duvall were the two toughest, most fearful guys in the north woods, pack leaders in a clan of seven brothers who had attained what big-city reporters would describe as urban-legend status, never mind the lack of anything urban for miles around.

The family patriarch was Raymond Duvall Sr., who'd died in prison. The matriarch was Shirley. J.R. was also known as J. or the Bird. He had a crude "JR" tattooed on his left arm. Coco had a tattoo that said "COKE" on his right hand. Tommy was known as the Worm, the quietest of the bunch, but tough when need be. Frank was called Fin. Rex Wayne, known as Rexy, was 32 and at the time of the big police conclave was serving time for criminal sexual conduct with a friend's 15-year-old daughter. The two youngest brothers were Randy, a.k.a. Nin, born in 1961, and Kenneth Ray, a.k.a. Ed, born in 1964.

There was one sister, Charlene, known as Sissy.

The Duvalls were legends both up north and in the tough-as-nails town of Monroe, down near the Toledo border along the Detroit River. As kids they spent most of their time in Monroe, where other kids learned as early as elementary school to fear them. Their classmates' parents called them the Monroe Mafia.

J.R. got married as a teen-ager to a girl named Kate and went off to Vietnam. He didn't have to wait till 'Nam to shoot anyone. One day when he was 13, Raymond Sr. started stabbing his wife, so J.R. took aim and fired with a .22. Father and mother both survived. The authorities decided that Junior had acted in self-defense. It was one of those things they talked about in the family for years. Still do. Made J.R.'s reputation. If they were the Monroe Mafia, that's when he made his bones.

When he wasn't stabbing his wife, Ray Sr. was beating her. Family lore was, two of the boys were born with black eyes. "I'm glad the son of a bitch is dead," said a young Coco when he got the news.

J.R. finished his four-year stint as an MP, something law enforcement officers later would find a combination of baffling and highly ironic. Late in the 1970s, after giving birth to two sons, Kate divorced him. Her sister, Georgia, who married Coco, said J.R. was a different person when he came home from Vietnam. Who wasn't?

Georgia married Coco in 1970 and divorced him six years later, tired of his drinking and his fists. He broke her jaw the year they got married, her nose another time. The jaw wasn't his fault, he said. He was trying to hit her uncle and she just got in the way. He and his brothers were a pack, she said. "If you deal or fight with one, you deal or fight with all of 'em."

In adulthood, the Duvalls moved back and forth between the two extremes of Michigan culture, the blue-collar city where a job in an auto plant meant you'd made it, and the northeast woods of white and red pine, stands of oak, cedar swamps, few people and many deer. Some of them lived up north year-round. Others wintered in Monroe. Some called Monroe home, but spent much of the summers and every deer season up north.

J.R. and Coco were shining examples of evolution (or of intelligent design, if you thought the universe was Satan's idea), perfectly adapted to both of their worlds—they could steal cars, chop them into parts and have them sold in a day;

they could track deer and run trap lines and knew where the best hardwood was to chainsaw into loads of firewood; they could run salvage yards one week and poach all manner of fish and wildlife the next. They were good mechanics, roofers, welders and electricians who thought nothing of climbing a Consumers Power pole and rigging up a line to run free electricity down into their houses.

When asked years later what he did for a living in the 1980s, Coco answered, "Firewood and welfare."

Southeast Michigan is home to three or four million, depending on how large you define it. The Duvalls' northern base of Oscoda County had just 10,000 residents. The county seat of Mio was the nearest thing to a city, and it had just 2,016 residents according to the 2000 census, and likely fewer in 1985, when the hunters disappeared. It also had the only stoplight in the county.

Because of the lack of trains, Oscoda and the other counties of northeast Michigan were among the last areas in the Lower Peninsula to be settled. Mio wasn't founded until 1881 and was originally named Mioe, after the wife of one of the town's founders, Henry Deyarmond. Along the way, the "E" was lost.

It was a hardscrabble place for many. There was no industry, except for what folks euphemistically called "the tourist industry." Not much of an industry. Good if you owned a motel. Meant decent tips during summer for waitresses, during deer and snowmobile season for barmaids and bartenders. If you didn't work for the county, high-paying jobs were nearly nonexistent. Median household income in 2000 was just $26,831.

Mall citizens they weren't, but the Duvalls had status all right. J.R. and Coco were as ferocious and nasty as the wolverines Michigan claims as its state animal, though scientists doubt any wolverines ever trod its woods. They'd been drinking and brawling most of their lives. They poached deer and fish in all seasons in the forests and swamps that surrounded them, all the land bisected by dirt roads and firebreaks and two-tracks that usually kept them far away from prying eyes.

The bureaucrats who run the state's two-week deer season always refer to it euphemistically as "the harvest." Sounds more peaceful than "woods full of hunters firing high-powered rifles all day and hundreds of thousands of deer bleeding out over the snow or rotting leaves."

J.R. was a year-round harvester. He knew the woods the way some people know the way to work, and friends and family swore he killed a hundred a year—buck, doe, fawn, it didn't matter to him. One year, he hired on with Consumers Power to cut down trees or trim them with a chainsaw. Got pretty handy with one, good enough he started using a chainsaw to quarter his poached deer.

They weren't imposing, not visually—if you exclude the times when J.R. had just chainsawed a still-warm deer or a cow in half; then you might be a little put off by the coating of blood and viscera, bone chips, bits of fur.

At one of their Fourth of July pig roasts, it didn't look like the pig they were roasting was going to be enough for the crew that showed up. If typical, it would have included motorcycle gang members in their colors, the Highwaymen or the Penetrators or both, and all sorts of friends, relatives and neighbors. So J.R., Rex, Randy and their mom's boyfriend, James McBee, reportedly drove off down the road to a neighbor's farm. Someone shot a cow, and J.R. cut it in half with the chainsaw right where it fell, so they could drag it over to the road and wrestle it into the back of the Jeep.

They weren't big. Baths weren't a daily concern. They had scraggly beards and unkempt greasy hair that settled down on their shoulders. Coco was 5–5, a bit stocky at 165 pounds. J.R. was thinner, four or five inches taller. If you didn't know better than to mess with them, though, you'd soon learn the error of your ways.

Conservation officers for the DNR frequently targeted the Duvalls, largely without success, though Coco and J.R. had been part of a ring that was broken up temporarily and convicted of illegally selling salmon eggs in 1982. They sold fish, too, mostly out of season. They set out turtle traps in the cedar bogs and swamps. They cut wood and sold it by the face cord, paying down-on-their-luck friends $10 a day to help them, and the DNR folks figured a lot of that came illegally from state-owned land.

It was alleged J.R. and Coco stole cars and chopped them into sellable parts, and if locals knew anything or suspected anything, they kept it to themselves, either out of fear or out of the antipathy toward police and authority that runs in the blood thereabouts. One or two of the brothers owned legitimate junkyards off and on, and all of them were good at dismantling cars into parts they could sell or trade.

They weren't above legitimate work. They'd paint the occasional barn for someone, or put in fence posts for some farmer. They'd re-roofed some restaurants in the area. J.R. had bartended at Timber's Steak House in South Branch, where he doubled up as a very effective bouncer. Coco had a tow truck for years down in Monroe—some of whose owners even wanted to be towed—and fought the city for years over running a business out of his home.

At the time the police task force convened, both Coco and J.R. worked at the Union 76 station next to Timbers, a weathered little hole in the wall that served good food—and when you were done eating you might get to see one or another of the Duvalls duking it out with each other or someone else.

Coco's current live-in girlfriend, Connie Sundberg, worked there, too. One time, during one of her break-ups with Coco, Connie agreed to a date with the son of a local deputy sheriff. When the guy came by to pick her up, a couple of the Duvalls and one of their friends jumped him. The friend had a metal pipe and busted his head up good. The deputy sheriff came by later and raised holy hell over what they'd done to his boy, but no charges were ever filed. Deputy sheriff or not, it paid to be discreet when it came to the Duvalls.

J.R.'s live-in girlfriend at the time of the police meeting, Donna Loreen Meakin, in the midst of a divorce and pregnant by J.R., was Connie's sister. His girlfriend at the time the hunters went missing, Eileen Seitz, had left him by then, tired of the beatings. Eileen and J.R. used to live in an earthen home near Curtisville, almost a sod hut, the kind of thing you might have expected to see on the prairie in the mid-1800s, with dirt floors. It was surrounded by litter and junk and had quite a reputation in an area where reputations were hard to come by.

(Eileen's luck didn't get any better leaving J.R. She married Nelson Bolzman, who in 1994 was convicted of beating her to death and got sentenced to 18 to 30 years.)

Donna, who wasn't quite 24 when the task force met in early September of 1988, had known J.R. since she was 14, but hadn't moved into his trailer till the previous March. They wouldn't remain together long. Things started going downhill after the baby was born in March of 1989. He beat her up pretty badly one day in May, then over Labor Day weekend he got pissed off about something and dragged her through the mobile home by her hair. On September 16, while he was out fishing or drinking, or both, she packed up her things and the baby and got the hell out.

When the weather got bad up north, you could often find the Duvalls in Monroe. Most of the brothers at one point or another worked for Bentley's Nursery in nearby Belleville; Coco, Frank, Kenny and Tommy all worked there at the same time in the winter of 1989. The owner remembers mentioning once that she was having problems with her 1978 Ford Bronco, and Kenny told her he could get her a replacement at a very good price, which she took to mean stolen.

Up north, their yards were shrines to fenders, boat parts, refrigerator parts, old iron wood-burning stoves rusting at odd angles, rubber tires collecting water in the spring and breeding mosquitoes, mouse-chewed mattresses, dog shit, horse shit, cow shit, pig shit. Especially pig shit. God, those Duvalls loved their pigs. Rex's favorite pig lived in the house with him and Sharon. J.R. was known to pass out next to it on the bed.

One neighbor girl, who was 8 or 9 at the time, used to come over to play with Sharon's daughter, Nicole. She'd remember years later watching the Duvalls heading down the steps to the basement, hearing them fire up a chain saw, hear the motor revving up and down as the teeth did their work, then the brothers coming back up, white five-gallon plastic buckets dripping red, filled with raw meat they'd go out and toss to the pigs.

They were, said one law official, "three levels lower than *Deliverance*."

They lived in houses or shacks or little trailers. Some of the houses had dirt floors. In the winter, for those who hadn't fled to Monroe, winds howled through cracks in the walls or through dry-rotted window sills or through gaps in the putty that left the windows rattling and curtains wafting back and forth in front of the glass.

Congenitally quick with their fists, J.R. and Coco earned equal measures of fear and respect in the bars of northeast Michigan, around Mio and Luzerne and Curtisville and Rose City, where their exploits fueled drunken gossip. They'd show up at a bar and regulars would start thinking of ways to sneak out without being seen, wanting to bolt, but not wanting to give offense. Always a good idea with those guys to avoid eye contact and keep your voice down until you could judge what mood or state of intoxication they were in.

Even the cops trod lightly. Sheriff Doug Ellinger of adjacent Alcona County said if you pulled one of them over for something, you knew to call for backup, first.

It was a big family just counting the siblings, huge when you figured in all the McMullen first cousins, the second cousins, the children, the illegitimate children, the wives, ex-wives, girlfriends and ex-girlfriends. It was the kind of close-knit-by-blood family that, when a cousin was asked if he was a cousin on the mom's side or the dad's, he could very well answer, "Both."

17
FALLING APART

Cops learn early on in their careers not to fall in love with informants, and not to trust their information.

On December 15, 1988, Schram and State Police Detective Sergeant James Gavigan, of the state police's Western Wayne County Auto Theft Unit, met with Anderson's informant. Things were not quite as he had portrayed them.

For one thing, he hadn't overheard J.R. Duvall confess to anything. He knew the Duvalls, all right, but hadn't been at the celebration. Turned out it was a friend of his, Rocky Harmon, who said he'd overheard talk of murder. And the informant didn't believe any of it.

J.R. and Coco were tough as hell, very violent, but he had never seen them, or known of them, to carry guns or knives. They were brawlers who settled things with their fists. If Rocky said he'd heard J.R. say he shot someone, it was his opinion Rocky was full of it.

There was, however, a Ford Bronco, and the renowned "re-tag" man and a guy in South Lyon he had sold the Bronco to. It was a Bronco that had later had extensive work done to it. The wheels were changed, it was painted a different color, it was converted to a pickup.

But that part of the story began to break down, too. The guy who'd bought it lived in South Lyon with his employer.

The two officers interviewed the employer, Dewey Deckle, who told them that the South Lyon man was a whiz at fixing cars, that he had bought the Bronco from a guy up north for $1,300, then rebuilt the motor, put in a new crankshaft and bearings, a new tailgate and a new passenger door. As for the paint job, he had primed it and for a while it was a different color, but he repainted it the original silver.

He had it a month and resold it for $3,600.

A state police detective contacted the re-tagger's wife. She produced a pink copy of the title, showing it had been purchased from Boyce Motor Sales, a purchase confirmed by Boyce. The LEIN network produced a complete title history and everything was legitimate.

Schram's report of January 20, 1989, summing up the incident closed with:

> The vehicle is that of a 1978 Ford Bronco, not that of the 1980 Ford Bronco belong to the missing hunters. The vehicle in question at no time belonged to the missing hunters, nor was it in any type of possession by the Duvalls.
>
> No contacts will be made with the possible suspects, the Duvalls. Both Duvalls have extensive criminal histories. It is believed that no information will be gained by any type of interview with the subjects.

Another dead end in a maze filled with them. Or, maybe not. The "re-tag" man was off the hook on this one. It was the wrong Bronco. But they had two names of known up-north bad guys, now, and that was better than nothing. Just because they weren't known to go around shooting people with guns or stabbing them with knives didn't mean they were innocent of other dark deeds.

18

REWARD POSTERS AND
A BIG STORY

The case was officially open, again, but that didn't mean much, mostly just a brief monthly review and a one-line note in a report.

> 2/15/89—Reviewed. Pending any new information.
> 3/20/89—No new information. Check for informant. Nil.
> 4/19/89—Reviewed.

And so forth.

On August 14, Schram reinterviewed Detective Anderson's informant on the 1978 Bronco and the Duvalls.

The story had a big change from the last time he'd told it in December. This time he said he had been in O'Shea's Tavern in Wixom about two years earlier, and had heard J.R. telling family members about himself and his brother Coco getting into a fight with two deer hunters outside a bar and killing them. He didn't know where the bar was or what the Duvalls had used, but since then he'd heard other family members telling variations of the tale, too.

The informant told them that if anyone knew anything of value, it would be a guy named Raymond Metcalf, a good friend of the Hoffmans', related by marriage, who lived up in Kalkaska.

On September 7, Curtis Schram, Detective Sergeant James Gavigan and Detective Sergeant Bruce Gualtiere of the Kalkaska County Sheriff's Department met with Metcalf. He told them he knew J.R. and Coco well, but had had nothing to do with them in about fifteen years, and that they were heavily involved with drugs.

Hoffman told them that two or three years earlier, one of the Duvalls' cousins, Lonnie McMullen, was visiting him and said that J.R. had told him about killing some guy and feeding him to his pigs. He said he hadn't asked him more about it, and had no idea when it happened. And he said he knew nothing about any 1980 Ford Bronco.

Good news for the police: Hoffman's wife, Debbie, was Lonnie's sister. She was one of the Duvalls' cousins, too. Maybe she'd know more.

Debbie remembered the incident. She thought Lonnie was just bullshitting or joking and hadn't taken him seriously. Coco Duvall was very close with her sister, Susan Yonkin, who lived down in Florida. If anyone knew anything, it'd be Susan.

A couple of days later, Debbie called Schram. She'd called her sister in Florida, saying her kids had been arguing about details of something they'd heard Lonnie talking about a while back, something about J.R. and Coco feeding some guys to pigs. What'd she know about it? Was it true?

Susan told her it was. The story J.R. had told was that three or four years ago, he'd gotten drunk at some bar and was beaten up by five guys. J.R. had left and come back with Coco and someone else. Only two of the guys who'd beaten him up were still in the bar. They dragged them outside, beat them up, killed them and fed them to pigs. She didn't know what bar or what town.

What to make of it? No one had seen Tyll or Ognjan in a pack of five. Maybe the Duvalls had killed some other guys they didn't know about. Was it a dead end? Who knew? It was something they could keep picking at, see what developed.

On September 11, Schram and Maxwell met with a reporter from the *Detroit Free Press*, along with the Ognjans and the Tylls. The *Free Press* was doing a big piece recounting the mystery. In conjunction, a flyer had been made up offering a reward of $15,000 for information that would lead to the location of David or Brian. The flyers were being sent to the West Branch, East Tawas and Alpena State Police posts, as well as to the Monroe Police Department.

The flyers didn't mention J.R. or Coco, but the police were hoping they would get into the hands of people who knew them and who knew more about who they'd been fighting with, who they'd been bragging about killing.

There was nothing to do now but wait for the newspaper, which sold about 800,000 copies statewide during the week and nearly double that on Sundays, to hit the stands.

19
HEATING UP

The *Free Press* appeared on September 18, 1989, filling the yellow coin-operated boxes that were ubiquitous around the state. The flyers started going out and getting taped up or thumb-tacked up in police stations, post offices, bars, restaurants, gas stations and convenience stores.

And almost immediately the action began. It was what Schram had been hoping for.

On September 17, Schram got a call at home from the East Tawas post. One of their informants had something good on the Duvalls. The informant had provided good information in the past that checked out and was considered reliable.

He said he'd been at a party at a gravel pit near the Alcona Dam with J.R., Coco and members of the Highwaymen motorcycle gang. Everyone was drinking heavily. At one point, J.R. told the informant that he had killed two people and fed them to some hogs. And that their vehicle had been cut up and part of it rolled down the high banks above the dam into the water.

On September 21, the Michigan State Police dive team spent a long time searching two deep-water spots behind the dam, criss-crossing the waters methodically, but they finally gave up, convinced there was nothing there.

On September 22, another tip came in. Schram had wanted to rattle the Duvall family cage, and it was rattling big-time. This one, even given cops' long-ingrained mistrust of informants, in general, and the wasted dive just the day before, in particular, had a feel to it that resonated with Schram. Maybe because this informant was a woman.

He set up an interview. The informant said she had been at Shirley Duvall's house in November of 1985 when a call had come in.

J.R. was in trouble and needed the family's help. A little later, Coco and four others that she named grabbed some sticks and some knives and raced out. The problem was other informants would later tell nearly an identical tale, but with a different cast of characters in a different year.

At daybreak, they all returned. The informant saw them, but not closely. She didn't notice any blood on their clothing. She didn't hear any talk about what had happened.

Months later—around the Fourth of July in 1986—a family friend's pickup was seen with the front and rear axles of a Ford four-wheel drive vehicle and possibly the transmission, too. The parts had come from a guy over in South Branch.

The parts were then delivered and sold to another guy named Mike.

Best yet, said the informant, three days earlier, on the 19th, one of the Duvalls' wives had called her. The wife had seen one of the flyers asking for information. Seemed like they were everywhere. The wife said she had just talked to Coco, and he was warning the family "They better get ready because the police are coming after us." He was sure the cops would be asking friends and family about what they knew of the two men he and his brother had murdered. The implication was: Get your stories straight.

It was time to talk to as many family members as possible, see how straight the stories were.

20

THE EX-GIRLFRIENDS TALK

State Police Detective Sergeant Halleck of the West Branch post tracked down J.R.'s ex-girlfriend, Donna Sundberg, on September 23. She was the one who'd had a child by J.R. earlier in the year, gotten dragged around by her hair in one of his rages over Labor Day and had moved out just a week earlier.

It may have only been a week, but Donna wasn't letting the grass grow under her. She already had a new live-in boyfriend in Cheboygan, her sister's husband's uncle.

She told Halleck that right after the Labor Day weekend, J.R.'s mother's boyfriend, James McBee, had come by looking for J.R. He wanted to warn him that his brother Frank had just called to warn the family that cops down in Monroe were asking questions about the missing deer hunters.

A couple of other buddies stopped by and they talked long and loud about the hunters and the renewed investigation. One buddy called Cricket said no one could blame him, he was in jail at the time. At one point, J.R. seemed to make up an excuse to get Donna to go to the store—seemed to her he wanted her out so they could talk more freely.

Nonetheless, she'd heard some good stuff she was only too happy to pass on to Halleck. One of the lines she'd heard was "There's a snake in the woodpile," meaning, Donna thought, there was a stool pigeon out there talking. The cops seemed to know too much. They'd bandied about names for the snake—was it Red? No, couldn't be him. Could it be Eileen Seitz, J.R.'s former girlfriend? No, J.R. said, Eileen would know what'd happen if she talked. Could it have been Sharon Russeau, Rex Duvall's ex-girlfriend?

They knew someone had to be blabbing, because one of the cops, according to one of the many phone calls going back and forth amongst Duvall friends and family, had asked about a party at Sharon's back in 1985 or 1986, the one that had become a family legend. Donna didn't know the details—it'd had to do with someone challenging someone: "I'll bet you five bucks you won't kiss that pig's pussy"—but other than that, she didn't know.

Anyway, a day or two later, lying in bed together, Donna, wanting to find out more about what was going on, but not wanting to press too hard, joked with J.R., "You know, pigs don't eat skulls."

"If you don't shut up, I'll feed you to the pigs," he said.

As for missing cars, Donna said it was common knowledge some family members or friends used to bring cars up from southeastern Michigan to be cut up and sold off.

The next day, the Cheboygan State Police post called Halleck at home. Donna had come in and was nearly hysterical and needed to talk to him.

She was worried about her sister, Connie Sundberg, Coco's ex-girlfriend. Coco had a new girlfriend named Terri, and Donna had heard that Coco'd told Terri he thought Connie was shooting her mouth off, and he was going to kill her.

~

On September 25, Halleck interviewed Sharon Russeau. She'd moved to South Branch in 1981 with Rex and lived in a house on Curtisville Road with Rex, J.R., Eileen Seitz and the various kids the women had had by their boyfriends or previous partners.

She and Rex had broken up the previous year, with pretty good reason. On September 19, 1988, Rex had been sentenced to 36 to 42 months at the Southern Michigan Correctional Facility in Jackson, the world's largest walled prison, for criminal sexual misconduct with a 15-year-old girl.

Russeau was now living in Monroe and had a boyfriend named Richard Goode. Goode's ex-wife was now living with one of the Duvall brothers, Kenny. 'Round and 'round it went.

She said she'd been working at Timbers Steak House in 1985. That year, like all others, all the Duvalls and a lot of their friends were up for deer season, and drinking heavily on a daily basis. She said she had no direct knowledge of the missing hunters, but had heard tales of the brothers cutting up cars and disposing of parts. It was common knowledge, she said, that with J.R.'s knowledge of the local woods and swamps, he had no problem knowing where to go and hide things.

What about the party where somebody challenged someone to kiss a pig's pussy? Probably was at her house, she said. Over the years she'd kept many a pig out behind her house. In the mid-1980s, she'd had three sows that had at least three litters of pigs. The Duvalls were always out poaching deer, and they'd feed the remains to the pigs. What the pigs wouldn't eat, they incinerated.

She was always hosting pig roasts. The party where the line about kissing a pig's pussy entered the family lore was the same one where J.R. ate pig shit on a dare for $5, then passed out in the house next to where her pet pig was sleeping. When J.R. woke up, his face was down by the pig's genitalia. She thinks what happened was, one of the bikers had seen J.R. waking up and asked him if he'd kiss a pig's pussy for $5, too.

~

When Halleck made an appointment to talk to Eileen Seitz at her house in Cass City on September 29, she thought he wanted to talk about J.R. not making his child support payments. She'd broken up with him in 1984 and didn't have direct knowledge of any events the next year, but said he used to beat her up a lot and was capable of anything.

Stolen cars were always being cut up, she said. She remembered parts being buried in a hole behind their trailer, and she remembered them once setting fire to a car and then pushing it over the high banks and into the AuSable River.

Later, she called Halleck back. Her mother had reminded her of an incident she'd forgotten. It had been the evening of November 24, 1985. She had moved in with her mother in Cass City and her mother was having Thanksgiving a few days early. J.R. stopped by with Larry Sundberg. Both were very hungover. A day or two later, she was at Randy's house, and the Duvall brothers and some friends were sitting at a table.

"Just forget the subject and we'll never talk about it again," someone said.

Coco responded, "I know we're gonna get caught."

~

On September 29, Schram briefly talked by phone to Connie Sundberg, Coco's ex-girlfriend, who'd managed nine years with him before running off to Virginia with a construction worker. She remembered hearing about some fight the boys had gotten into over one of J.R.'s former girlfriends, but didn't know anything about any murders or a missing Bronco.

Schram reached Susan Yonkin down in Kissimmee, Florida, the same day. She told him Coco had told her about the fight in question and it was revenge for a beating suffered by J.R., but that no one had gotten killed. She'd been at O'Shea's, too, and hadn't heard any talk about murders or pigs.

Her husband, Tom Yonkin, said he'd heard rumors about the brothers killing some hunters, but didn't know anyone who'd have direct knowledge.

Also on the 29th, Schram called Lonnie McMullen in South Lyon. He said he'd heard through the grapevine that J.R. and Coco had supposedly killed some guys, but he had no direct knowledge of the hunters or the Bronco.

Emily Duvall, Frank's wife, said she'd heard rumors, but nothing more than that. Coco's current girlfriend said she hadn't heard a thing, didn't know anything.

21
FAILING THE TEST

On October 19, J.R. was arrested by state police on a warrant out of Alcona County for failure to pay child support. The arrest was pretext to pressure him into a lie-detector test, which he agreed to, and it was administered that day after a drive down to the State Police Crime Lab in Bridgeport, near Saginaw.

He said he was probably living in Curtisville in 1985, in a trailer across from the community center, but that when the hunters had gone missing, he was camped out in the woods, like he did every year, on a two-track that ran east–west just behind his trailer, and bearing the unlikely name of Trees for Tomorrow Road.

The only fight he could remember was one in Cass City, two guys beating him up when he'd started hitting Eileen. But by the time his brothers had gotten there, it was all settled and done and they just took him home. He was the only one to get beaten up.

He didn't know about any missing hunters. Didn't know about any Bronco.

Lieutenant Charles Allen administered the test. He called Schram after it was over. J.R. was lying, he said. He was either directly responsible for the incident, or at least involved.

◆ ◆ ◆

On October 25, Schram interviewed Rex Duvall, who was in the Carson City Temporary Correctional Facility, scheduled for parole in July of 1991 for the third-degree sexual misconduct felony involving a 15-year-old daughter of a friend.

I'll be happy to talk to you, said Rex. But you gotta get me out of here tomorrow.

Not possible, said Schram.

In that case, I know nothing, Rex responded.

Schram kept him on the line for the next hour. Duvall told him he was well aware of the investigation, that it was all the talk of the family. Rex told him he didn't think his brothers or anyone else had killed the hunters. Schram asked him if he'd ever reveal any information about his brothers if he had any. Never, said Rex.

On October 25, *Unsolved Mysteries* aired a segment on the case. Over the next six days, twenty tips were phoned in. On the last day of the month, headed toward the four-year anniversary of their disappearance, Schram wrote:

> *Most [of the tips] can be discounted. However,*
> *some tips will be investigated at a future date.*

One particularly interesting one came in on November 15 and took a while to investigate and figure out.

It was a tip from Kesterville, Texas, no phone number given. The tip said:

> *South Branch, Michigan. They were at the Timbers*
> *Steak House. There's a guy in jail named Russeau.*
> *They were murdered and fed by him to the*
> *hogs. David and Brian were murdered by this guy*
> *Russeau.*

At the time, the show didn't use any technology that could actually pinpoint where a call had come in from. First step was to find Kesterville. Turned out there wasn't any, at least not in Texas.

There *was* a Russeau in jail. Schram knew who he was. Knew he couldn't have been the killer. Schram was convinced, in fact, that the mystery caller was either one of his two prime suspects or someone they'd put up to it.

Keith Russeau was Sharon Russeau's son. Just a few weeks before the phony tip was phoned in, he had become one of the state police's best informants. He was in the Iosco County Jail on a B&E and sent word through his attorney that he wanted to talk. He knew a lot about the Duvalls, not just in relation to the hunters, but to a lot of other stuff they'd been up to over the years. The main reason Schram knew he couldn't have been the killer, though, wasn't that he was so cooperative. It was because he was only 18, then. At the time the hunters had gone missing, he'd have been 14, a little young for a double homicide. Probably not strong enough to feed a couple of adults to the hogs.

If it was the Duvalls who'd called in the tip, they obviously had good intelligence. They knew Russeau was talking.

22
CLOSING OUT THE YEAR

Not that he had any confidence it would do any good, but on November 1, Schram finally had his first talk with Coco Duvall. He'd been living out on East County Line Road in South Branch in 1985, he said. He was well aware of the accusations swirling around him, but was in no way responsible and didn't know squat.

Would he be willing to submit to a lie-detector test?

Not at any time, he said.

He did admit to frequenting a number of South Branch establishments, both in 1985 as well as now, including Timbers, McKinley's Bar, the All Seasons Party Store and Doug's Trading Post.

Meanwhile, Doug Halleck had gotten departmental approval to go down to Virginia to talk at length with Connie Sundberg. Her name kept being mentioned as someone who had to know more than she'd let on. She and her construction-working boyfriend were staying at the Best Western Hotel while he was on a job. It wasn't an interview Halleck thought should be done over the phone.

They got together during the early evening hours of November 8 and she recounted her tumultuous years with Coco.

They'd met during the deer season of 1979, when she was 16 and Coco was 27. She'd moved in with Coco in Monroe in

January of 1980, and in June they'd moved back north to the South Branch–Curtisville area, where they remained until the previous May, when she met and took off with John Brown.

Junked cars and pigs seemed to be constants of the Duvall brothers' existence. Coco always had dogs, chickens and calves running around, and often pigs, too. J.R. and Eileen always had pigs at the trailer and yard across from the Community Center in Curtisville, as many as thirteen at a time, and at least six.

Rex Duvall and Sharon Russeau had pigs, too. One lived in the house, some stayed in an old junk school bus behind the house and some lived in a pigpen.

J.R. fed his pigs any and everything—poached deer parts, fish, even small live animals like possums and raccoons. The pigs got such a taste for meat that people would joke that they were cannibals. She never heard about them feeding any people to their pigs, but it wouldn't have surprised her. Not in the least.

J.R. and Coco were both alcoholics. Coco would get plastered and beat Connie up, then pass out and have no recollection of how she'd gotten her bruises or cuts when he woke back up.

J.R. was a very heavy drug user, too, but Coco thought he'd had a heart attack once and was too afraid to use drugs anymore.

She didn't know about any specific fights that had caused the brothers to rally to J.R.'s cause, but she said various combinations of the brothers were always fetching each other in the middle of the night to go out and do who-knows-what. The Duvalls, she said, were in many, many bar fights over the years, usually over at Timbers. They always fought together and went to each other's aid.

As for cars, she knew of at least five different stolen vehicles that had been completely dismantled. The parts that couldn't be re-used or sold for junk were set afire or buried. Some of the frames had gone into a big hole they'd dug up and later covered at a neighbor's house. The back seat of one of the Blazers they "parted up" ended up decorating his porch for years. There were a lot of cars stolen down in Monroe and brought up.

It had been going on about as long as she knew them all. She said she remembered being 16 or 17 and watching her brother, who was a year older, just about dismantle a Blazer all by himself, using a big power saw with some kind of monster blade that did up about everything except the engine.

Halleck might want to look into some arsons-for-hire, too, she said.

One time a house J.R. was renting burned to the ground. The owner had ordered it torched, she said, and had given the money to an intermediary to pass on to J.R. A little while later, the house burned to the ground. It was all common knowledge in the family, she said.

When Halleck got back to Michigan, he looked up the police reports. One of J.R.'s residences had, indeed, burned to the ground in 1984. An investigation found it was likely arson, though no one had been arrested and the case was considered open. The insurance company had paid off.

A few days later, Sharon Russeau, who had been living with Rex Duvall at the time, confirmed the fire.

The more Halleck nosed around, the more people he found out who told the same basic story about the fire. On November 28, it was time to talk to the owner, who told him he'd heard all about this new investigation, that there'd already been an inquiry into the fire and he'd been cleared. He'd taken a lie-detector test administered by the Iosco County Sheriff's Department and had passed it. He did admit to giving the Duvalls money related to a fire, but only to purchase firewood.

The same day, Halleck got the report from the lie-detector examiner. The owner had taken a test, and it had come back inconclusive. He hadn't passed it. He'd been told he hadn't passed it. He was lying, now, to Halleck.

~

On November 27, just after the anniversary date of the disappearances, Schram interviewed an informant in Monroe who had offered up the information originally to Detective Lieutenant Dan Reed of the Monroe drug unit.

Reed's informant was living temporarily up north in Curtisville and had heard a couple of things since arriving there in October—one, that some guys named Duvall had been involved in the disappearance of the hunters they were looking for, and, two, parts of the missing Bronco were on a Bronco now belonging to a guy named Charles Essary, and that some parts likely could be found as well at the residence of a guy named Mark Beach in Rockwood.

The next day, wasting no time, two members of the Western Wayne County Auto Theft Unit found Essary's 1978 Bronco in a Ford Motor parking lot in Monroe. They got under the vehicle and were able to determine that all the parts were original, including the transmission and the transfer case.

On December 1, Schram interviewed Essary. He had, in fact, bought a transmission and transfer case, a front and rear axle and two drive shafts from Randy and Kenny Duvall in the spring of 1986, thinking they'd fit on his 1978 Bronco, but they hadn't. He'd held on to them for a year, then sold them to Beach. They hadn't come off a 1980 Bronco, though, they were from a 1979 model.

On December 12, Schram got Randy Duvall to agree to a lie-detector test, which was administered the same day. He passed it with flying colors, claiming he was not involved in the disappearance of Tyll and Ognjan, and, moreover, that he had no direct knowledge about it.

As for the Bronco parts, he was candid in an interview with Schram following the lie-detector test. Randy got a stolen 1979 Bronco from a guy in Monroe, either in the summer of 1984 or 1985, and he and Kenny had cut it up into parts out behind someone's place in the woods near North Branch. Some of the parts had been sold to a guy up there, some to a guy in Monroe, and the rest of the thing was dumped in a field and pond in Monroe. The car was brown or beige and had an automatic transmission.

Two days later, Randy took Schram to a field in Monroe and they found some of the vehicle's remnants.

On December 11, Schram interviewed Allen Snedegra, a swine expert at the Department of Agriculture at Michigan State University. Two grown men getting fed to pigs? Well, he supposed if you had five or six big pigs, and you hadn't fed them for a few days, they could consume two men in three or four days. They wouldn't do it faster because, unlike cows or horses—and, despite their reputation—pigs will only eat so much before stopping.

It would be highly unusual for them to eat bones, either. And having eaten human flesh, it would take them about seventy-two hours to excrete it.

~

It was back to interviewing more cousins and in-laws, focusing on the party at O'Shea's Tavern in Wixom in October of 1986.

The same day he got the lowdown on swine, Schram interviewed three attendees.

Charles McMullen Jr. said he knew what was being said about the boys, but he hadn't heard anything that night at the bar. He did say, though, that his sister, Susan Yonkin, had told him both J.R. and Coco had confessed to her that they'd killed the missing hunters and gotten rid of their truck. And he said his brother-in-law, Tommy, had told him J.R. had told the same story to him.

Connie McMullen said she didn't hear anything at the bar, but then, she'd spent most of the night out on the dance floor and out of range of any conversation.

Tammy Harmon, Connie's sister, said she was at the bar, but she didn't hear anything. She spent most of the night out on the dance floor, too.

Her husband, Lloyd, known as Rocky, was at the bar, as far as he knew, the only sober one. He and his wife took turns drinking on nights out, so one of them would be street-legal on the ride home. Lloyd didn't hew to the family line. He hadn't danced the night away, either.

Harmon said J.R. and Coco had started talking about killing the two hunters, "right out of the clear blue." He took

J.R. seriously, didn't think it an embellishment or bullshit just to impress. And he was sure others at the long bank of tables they'd pulled together had heard it, too.

The string of reports for December ended with one short, understated paragraph, one that had huge implications.

Under the heading "ADDITIONAL INFORMATION," *Schram typed:*

> *Undersigned officer is currently involved in the Grand Jury in Oakland County concerning the missing hunters. Testimony has taken place on 12/5, 12/12 and 12/14 concerning the disappearance of the two men. Additional testimony will be conducted in the future.*

A grand jury? They could be fearsome things even for sophisticated types knowledgeable of the legal system. For a bunch of north-woods miscreants? Obviously the system was ratcheting things up a few notches. The way some members of the extended Duvall family had aleady started singing under Schram's recent pressure, it seemed inevitable a grand jury would have a chorus going quickly into the new year. Indictments couldn't be far off. That was one thing Schram was sure of as the 1980s gave way to the last decade of the millennium.

Under the standard last line of his reports, the one saying "COMPLAINT STATUS," Schram no longer had to decide whether to call it closed or open. That was at least one sign of progress, a big one.

"Open, pending further investigations," he typed.

23
LIE DETECTORS AND PIG FOOD

Schram got another Duvall to take a lie-detector test on January 2, 1990. Kenneth Duvall was only 25, more than a decade younger than his notorious older brothers. He told Schram before the test that he was close with his brother Randy, but wasn't close at all with either J.R. or Coco.

He said he wasn't up north in 1985 and knew nothing about the missing hunters or their vehicle. The lie-detector test confirmed it. On the way back to Monroe after the test, Ken told Schram he had asked his brothers a couple of months ago, when this latest round of investigation began, what was going on, and they both claimed they had no idea. He said he didn't want to know, didn't want to be involved in their business and if he did know anything, he wouldn't tell the police, anyway. At least he was being honest.

The next day, Schram met with Gerald Drewior Jr. at the Monroe police station. An informant had said Drewior might have been there when the hunters were killed. He hadn't been part of their murder but had helped get rid of the bodies.

Drewior said it was all a pack of lies being spread by J.R. and Coco, trying to shift the blame. He said he was up north for deer season in 1985 and likely was at Shirley Duvall's when the hunters went missing, since that was where he often stayed when he was up north, but he knew nothing about the hunters or the car.

He, too, said he would take a lie-detector test. He'd take one, he said, even though Coco had told him at least twice not to take any lie-detector tests and that the police couldn't make him.

On January 4, Drewior took and passed his test. After the test, Drewior told Schram he had a pretty good tidbit for him. Three or four years earlier he had been at Rex Duvall's house up north, near the pigpen, when out of the blue Rex said, "Wouldn't that be something to put two people in there for the pigs to eat?"

(In August of that year, his father, Gerald Drewior Sr., 64, passed out and choked to death, his blood alcohol count at .31. In July of 1996, Jr. would be struck by a train in Monroe and die at age 40.)

24
WEIRD AND WEIRDER

It was a frustrating investigation because it hadn't turned up Tyll or Ognjan, either alive or dead. It hadn't led, so far, to any arrests or indictments. But Schram would never be able to say it was boring. It was getting to where not a day seemed to go by without something else popping up you'd never find in any police manual.

Take Dolly Duvall, for instance. She'd been married to Frank Duvall and had four children by him, but had the good sense to divorce him after he got incarcerated.

When Schram interviewed her on January 3, she was living in Monroe with Billy Price. Price at one time had been married to Sissy Duvall, who had been Dolly's sister-in-law before she divorced Frank. Enough to make Schram's head hurt trying to keep track of it.

Anyway, Duvall told Schram she'd heard all the rumors about J.R. and Coco killing those two hunters, and she had no doubt at all the rumors were true. She'd just recently heard in a bar, in fact, that the victims' heads had been cut off and J.R. and Coco had drunk their blood before disposing of the bodies.

If she or Billy heard anything, don't worry, she'd let him know. Neither one of them had any use for J.R. or Coco, and he wouldn't have to worry about her withholding any information that came her way.

No doubt.

Billy had a different story to tell, though, on January 9. It was one of nine interviews with various Duvalls, their in-laws or friends that the hardworking Schram conducted that day. Billy, who was 33 at the time, told him he had known J.R. and Coco for twenty–twenty-five years and that if he had any information, he sure as hell wouldn't share it with the cops.

However, he said, he had heard from a woman named Opel Sams that J.R. was shooting his mouth off about the killings. Schram ought to go talk to her. And he did.

Sams told him she'd been leaving a bar one night around Thanksgiving of 1989 just as J.R. was walking in. Later she was told that J.R. had been overheard bragging about being involved in killing the two hunters. But she couldn't remember who in the bar had told her.

~

On January 9, Schram interviewed J. R. Duvall. Not *the* J.R., but his 17-year-old son, J. R. Wilbur Duvall, a.k.a. Doobie. Doobie was interviewed in Monroe County Youth Home, where he was being held on criminal sexual assault and other charges.

He said he'd been living with his dad in 1985 and knew nothing about the hunters and never saw the Bronco.

As for tough Duvalls, his dad and Coco weren't so tough, he said, not compared to Rex.

He said he hadn't had any contact with his dad in more than six months. Coco was the one he was close to.

(In 1998, Doobie would become a homicide suspect. A body was found on the railroad tracks in Monroe, an apparent suicide victim. But a cellmate of Doobie's, who was once again in jail on one charge or another, told police Doobie claimed to have killed the man, and they'd covered it up by placing his body on the tracks. Doobie failed a lie-detector test. Later, the informant, wearing a wire, captured Doobie on tape talking about having violent streaks that he thought were caused by the way he was treated as a child. He said he had been raped by a male relative when he was little, was into drugs by 11 and that his family was straight out of *Deliverance*. But he didn't say anything incriminating and he was never charged.)

~

Next, Schram talked to Doobie's 15-year-old brother, Tom. He said he was very close with his brother and that they'd talked the whole situation over. Tom thought his brother might have more information than he was letting on.

Tom told Schram that Doobie had told him one time that if their father did kill someone, he certainly would be capable of killing someone else.

What do you think he meant by that? Schram asked.

That Doobie was scared. That if he ever said anything, his dad would come and get him.

~

Also early in January, Schram got a call from Andre Huybrecht, who worked at the Franklin Life Insurance Co. office in St. Clair Shores. Franklin Life was still carrying a $25,000 life insurance policy on Brian Ognjan. It was still in effect, and the premiums were continuing to be paid, every month, like clockwork, from an address in Florida.

Huybrecht was sure it was Brian Ognjan himself who was making the payments. He was alive and well.

Schram got a return address that turned out to be an apartment in Deltona. There was an Ognjan there, all right. Two of them. Mr. and Mrs. Ognjan were there for the winter. They told Schram they were indeed continuing to pay for their son's policy; in the event he ever returned, he could cash it in and use the money to go to college.

25

ANOTHER EX-GIRLFRIEND

There seemed to be no end to ex-girlfriends and no end to their tales.

On January 5, Vaughn Cobb, a 63-year-old temporarily wanting for transportation, was hitchhiking east out of Curtisville. J.R. pulled over, picked him up and accelerated away.

It wasn't a courtesy stop he'd made, however. He told Vaughn that Donna Holbrook, Cobb's stepdaughter, was running her mouth too much at the bar and she'd better learn to keep it shut.

Four days later, another friend of hers warned her that J.R. was offering a bounty to anyone who would beat her up. That she hadn't yet been assaulted probably was a reflection of the sum J.R. was offering—$20.

The next day, Donna called the state police. She'd heard, she said, that her ex-boyfriend, J.R., had taken a contract out on her life.

Halleck raced over to her stepfather's house in Curtisville to see what *that* was all about. They'd only dated two months, Donna said, from the end of October to the end of December. J.R. had warned her then not to talk to a neighbor named Bobby, one of his former friends whom he suspected of being a snitch for the cops.

Donna not only talked to Bobby, she told him what J.R. had said, and of course it got back to J.R.

Knowing J.R., she didn't trust that his desire to have her beaten wouldn't escalate into something far worse.

On January 11, Halleck called Donna Sundberg in Cheboygan, working his sources, seeing if anything had developed. Coincidentally, it had.

A few days earlier, J.R. had been by her house, dropping off their son, Ryan. As often happens with those kinds of drop-offs, the two former lovers made small talk for a few minutes, J.R.'s definition differing from the standard. He told her Donna Holbrook had been shooting off her mouth.

Donna, he said, I'll give you $20 if you beat her up.

Donna refused.

J.R. did the sensible thing: He upped the offer to $50.

She still said no.

26
LOOSE LIPS

They sink ships, and the loose lips of the Duvalls' friends and relatives kept Schram hopping in February as the grand jury, whose term was for six months, conducted its secret business in parallel with him. They were talking to a lot of the same people he was, presumably getting better, truer information under threat of perjury.

On January 30, Schram interviewed Larry Asher, one of Coco's seemingly endless supply of drinking buddies.

Two weeks earlier, Coco had been over with another friend drinking beer. As Coco got drunker, he started talking about the damned police investigating him for killing those hunters. Up till then, Asher was pretty sure all the talk was just that. For all their wild-ass ways, he didn't think J.R. and Coco had killed anyone. Disposed of a car? No problem. But murdered two guys and fed them to pigs? Didn't ring true.

Coco told him that Lonnie McMullen had been picked up and questioned. Waste of time, Coco said. Lonnie didn't know anything. He didn't know, for instance, that the bodies and their car were in a lake up in South Branch. Or maybe he said it was a river. Anyway, under water.

Coco said there'd been a tiff in a bar, five guys beating up J.R. J.R. had left, gotten Coco and some other backup and returned. By then, only the two hunters were left. The brothers had hauled their asses outside and beaten 'em to death.

Asher told Schram he hadn't asked which lake or river it was. Next time he saw J.R., he'd try to get it out of him. If he did, he'd get back to Asher.

It was a recurring theme. J.R. beaten up by a gang, retribution paid back on two of them. It didn't fit what they knew, though. Ognjan and Tyll hadn't been with anyone else, had they? None of the sightings they relied on had included three others. People had seen Brian and David getting drunk, even a bit rowdy, but nothing close to fisticuffs or beating up on a single target.

Were there two separate incidents that had gotten conflated over the years? Was there another couple of guys the Duvalls had done in that the police didn't know about?

~

The next day, a cop with the Warren P.D. called Schram to let him know that one of his informants had told him that he hunted up in South Branch every year. Last year, he was hunting with a buddy who lived up there who told him the hunters had been killed by Coco and four other men who the informant named. Unfortunately, it was a different four "others" from the ones Schram's earlier informant identified.

And the Bronco was in a pond in Plainfield Township.

Schram had to wonder: Was there anyone who hunted in the Mio area who didn't have an opinion on what pond, stream, lake, river or creek the Bronco was immersed in? Who didn't know which bridge or dam it was under? Who didn't know which combination of north-woods shitbags named Butch or Jake had helped Coco and J.R. do the deed?

Apparently not.

~

In 1990 there was only one scrapyard in Monroe, bearing the fancier-than-it-deserved name of the Magniment Corp.

On February 6, Schram checked its records for activities by the Duvalls there at the end of 1985, the beginning of 1986. From December 25, 1985–February 2, 1986, Kenny Duvall had scrapped five cars. He'd also scrapped two radiators, a motor, something just described as "scrap iron" weighing 860 pounds and something else described as "scrap iron" weighing 2,760 pounds.

From January 1–May 23, 1986, Randy Duvall had scrapped 6½ cars, a motor, a radiator and something else described as "shreddable" weighing 2,060 pounds.

J.R. had scrapped something described as "cast iron" that weighed 1,260 pounds.

Drewior had scrapped three cars.

A worker told Schram that if employees could see a VIN number, they were supposed to record it and send it to the secretary of state's office in Lansing. Sometimes they did.

But he said if the vehicle was cut up or all bent up and battered, no one was going to make an effort to get the VIN number off the motor or frame.

Types of vehicles were not recorded. They could have scrapped fourteen Broncos for all Schram knew. What he didn't know, yet, was that one of the Duvalls' uncles had helped run the place in 1985 and 1986, James (Mike) McMullen. Later, they'd ask McMullen if he thought J.R. or Coco were capable of murder. "No, they were always good kids," he'd said.

~

As February passed the halfway mark, Schram finally ran out of Duvalls, Duvall cousins, Duvall in-laws and Duvall drinking buddies to interview.

His last interview was with Charles McMullen Sr., the boys' uncle, who was married to Shirley Duvall's sister, Joyce.

On February 15, McMullen told Schram he had heard all the rumors, but had no direct knowledge of anything. He'd been in O'Shea's Tavern, all right, but didn't hear Coco or J.R. telling anyone anything about the hunters or their car.

He also told him that if he did know anything, he wouldn't tell him, anyway.

The episode of *Unsolved Mysteries* aired in February. It resulted in eight new tips. None of them panned out.

The rest of February and all of March, Schram worked on his active caseload. He'd followed up every angle he could think of, shaken all the trees, interviewed all the nuts that fell out, had learned more about the geography of northern Michigan than he'd ever imagined.

It was time to give it a break.

~

Detective Sergeant Halleck got one of his more interesting tips on February 27, in a phone call from Sharon Roque in New Jersey. She'd had a premonition, she said, about the missing hunters. She said she was a well-known psychic and had been contacted from friends of the hunters' families to help solve the mystery.

The image she was getting was of David killing Brian during a lovers' quarrel, and that he probably had fled to the Michigan town of Hobart. She had checked, and there was a Steven Tyll living there.

It turned out she was at least right about Steven Tyll. He did live in Hobart. He was a distant relative of David Tyll. He seemed cooperative. He claimed no involvement or knowledge.

~

The lengthy investigation into the disappearance of Tyll and Ognjan finally began to pay off on March 14.

Based on new information Halleck had dug up, J.R. and Randy Duvall were arrested on March 14 and charged with three counts of arson involving the 1984 burning of the house J.R. had rented.

27
THE MOLE

On April 5, Schram got a call from Detective Lennie Boguicki of the Monroe County Sheriff's Department. He had an informant who had told him that Emily Duvall, Frank Duvall's wife, had not disclosed all she knew in her recent testimony before the Oakland County Grand Jury. She'd told them she didn't know where the bodies were. But supposedly, she did know something.

The next day, Schram, Boguicki and Detective Mark Porta of the Monroe City P.D. talked to her at the sheriff's office. They worked her hard. With great hesitation, she admitted she hadn't told the whole truth. She didn't know where the bodies were first-hand, but she did know something. She knew what Frank had told her the previous fall, that Coco had told him that the bodies were buried one on top of the other.

It was Frank's turn for a grilling. He finally admitted he'd lied to the grand jury, too. It was after Thanksgiving, before Christmas, he was over at Coco's trailer. Coco was worked up about the investigation, drinking heavily. At one point, he said, "Cops are so dumb. If they find one, they'll find the other body right underneath."

A bunch of guys were there. All of them had heard Coco, including Tommy and Kenny, he said.

He told them that back in 1985, he'd gotten a call in prison, couldn't remember if it was Riverside or Northside, one of the two, but he'd gotten a call from Randy, or maybe it was his mother. J.R. had gotten in a fight with a motorcycle gang and got his ass whipped.

Schram looked into it. Turned out Frank was in Riverside from January 20, 1983, through June 11, 1985, then spent the next month at Northside. If J.R. got beaten up while Frank was in one or the other, the hunters couldn't have been involved. Seemed like J.R. had done nothing else but get beaten up by groups back in '85.

Schram and Assistant Oakland County Prosecutor Larry Bunting called Rex Duvall in jail on June 13 to try to convince him to appear before the grand jury. They reminded him of his last offer to Schram the previous fall, that he'd tell what he knew if they'd spring him from prison the next day.

There was no such request by Rex this time. He said he must have been lying earlier, since he didn't know anything except what Schram had told him. None of his family or friends had ever told him anything about any hunters.

He also said he wanted an attorney and said he'd decided he would take a lie-detector test.

On June 18, Rex was allowed to leave the Mid-Michigan Correctional Facility so he could take a polygraph. Two days later, he was scheduled to appear before the grand jury.

Examiner Richard Torongeau jumped the gun on the exam. State police policy required three rounds of questions before a determination of lying could be made. After round two, it was Torongeau's opinion that Rex was lying and did, in fact, have some knowledge of the hunters' disappearance. The fourth question in round two was, "Did you help dispose of Brian and David's bodies?"

He answered, "No."

When he was done with round two, Torongeau asked him if he could remember the first question. He did, and repeated it accurately. The same with questions two and three. What about question number four?

"Did I help bury the bodies of the missing hunters?" said Rex.

"I never said anything about the bodies being buried," said Torongeau.

Rex flared up, told him he was done taking any tests and wanted a lawyer.

The test had to be stopped. Because the third round of questions went unasked, Torongeau had to mark the test as incomplete.

On June 20, the grand jury, which had started its work on December 5, heard its last witness. Members had heard hours of conflicting testimony about bar brawls, pigs, motorcycle gangs, various lakes and ponds, all manner and color of Broncos, names of various supposed accomplices with a wide range of colorful nicknames. They'd heard half-truths, truths and bald-faced lies. But which was which?

~

Witnesses weren't the only ones lying. The authorities had lied, too, inadvertently, when they promised Connie Sundberg that her testimony before the grand jury would be confidential.

Among other things she told the grand jury was what she'd told Halleck about arson for hire.

Soon after her testimony, on April 28, she was back up north in South Branch at her dad's place. Sherm (the Worm) Heilig, a long-time buddy of the Duvalls and a long-time suspect as an accomplice in the hunters' disappearance, had shown up knocking at the door.

He told her that he'd been downstate and a guy he knew had opened up the trunk of his car and gotten out some papers from his briefcase. They were, said Heilig, copies of grand jury transcripts. He said he had read them. In case she thought he was bluffing, he described in perfect detail the sequence of events she'd told the grand jury.

Heilig left. Connie, of course, freaked out. She called the state police in near hysterics, scared and mad. If Heilig knew, the Duvalls knew. She'd been promised anonymity, she'd co-operated to the fullest and this was the payback. They might as well have drawn a goddamn target on her back.

The Duvalls had a mole deep inside the Oakland court system.

28
WHAT TO BELIEVE?

Thirty-six witnesses testified. Here's some of what jury members heard:

Connie Sundberg said Coco had drunkenly told her one night, "We killed them."

Rocky Harmon said he'd overhead J.R. and Coco tell family members at O'Shea's that they had killed the hunters.

Rodney Sundberg said that J.R. had said at a party that a good way to get rid of bodies was to feed them to pigs.

Lonnie McMullen said he'd heard from two of J.R.'s friends that J.R. had admitted killing the hunters to them.

Donna Sundberg said J.R. had threatened to feed her to pigs when she asked him what he and his friends had been saying one night about the hunters.

Eileen Seitz, another of J.R.'s ex-girlfriends, said she'd seen Randy Duvall driving a Bronco the weekend the hunters disappeared. Once she heard J.R. and Coco talking, and one of them said, "I know we are going to get caught."

Gerald Drewior said Rex had once told him, "Wouldn't it be something to feed people to pigs?"

Larry Asher said Coco had told him once that J.R. had been beaten up by five guys, but Coco and J.R. had later jumped two of them and beaten them to death, chopped one of them up and fed them to the hogs. And another time,

Coco said if they went fishing in a particular spot, they'd be near the Bronco.

Jody Duvall said she was at Shirley Duvall's up north the weekend the hunters went missing. Rex called and said J.R. had been in a fight and needed help. She thought Coco and four others she named had gone to Cass City, armed with knives, and returned early the next morning. It was a variation of a familiar story—the "others" changing from witness to witness. The location now Cass City instead of Mio.

Emily Duvall said she and other family members had been in Timbers over Thanksgiving of 1989. Coco saw a poster of the missing hunters and said, "They deserved it." And that she'd been told by Frank that Coco had told him they'd buried the hunters.

Ken Duvall said they'd gotten a call from Rex saying J.R. had been beaten up by five or six motorcyclists. They drove for an hour and a half to Caro, but when they got there, J.R. was sitting on a curb. He didn't look as if he'd been beaten up. He said he was okay. They went to a coffee shop, bought cigarettes, got some gas and drove home. They didn't see anyone or fight anyone.

Randy Duvall said J.R. had been in a fight with two guys. The brother drove to Cass City to help him, but when they got there, he was sitting on a curb, looking okay. They took him back to Shirley's.

Tommy Duvall told Randy's story, almost in the same words.

Shirley didn't know anything.

Glen Lumpkins said he was at Rex's house when J.R. had called, saying he'd been in a fight in Cass City. They gathered up the family and drove over there in Randy's black Blazer. When they got there, J.R. was on the sidewalk with his sleeping bag. The round-trip took three hours. They stopped at a restaurant, got coffee and doughnuts and got back to Rex's about 6:30 a.m.

Frank Duvall said they'd been drinking one night when Coco told everyone that cops were dumb and "If they find one body, they will find the other one underneath."

J.R. Duvall said there was no fight in Cass City, that he might have gotten pushed by someone, but that was all. He denied saying what others were reporting he'd said.

Coco Duvall said J.R. got beaten up by five guys down at Eileen's place and complained the day after about sore ribs. He denied saying any of the incriminating statements others claimed he'd made.

Rex Duvall said he wanted a lawyer. A week later, he reappeared with one. He said the call about the fight was in 1986 or 1987. He said J.R. had been in a fight in Caro with his ex-girlfriend's boyfriend and two others and he needed to be picked up to avoid further trouble. Rex, Glen, Randy, Kenny and Coco drove to Caro in Kenny's car. They found J.R. on the sidewalk, went to a coffee shop, got doughnuts and coffee and drove home. He denied making any statements about pigs, and said he'd lied to Schram in order to get out of prison.

All in all, a pile of horseshit. The grand jury told Assistant Oakland County Prosecutor Brian Zubel that it didn't have enough to issue indictments. If and when any concrete evidence was found—whether it was the bodies or identifiable body parts of Tyll and Ognjan, or car parts that were conclusively from the Bronco, or an actual eyewitness willing to talk—indictments would be issued. Until then, nothing.

It was a sad commentary that Schram waited nearly six months, till December 4, to write a report about the end of the grand jury.

"It would certainly appear that after all testimony, that indictments are certainly possible should any type of evidence be recovered at any future date," he wrote, trying to put a happy face on a bitter disappointment, the cup being one-twentieth full and not nineteen-twentieths empty.

At the end of 1989, it had seemed sure indictments would be forthcoming. By the end of 1990, none had been issued, none were forthcoming. J.R. and Coco were free to keep on poaching deer, scrapping cars, brawling and drinking.

29

GRASPING AT STRAWS?

Four Point Productions out of California taped some of the principals, including the Tylls and the Ognjans, for a nationally syndicated TV show, *Missing: Reward*. Schram didn't hold out much hope, but *Unsolved Mysteries* had generated a few good leads and maybe this show would, too.

It was scheduled to have its first airing in Traverse City over Labor Day weekend and to run on other local stations around the state and around the county in the tail end of 1990 and the early part of 1991.

By mid-October calls were coming in from all over. A mountain man named Brian in California who only came in to town to wash laundry matched Tyll's description, said a caller. An Iowa man had seen black Bronco parts on a trail near Mio when he was in Michigan the previous June. A guy calling himself Thomas who looked like Tyll was living in South Carolina.

A guy in Washington State called to say a Brian he played ball with was the Brian they were looking for. Unfortunately, his Brian had been playing ball with him since 1980 and was 6–2 and 200 pounds.

A woman in Minnesota saw Brian eating at an Old Country Buffet the day before the show aired in St. Paul, but he had gained a lot of weight. A caller from Pittsburgh said Tyll was working at the airport there. A caller from Desert Shores, California, called to say Brian was working out there, but his eyes were blue, now, not brown.

And many more of the same. Nothing panned out.

Schram seemed almost obsessed to keep the investigation moving by trying just about anything.

He asked the Ognjans about what jewelry Brian might have been wearing. A Timex watch. No rings. He asked his dentist about dental records. Yes, he still had them. What about X-rays? Brian had broken his right ankle. St. John Hospital in Detroit still had them.

He called the Tylls. David had never broken a bone. No X-rays. He called his ex-wife. He didn't wear a watch. He didn't wear rings.

What was that about? An informant, given a number in the reports instead of a name, 89-02, had reported that he'd heard from several sources about a brother and sister, Sherm and Katie Heilig, who had buried the hunters on their property, and had helped submerse the car in Alcona Pond, a sizable lake, despite its name, formed by the Alcona Dam.

Schram arranged a sting. On November 29, the informant went to the couple's house, wearing a wire and a transmitter, and pretended he was pissed at his girlfriend's ex-husband and wanted him dead.

"Would you have room to bury him with the others on the property?" the informant asked.

"Yes, we do," Katie was allegedly recorded as saying. The grave would have to be deep enough so the dogs wouldn't dig it up, she reportedly said. You'd have to make sure the bodies didn't have any metal to set off any metal detectors.

Sherm Heilig, one of the Duvalls' best friends, whose name had come up repeatedly as someone who had either taken part in the hunters' disappearance or knew what had happened, was a knowledgeable woodsman, so much so in fact that he worked freelance as a scout for Maple Ridge Hardwoods of Sterling, helping the firm find suitable trees for its veneer and other products. Maple Ridge paid him $21,000 in 1988 and

$23,000 in 1989 for his expertise, a lot of money for part-time work scouting around through the woods.

Heilig had been questioned before and, denying any involvement or knowledge, had taken a polygraph on October 27, 1989. He'd come down to the Bay City post to have it administered, telling Halleck he had all the time in the world and would use the trip down to visit a brother who lived in the area. But two hours into the test, he said he had to get going, that he hadn't realized it would take that long and had made other plans.

The results were inconclusive, though Heilig admitted he'd camped with the Duvalls during deer season of 1985.

At the time the tip had come in, Heilig was being investigated by the State of Michigan's Tax Fraud Division. Halleck started calling area police and sheriffs' departments to see what they knew about him. He found out Heilig had been arrested in Oscoda County for leaving the scene of a personal injury accident in 1974 and had been jailed in Iosco County in 1985 for operating under the influence and having a loaded firearm in a motor vehicle.

On November 1, Halleck reinterviewed Heilig, who reiterated his ignorance of anything relating to the hunters. Halleck told him he had until November 9 to get back with Treasury agents on the tax matter or an arrest warrant would be issued. Heilig ignored the deadline.

~

Near the end of his five-page report of the year, Schram wrote up his best guess of what had happened to the hunters. On November 24, 1985, he had them in a bar in Mio, then heading over to Timbers in South Branch. There, they'd gotten into an argument and been killed either in the parking lot or down the road.

He wrote that he believed the informant who'd said the bodies were buried somewhere on the Heiligs' thirty-eight acres. But there wasn't much he could do about checking it out. The parcel of land was too big and too dense with trees and bushes to walk through it all, for one thing; for another, he'd need to get permission, which wasn't likely.

One state cop he knew told him there was an officer with the Cook County Sheriff's Department who was an expert at taking and interpreting aerial photographs. Maybe they could do a flyover. But the Cook County cop, he found out, had moved to Oregon and no one in Cook County or the Illinois State Attorney's Office could give him any leads on where to find someone else.

On the last line of his report for 1990, under "STATUS," Schram wrote—Optimistically? Out of habit? A bulldog, refusing to give up?—"Open, pending further investigation."

30

BY SEA AND BY AIR

It ate at Schram that those bodies might be out there, right where he was told they were, and there was nothing he could do to check it out. He kept in touch with informant 89-02, who was still trying to dig up new information. The informant had even told the Heiligs the cops knew what they'd been involved in, trying to rattle them, see if he could get them to talk about it.

Technology might help. Schram started asking around dive shops and found out there were two businesses in the state that rented out magnetometers to divers to help them find treasure. The treasure the state police dive team had been looking for off and on in various lakes and rivers was a Ford Bronco, not pieces of eight. The next body of water to search was Alcona Pond, which was murky and swampy, with little visibility.

The cost for the device, known as a JW Fishers Mfg. Inc. Proton 2 magnetometer, was $200 a day. It was a torpedo-shaped sensor about six inches in diameter and four feet long and could be towed up to 16 miles an hour at depths of 200 feet. They'd need one for about five days. Schram had no budget for it, but the Tylls and the Ognjans agreed to put up $500 each. In April he reserved the device for May 5–10.

That might take care of underwater pursuits, but what about aerial? Schram came up with something there, too. In

March, he called U.S. Army Intelligence officers at the Redstone Arsenal in Huntsville, Alabama, asking what he'd need to do to get hold of satellite photos that might show suspicious displacement of ground, something that would look like a gravesite.

No can do, he was told. You'd need a security clearance just to look at whatever the photos produced, and you don't have one.

Schram wrote a letter on March 27 to a commanding officer at Redstone, filling him in on the case and asking him how he would go about getting the clearance he needed. Schram had by this time amassed cardboard boxes full of details. He told the commanding officer just where to aim the satellite: longitude of 83 degrees, 51 minutes, 37 seconds, latitude of 44 degrees, 33 minutes, 37 seconds. Or, in old-fashioned terms, Section 17 of Curtis, Alcona County, northwest corner of Bamfield and Brodie Roads.

Meanwhile, he also contacted officials at Selfridge Air National Guard base northeast of Detroit, asking how he might arrange for Air Force planes to fly over a possible burial site involved in an ongoing murder investigation. In mid-April word came back—he'd been granted clearance to use the Air Force's best, high-flying photo technology. Retired Colonel Tom Reams and Captain Dan Addis at Selfridge had been told to make photo runs over the thirty-eight acres. They were going to use high-resolution infrared film. And just as soon as they had results, they'd get them to him.

Early in May, he got word back from Redstone. The satellite photos he was interested in were no longer kept there, but should be at an Army Intelligence facility in Washington, D.C.

Assuming he tracked the photos down, though, he still needed someone with clearance to look at them. He found a University of Michigan engineering professor who had some government contracts and a clearance to see the secret photos and asked if he would look at them when and if Schram could get them.

May 5–8, the dive team, using the magnetometer, worked every cubic inch of Alcona Pond. Nothing. The only bit of good news was that they got done in three days instead of five, so the families only had to pay $300 apiece.

A week later, an informant told them they had wasted their time looking for the car in the water. He'd heard that a friend of the Duvalls had taken care of the car some other way, heard it from a guy named Cricket, and that a girl named Sunshine who was dating Cricket's brother, Corky, knew something, too.

Tips and informants were ubiquitous. Everybody up north, even people who went by their given names, knew something, or thought they did. Schram took them all seriously. He made a note to try to track down Cricket and Sunshine and put their names in his report of May 29, 1991.

His next report on the case wouldn't be written for fourteen months. Tired of jotting down gossip and speculation from so-called informants, frustrated with dead ends, busy on a perpetually heavy caseload, Schram didn't update his reports until July 24, 1992.

It didn't take him long to sum up the intervening months, just seven paragraphs. Kevin Tyll, David's brother, had heard rumors that some guys up in Rose City had been bragging about the killings. Schram and Halleck had tried without success to get the state attorney general to issue a warrant for income tax fraud for Sherm Heilig, thinking a felony warrant might be the leverage needed to get at the bodies or the Bronco. The attorney general didn't think there was enough evidence; one was never issued. Heilig avoided prosecution and died of a heart attack in 1998.

(A nephew would later tell Bronco Lesneski that everyone knew Heilig was a shyster who had conned a lot of people out of money. "He'd screw anyone, given the chance," said the nephew. But he wasn't the type to kill someone, the nephew said, though he'd easily be capable of helping a friend cover it up. By the time of his death, the reward had grown to $100,000. That was the puzzling thing, said the nephew. Heilig'd turn anyone in for a reward. "He even turned me in to the DNR one time for stealing Christmas trees from the forest." But then, the nephew wasn't likely to kill him for being a stool pigeon. The Duvalls?)

As far as high-tech by air, nothing had panned out. There were no signs, either by satellite or by high-resolution film shot on a flyover, of anything resembling a gravesite on the thirty-eight acres in Alcona County.

Halleck was busier on the case than Schram in those months. He had more people in his area of northeast Michigan to track down or reinterview, more tips to pursue. Two of the tips involved Broncos or bodies in lakes. On August 20–21, 1991, the state police dive team searched the waters of Horseshoe Lake and O'Brien Lake. Like previous dives, it was without success.

On March 10, 1992, Frank Duvall was charged with felonious assault and being a habitual offender in Alcona County. Halleck thought he might be able to leverage the charges, but Duvall's attorney said he knew nothing about the hunters and had no information to trade. He had been in prison in 1985 and couldn't have been involved.

On May 28, though, as sentencing grew near, Frank was more willing to talk. In a meeting with Halleck—with his attorney and the prosecutor present—he said that on Thanksgiving the previous year, he was driving the back roads of South Branch with J.R., Coco, Rex and another guy.

Frank was driving because he was the only one sober. Someone brought up Detective Schram's name and the ongoing investigation, and Rex blurted out, "All I did was transport the bodies."

At the end of the meeting, Frank said he'd try to find out more useful information for Halleck.

31
LET'S MAKE A DEAL

Another year went by. Schram stopped writing the little bits and pieces of stuff that came to him directly in Northville, or filtered through cops in Monroe, county sheriffs up north or state police in East Tawas or West Branch.

On August 27, 1993, he suddenly had something to write about. The Monroe P.D. called. Ken Duvall had been arrested for spousal abuse, stalking his wife and breaking and entering his own home. Unable to post bond of $1,000, he'd been in jail a week, and was scheduled to be sentenced on September 29, and he wanted to make a deal. He'd talk about what he knew about the deer hunters in exchange for a break on the charges.

Schram drove straight there and read Ken his Miranda rights off the printed card he always carried.

Ken said he understood that what he said could be used against him, and told this story:

Just before Thanksgiving in 1985, down in Monroe, he got a call from his brother Rex, telling him they had some stuff to get rid of and they needed him up north pronto.

Ken did as he was bid. When he got to Rex's several hours later, Rex and a friend were in the garage, working on a black 1980 Ford Bronco. Rex's live-in girlfriend and her kids were in the house and the door to the garage was locked to prevent anyone from accidentally wandering in.

Rex told him the car belonged to a couple of guys from "down under."

Over the next couple of hours, in Ken's words, they "parted out" the Bronco. The interior was light blue. It had bench seats, a modified 351-cubic-inch engine, and an AM/FM radio and cassette player. They took off the doors and got out the torches and cut the body in half. The three of them loaded the front half in his pickup, including the VIN number, drove it to the back of Rex's property and dropped it into the creek.

They dumped the back half into the woods off one of the less-traveled roads in the area, then loaded up the motor, the transmission, the steering box, the steering column and the axles into Ken's pick-up. He drove down to see a guy in Saginaw, who paid them $400 for some of the stuff, and Ken continued on to Monroe, hid the transmission in his garage, mailed Rex $200 for his share, and a few months later sold the transmission to a guy named Garth.

It wasn't until Schram's investigation really heated up that Ken put two and two together. Maybe the guys from "down under" weren't from Australia or New Zealand. Maybe they really were down under, dead and buried.

There was more. Ken said two–three years ago he was over at a guy named Cricket's house—apparently the same Cricket an informant had talked about back in May of 1991 when they were diving in the Alcona Pond—and Cricket had mentioned that the cops would never find the hunters.

"What do you mean?" asked Ken.

"We used the chainsaw on them. They will not be found."

Ken asked Cricket if his family was involved. Cricket looked at him, smiled and nodded.

Schram asked him why, if he knew all this stuff, had he told the Oakland County Grand Jury that convened back in 1989–1990 that he knew nothing about any Ford Bronco.

"I lied," he said.

It was good stuff, but there were major problems with it. The chain saw? That Schram could believe. But a 351 engine meant eight cylinders. Tyll's Bronco only had six. Maybe Ken was mixing up his engines.

~

Next, it was on to Garth's house. Garth was 35, his real name was Michael Slatinsky—who knew where all these nicknames came from? must be a requirement for residence both in the Mio area and Monroe—and he said he had, indeed, bought a transmission from Ken Duvall and put it in his 1972 Bronco. He still had the car. The transmission's VIN number didn't match the Tylls' Bronco. And it was an automatic. Tyll had driven a shift.

The account of the transmission rang a bell with one of the Monroe cops. He went back through his notes and found that in 1989, a guy named Michael had told him about buying a manual transmission from Ken Duvall in 1985 or so.

They asked Ken about it. Could be, he said, but he had no memory of any specific transmission. He'd sold stolen parts to Michael six or seven times.

The Monroe police said there was a good reason Ken's memory might be less than reliable. He'd been on a crack-cocaine binge when arrested by the police a week earlier and was just now coming down, and calming down.

~

On September 3, Schram signed Ken Duvall out of the Monroe County jail and drove him three hours north to the West Branch State Police Post, and from there on to Rex Duvall's former home on County Line Road.

Duvall led them to the rear of the property, which was littered with rusting parts from several "parted-out" cars. He showed them where the creek ran into a small lake and said that was where they had dumped the front half of the Bronco.

Hard to tell the exact locations, it had been 2 in the morning and dark out.

A search of the creek and lake would be arranged. Frank was driven back down to Monroe. On the way he said he'd be willing to wear a wire and go visit Cricket in an effort to get him to incriminate Coco and J.R.

32
THE YEARS FLY BY

Every once in a while a new tip came in that had to be checked out. In December of 1983, a guy remembered seeing a hunter in the woods who had parked a Bronco nearby. Had a clear memory of the scope on his rifle. Wrong rifle.

In March, two brothers said they'd been hunting on November 24 and 25, 1985. They talked to a tall hunter in the woods. After he walked away from them, they heard him having what seemed to be an argument with another hunter, followed by gunfire.

They were great witnesses, had photographic memories of the event. The hunter had on hunter's orange, boots and a gray hat. He had a 7-mm rifle with a scope on pivotal mounts, and a deer license pinned to the middle of his back.

Wrong gun. And neither Tyll nor Ognjan had a license.

In April of 1994, a woman turned in her ex-boyfriend, a ne'er-do-well who she said was a car thief and had probably killed the hunters. He had been arrested in 1989 for having a stolen Bronco, all right, but his was stolen out of Ann Arbor. Wrong car.

In September a guy in Trenton said he'd heard through a friend, or maybe a friend of a friend, that a guy named Scott had seen two hunters poaching deer and had shot them. It went nowhere.

In October, an attorney named Robert Betts subpoenaed the State Police for records on the deer-hunter case. Schram called the attorney, who told him he was representing Nelson Bolzman, who was accused of murdering Eileen Seitz, one of J.R.'s former girlfriends. The attorney wanted to make the claim that there were others besides his client who might want her dead—such as Coco and J.R.—to keep her from telling what she might know about the hunters.

That was it for 1994. And that was it for Schram, too. In early 1995 he was promoted to detective lieutenant and transferred to the Sixth District in Grand Rapids. Detective Sergeant Alison King inherited the case from him.

The Tylls and the Ognjans thought the world of Schram. Maxwell had always rubbed them the wrong way, despite his hard and continued efforts. "Curtis Shram was great. He gave us hope," said Cathy Tyll.

When he first introduced himself to them, the Tylls told themselves, buoyed, "This guy is great. He's gonna do it for us."

Over the years, he called them weekly with updates, or just to talk, to keep their hopes from flagging. And then one day he called them to give them the bad news that he'd been transferred to Grand Rapids.

"I always had it on my desk," he told them of his ever-growing case file. "I wanted to solve it before I left." When they got off the phone, Cathy sat down and cried. Another dead end.

33

AN EMPLOYER TALKS

In November of 1995, Channel 4 ran a story on the case, the mystery having hit its tenth anniversary, and asked viewers who knew anything to call Halleck in West Branch. On November 27, he got a call from Christine Bentley, the owner of Bentley's Nursery in Belleville, which had employed a lot of the Duvalls and a lot of their friends over the years.

There was one lead Halleck ought to follow for sure, she said. One of the Duvalls' best friends was a guy named Chipper Curley, a Vietnam vet, alcoholic, big-time brawler and bar fighter who had died in 1987 or 1988. Halleck ought to track down his ex-wife and, more especially, his daughter, who had heard a lot of tales growing up in that household.

She told Halleck that she'd once confronted Rex about his involvement in the case and his sarcastic reply was, "They haven't found any bodies, have they?" And then he laughed and walked away.

Halleck ought to talk to J.R.'s son, too. The one they called Doobie. Word was that Doobie had been talking too much. Halleck knew that Doobie had talked to Schram five years earlier, though he hadn't been very forthcoming. And Doobie's brother, Tom, had told Schram that Doobie was afraid if he told what he knew, his dad would kill him, too.

Anyway, said Bentley, word was that J.R. and some of his brothers had severely beaten Doobie to get the message across to quit talking, whether it was to the police or anyone else.

This was the code of the Duvalls and their associates, she said, that nobody talk about this case or their other activities.

Halleck drove down to Monroe and he and King went a'calling on Chipper's wife, Cynthia Dingus, and his daughter, Crystal. Crystal, 21, grew almost hysterical when they identified themselves at the front door of her home in Monroe and told her why they were there. After calming down, she said that she'd heard many rumors over the years, mostly through Sharon Russeau, Rex's ex-girlfriend, who had become her neighbor.

What she'd heard was that the two hunters had been killed in a drunken fight. The Duvalls had beaten one of them to death and had then had to kill the other one so as not to leave a witness. Eventually, they were fed to pigs. The Bronco went to Rex's house and was dismantled.

Cynthia Dingus confirmed all they'd heard about her husband, but she said he'd changed his ways in 1984 when she gave him an ultimatum that he either stop drinking and brawling or she'd leave. Her husband wouldn't have had first-hand knowledge of the incident because he'd gotten an insurance settlement of several thousand dollars just before Thanksgiving of 1985 and he'd stayed home instead of going hunting so they could celebrate their newfound wealth.

Chipper might very well have known all about the missing hunters from what the Duvalls had told him, but he would never have told her, because he would have known she'd go straight to the police.

34

"SPLIT LIKE A MELON"

In 1996 and 1997, tips were infrequent. A crazy Vietnam vet in a motorcycle gang might have done it. (Said crazy vet actually being, as it turned out, a state police informant.) A car body part was seen half submerged in the AuSable River. (Tips about it had been coming in for years.) A drunk arrested in Ohio claimed he had killed the two hunters, cut off their heads, hands and feet, and buried them. (When he sobered up, he said he was depressed over the breakup of his marriage and had made it all up.)

There was some excitement in May of 1997, though. The state was working a stolen car beef against Charles Mc-Mullen Jr., one of the Duvalls' cousins. He'd been arrested for being in possession of stolen property and was awaiting arraignment in Osceola County Circuit Court. McMullen, 35, a truck driver, had some information to trade. On May 15, with McMullen's attorney present, Detective Sergeant George Pratt of the Reed City post taped a chilling, eighteen-minute interview.

McMullen said he'd been living in Wixom in 1985, northwest of Detroit, across the street from his sister, Susan Yonkin. He said it was between 7 and 9 p.m. one Sunday night when he walked over to his sister's. Parked in the driveway was a black Ford Bronco, 1980, maybe 1981. J.R. and Coco were there.

Coco was very nervous, telling J.R. they needed to get rid of it. J.R. telling Coco to relax, don't worry about it. After an hour or so, the brothers drove off in the Bronco.

Some time afterward, McMullen was over at Coco's house in Monroe. Coco was drinking and blurted out how some guy's head had "split like a melon."

Split like a melon—no one knew, then, just how that phrase would come to resonate in the years ahead, how important it would be when uttered by someone besides Charles McMullen. At the time it was just another colorful phrase by another disreputable, if colorful, member of the Duvalls' circle of friends and family. Another tale in a long chain of tales told by informants with axes to grind or deals to be struck.

Eventually, Coco told McMullen that J.R. was out hunting in the woods, had shot a buck and was tracking its bloody trail through the woods when he heard a shot. Someone else had shot what he claimed was his deer. He ran to where he'd heard the shot, got in a loud argument with the hunter and shot him dead on the spot. The other missing hunter ran up and J.R. shot him, too.

Coco told him they'd cut up the bodies and fed them to pigs, which ate them up, bones and all. They then took the Bronco to McMullen's Uncle Mike, who ran it through his shredder.

McMullen said Coco had repeated versions of the same tale three or four times over the years. He said Coco seemed troubled by what had happened, but nothing bothered J.R., and Coco was scared of him.

Early on Pratt asked him if he knew the hunters were killed "for a fact":

"Yeah, I know that for a fact. The reason nobody ever found any bodies or anything like that was because they were cut up and fed to the pigs, and my cousin

Donald [Coco's given name] was in on that one because he was always going around bragging how the guy's head split open."

"How did you learn [the Bronco] went through the shredder at your Uncle Mike's place?"

"Because Donald and I painted a couple boats for him. And when he [Coco] gets drunk, he's got a real loose mouth, and he talks about it all the time when he's drinking . . . Like I said, when he gets drunk— he drinks a lot—he spills his guts on everything. Just me and him, we bent over the boat and I was painting the boat and he come up and he put his arm around my shoulder and he goes, 'You know, the guy's head split just like a melon.' And then he got scared and he loses all color, then he goes back doing what he's doing, grabs another beer. Few minutes later, he says something like, basically the same thing. You know, he goes, 'His head split like a melon.' Like he's scared to death. He's a real nervous person."

"Now, you expressed to me that there was a concern. You've got a concern?"

"Uh, if these guys find out I'm talking, they'd kill me. I guarantee it. Those guys are nuts. The oldest one, J.R., shot his dad before, over stupid shit. He shot him right in the head with a twenty-two.

"My mom called [Coco] and she told him, 'Hey, the FBI or somebody's here asking questions.' He goes, 'Well, nobody better say nothing. Otherwise they won't make it to court.' These guys, I would not put it past them. They're nuts. Like I said, J.R. is crazy. He'll do anything . . . I mean, he'd shoot his mom. If she pissed him off, he'd shoot her."

Chilling, and interesting. But it was all hearsay from a guy desperately trying to avoid felony charges. There was nothing to corroborate what he was saying. Coco certainly wouldn't. No one was going to sign any warrants based on what McMullen had to say. J.R. and Coco were no closer to jail than they ever had been.

On July 15, 1997, just shy of his 40th birthday, as a result of a petition by his mother, Brian George Ognjan was declared dead. It was thirteen days after a formal death certificate had been filled out and signed by Warner Spitz, a once-renowned medical examiner for Wayne County who was then in private practice. "Place of disposition: unknown," Spitz had recorded. "Method of disposition: body unrecovered. County of death: Oscoda." That was the one thing his mother thought she knew for sure.

The date Spitz filled out the certificate was recorded as the official date of death for a man no one had seen in nearly twelve years.

Years earlier the Tylls and Ognjans had put up a $15,000 reward for information about their sons, and the state police Crime Stoppers Program had added $1,000. On October 18, 1997, the Michigan Big Game Hunters Association offered an additional $15,000.

On November 1, the *Free Press* published a lengthy article on the case by Hugh McDiarmid Jr., which resulted in numerous tips. One resident of suburban Detroit called to say one or both of the hunters were living next to him. There *were* two people living next to him. One was a Canadian resident, the other was far too young. A Mackinaw City man called to say he'd seen the hunters eating breakfast with two girls. It had been years ago and he'd been meaning to call.

The Big Game Hunters Association called Doug Halleck on February 12 to say their members had responded to recent news stories by kicking in enough money that the total sum of the reward could be upped to $100,000.

On February 18, after all his years of plugging away, Halleck finally met the Tylls and Mrs. Ognjan. They drove up to West Branch to introduce themselves and discuss the case. He told them the new REWARD poster was at the printer.

The *Free Press* ran another lengthy piece on March 5, keyed to the new reward and the new posters. A flood of tips poured in, most of them, as usual, useless. But the volume alone was such that the case, which had officially been declared inactive the year before, was declared open, again.

One caller on March 6, who wanted himself identified by the code name of J.C., had information that rang all too true to Halleck.

He said he had known the Duvalls since the late 1970s and used to live near them in South Branch. The two hunters had gotten into a bar fight with the Duvalls and were killed. The Duvalls took the bodies to one of their homes, on County Line Road near Chain of Lakes Road, cut them up and fed them to pigs and dogs. The pigpen was out behind the barn.

The Duvalls, he said, had been cutting firewood in the woods for years and knew the back roads very well. He told Halleck to check out an ex-friend and roommate of Coco's down in Monroe, one Ed Lavere, and that Lavere's ex-wife might be helpful.

On March 12, J.C. called back with some more details and names of other people to talk to.

Soon after, Halleck found out that Ken Duvall had apparently gone legit, or at least was putting up a good front. Word was he now owned two different auto salvage operations under the name West Branch Salvage & Recycles—"You call we haul" was the motto on its business cards—and that J.R. was working for him at one of the locations, on M-33. County clerk records showed that forty acres on M-33 had been bought by Ken from James Bristol.

Both operations were actually partnerships with William Smith, 79, a retired General Motors worker who had moonlighted in the junk business for years. He told Halleck by phone on April 6 that Ken was a very hard worker and knew the business in and out, which was why he had gone into business with him. Ken's wife, Cheryl Ann, did the paperwork.

Smith said business was so good they had five wreckers, and a big metal crusher, thanks to all of Ken's contacts downstate.

No doubt, thought Halleck.

They had a follow-up conversation two days later. Smith said he had loaned/financed a lot of money to Ken and Cheryl, having met them at the funeral of a former operator of a nearby junkyard. Smith said he had saved a lot of money working for union wages at GM over the years and enjoyed helping out people who were hard workers. The Duvalls were that, he said.

The same day an auto-theft task force—made up of three state police detectives, a member of the state Bureau of Automotive Regulation and a member of the National Insurance Crime Bureau—conducted searches of the two junkyards, checking VIN numbers of all the vehicles they could, and interviewing the employees.

Randy was the only Duvall working. The first thing he told police was, "This is all Charlie McMullen's fault. He got himself into trouble on the west side of the state and now he's shooting off his mouth, trying to get us in trouble."

Randy said he was helping Ken get the business going, working hard as part of an effort to get back together with his wife, April.

And he said that all the business they were getting out of southeastern Michigan was from a deal Ken had struck with Hi-way Auto in Taylor. It was all on the up-and-up. Randy even took one of the new WANTED flyers on the hunters and put it up in the office.

A little while later Ken showed up, mightily pissed when he found out an auto-theft task force was going over the yard. He calmed down soon enough, though. He said he had gotten off drugs and booze and was trying to make a go of the business.

"Aren't you drawing Social Security?" Halleck asked.

"The business is in my wife's name. I'm not breaking any laws. She does all the books and stuff because I can't read or write."

He didn't know anything about the hunters, he insisted, and offered to take a polygraph.

Just about then, J.R. showed up, too, but he declined to chat.

36

SEARCHING FOR BONES

Brian Zubel, the assistant prosecutor in Oakland County who had helped lead the fruitless grand jury in 1989–1990, was, all these years later, on the state attorney general's staff, assigned to something called the Prosecuting Attorneys Coordinating Council in Lansing.

Halleck called him in early May and updated him on the investigation. Zubel put him in contact with an assistant prosecutor on the AG's staff, Mark Blumer. Blumer suggested meeting with Halleck and Dr. Norm Saur of Michigan State University to come up with a plan for searching for human bones in the areas were the various Duvalls had kept pigs in the fall of 1985.

They set up a meeting for May 15, and Halleck went to work in the meantime getting permission from the current owners of the various parcels of land. He got quick permission to search Sharon Russeau's old lot at 6810 East County Line Road in South Branch and Coco's at 7520 East County Line Road. J.R., at the time, lived just across the road from Coco and kept his pigs over at his brother's place's.

Halleck put in for expenses, $450–500 each for Saur and a forensic archaeologist, Bill Lovis, $200 a day for one of their assistants from MSU, and a fee yet to be determined for a backhoe and operator. Saur said they could do both sites in one day.

At their meeting, Halleck told Saur they had narrowed the possible dig sites down to two. Saur said the sites could be processed in a day. Zubel told Halleck that if they found human bones, he'd have enough probable cause to seek arrest warrants.

Magic, long-delayed words: "enough probable cause to seek arrest warrants." Going on thirteen years and until that meeting, no one had thought they were close enough to say them.

Now, they just needed some bones.

And they got them, at both locations. Small bones were dug up at Coco's old place, but Saur didn't think they were human. He kept two for testing at his lab back in East Lansing.

They didn't dig up any bones at Russeau's. But the previous owner had dug some up and had placed them at the base of a tree, where they remained. They didn't look human, either.

No human bones, no probable cause. Two more stay-out-of-jail cards for Coco and J.R.

On July 9, Donna Sundberg called Halleck. J.R. was in poor health. He might have diabetes. Never big to begin with, he had lost a great deal of weight. He was going to die of old age before they ever got this thing settled.

PART 3
BRONCO

37
HORSE'S ASS

Bronco Lesneski, an imposing physical specimen, thirteen-year veteran of the state police SWAT team, a triathlete and weightlifter who stood 6–2, chiseled but thick at 210 pounds, was teaching water safety and physical conditioning at the Michigan State Police training facility outside of Lansing.

Teaching with him was one of his best friends, Bill Darnell, who had troopered with him in Detroit. Many days they and the recruits played touch football on their lunch hour, which usually evolved into tackle by the time the hour was over. One day Darnell called him Bronco, as in Bronco Nagurski, the old University of Illinois fullback and football Hall of Famer, and the name stuck. Coincidentally—both for his nickname and for the vehicle at the heart of the missing hunters case—his hobby is restoring old Ford Broncos. He's had more than twenty over the years.

"I tell everyone Bronco is short for horse's ass," says Lesneski, self-deprecating, quiet-spoken. "I'm not the sharpest guy. I'm not a smart man. I'm really not," he says. "I'm a doer."

He works long hours in a job a little analogous to the old Western marshal who made the rounds of all the small frontier towns over many hundreds of square miles. For much of his time on the hunter case, because of hiring freezes and manpower shortages, Bronco covered four counties, some 2,500 square miles of northeast Michigan. "I just can't let go."

He still covers two counties. He starts early, stays late and works out on his lunch hour to reinvigorate himself. He is just minutes away from dozens of trails through the nearby state forest, where he loves to run and hike. He goes to Arizona on vacation each year to hike and run in the high desert plateaus, in Chiricahua National Park, Oak Creek Canyon, the Sedona trails and Montezuma Castle.

"I always thought, if I retire, maybe I'd be a guide in the Grand Canyon, hiking in and out of the mountains," he says.

Winters, he's been known to fly to Florida with a dentist buddy, rent Harleys in Key Largo and roll down U.S. 41 to Key West. Summer, after work and weekends, are reserved for his beautifully restored 1950 Cris-Craft and as much time as possible on Lake Huron.

Lesneski is employed in as pretty a setting as any state cop could ever find himself—in the northern Michigan tourist town of East Tawas, in a small brick, two-story building right on the shore of Lake Huron. He lives just around the bay, in a large ranch house on the water he can get to from work in several minutes. What was built as the front room houses a big Harley and two weight machines. There's a bike path just out the front door he can run on with his yellow Lab down to the lighthouse at the end of the point, or with his kids when they're home from college.

His wife, Tina, who has a rural postal route, "is my best friend. She puts up with my shit."

He is also, says retired State Police Lieutenant Mike Larrison, who solved a cold-case serial killing in 2002, just before his retirement, "the best detective in the state police."

The oldest of six kids, Lesneski grew up in the small town of Richmond, forty-five minutes north of Detroit, not far inland from Lake St. Clair. Richmond is a quaint place, with a historical downtown of 19th century brick buildings on a real Main Street, surrounded by beet and corn fields.

"There was such a sense of stability in the community and I wanted to share that with my family, provide that to my boys," he says. During a driver's training class a state trooper came in to give a talk. He was articulate, charismatic and, as Lesneski says, "much squared away." It planted a bug.

"It was instrumental in my coming into the state police," Lesneski would say years later. "In the back of my mind, it was always what I wanted to do."

His mom and dad had a cabin up north, where he nurtured his love for the woods. The summer after he graduated from Richmond High in 1974, his parents moved up north. Lesneski worked a series of menial jobs and spent two years as a lumberman. At 21, he applied to the State Police Training Academy. There was a hiring freeze, though, so he applied to the Iosco County Sheriff's Department.

They sent him to sheriff's school briefly, gave him a badge and a gun and said, "Here you go."

"I was scared. I made mistake after mistake after mistake."

But he learned his trade, thought quickly on his feet, had a wellspring of common sense that stood him well. People thought him fair and trusted him. He liked people. He usually even liked those he arrested. He tried to respect everyone and usually could find a kernel worth respecting.

"People accused me of being naïve and gullible. But what's the alternative? Being cynical?" he says.

He kept applying to the State Police, who had better cars, better uniforms, better benefits and much better pay. He scored 95 on his first test, not high enough for a white male in those days of playing catch-up for years of racial discrimination. He kept applying and he kept taking the test. He kept scoring in the 90s. He kept failing. Finally, in 1984, he scored 98, high enough, finally, to enter the 98th recruiting class of the Michigan State Police.

Be careful what you wish for. He was assigned to the Northville post in suburban Detroit, far from his north woods. "I saw more taillights in a day than I saw in six months up north," he says. At the big post, "I saw more patrol cars lined up in one parking lot than I'd ever seen."

Intimidated, "I kept my eyes wide open and my mouth shut."

From there, he got farther from his woods, assigned to the downtown Detroit post. To help Detroit's beleaguered, understaffed and underfunded city cops, the State Police had taken to patrolling the city's freeways, "policing crime in the ditch," they call it.

It was an assignment most troopers hated. They hated the crime. They hated the shabby surroundings of neighborhoods way past simple disarray. They hated the prostitutes and the drugs. A lot of them just hated blacks. Lesneski didn't hate any of it.

"I love it," he'd tell people who asked what he thought.

They'd respond, "You gotta be kidding."

"The people of the city of Detroit were respectful," says Lesneski today. "I loved the culture of the big city. The sports, the restaurants."

After two years, he was assigned to the training facility in Lansing, living in a barracks, schooling kids in the military life of the state police. The north woods kept beckoning. Tina grew up in Sand Lake, a little community a few miles inland from Lake Huron, just east of Tawas. He'd met her at a dance at the Sand Lake Fire Hall when she was 18 and he was 22.

About 1990 he got a transfer to Alpena, a fairly large town on Lake Huron not far from Tawas. Then on to West Branch, another up-north posting off I-75. It was what they call a complaint post, most of the work coming in the front door or by phone. Bar fights, B&Es, garage break-ins mixed in with freeway radar duty.

Finally came his transfer to East Tawas. "I felt like I was home."

Lesneski loved being a trooper, in uniform, driving those blue state cop cars. And he loved being back in Tawas, where he knew all the townspeople and the cops and sheriffs in the outlying communities.

His boss, Russ Smith, thought he'd make good officer material. Lesneski was happy doing what he was doing, but he took the sergeant's test and passed it. He didn't want to go anywhere they needed sergeants, so he turned down the promotion. They filled the slots, some time went by, he took the test, again. He told his bosses he'd only go to Alpena or West Branch, or stay in Tawas, and again they filled up the slots.

The next time the test came up, he said screw it, he didn't need the grief. The district inspector stopped by his house and told him to take the test. Lesneski took the test a third time, passed it a third time, told them he wasn't moving anywhere, and they did the unusual, told him he wouldn't have to and made him a uniformed sergeant right there in East Tawas. It was 1996 . . . and he was promptly bored to death. A uniformed sergeant is middle management. He dealt with budgets, paid bills, reviewed trooper complaints, processed payroll, updated files, ordered supplies and did all kinds of other stuff that had almost nothing to do with police work.

"I felt like I was stifled, sitting behind a desk. It was a hard detail for me. I thought about taking a demotion and going back to trooping."

Before he could do anything drastic, he got a call. Doug Halleck, the detective sergeant in West Branch, was leaving. Bronco had scored well enough on his sergeant's test to qualify as a detective. Was he interested?

Were they kidding? It was a field job, out from behind the desk, out of the office, doing real cop stuff, not pushing paper and watching the clock tick away. It was 1998 and he was finally and truly in cop heaven.

38
COLD CASE

When Lesneski inherits Halleck's beat in 1998, his territory covers some 2,500 square miles over Ogemaw, Gladwin, Arenac and Iosco counties, and his job entails investigating nearly every complicated or serious crime that occurs in dozens of small-town jurisdictions where the local cops are competent enough, but who haven't the time, manpower, equipment or expertise for most felonies or complex crimes.

As if that's not enough, he investigates the serious crimes visited upon each other by the maximum-security inmates at the state prison in Standish.

Requests come in all the time from county sheriffs or township and small-town cops. When they think they know who committed a more serious offense, they'll work it themselves. But if it's a who-done-it, they call him for help.

He works murders, of course, and robberies, arson, kidnappings, stalking complaints, suspected drug rings, serious complaints against local cops and civic officials, shootings and much, much more.

"I'm not plagued by drive-by shootings or bank robberies, but I'm one detective. There's a lot of job security up here. There's lots to do," he'd say. When the call comes from a nearby sheriff or cop asking for help, "I never say no to anyone. I never have and I never will."

Local cops often resent the State Police, the way city cops resent the FBI. But not Bronco. They like him and respect him. So they'll go out of their way when he calls with a request, in turn. "If I call and say, 'Hey, guys, canvass a neighborhood for me,' they do it."

There's barely enough time to keep up with the current caseload, none for clearing cases that were dated back to the Reagan administration.

At any given time, he might be investigating twenty-five to thirty active, unsolved non–garden-variety cases. "I'm not a cold-case detective. I'm a field detective," he'd say.

Almost immediately, though, he was about to prove himself wrong. It was July of 1998, and Lesneski inherited a small, empty office and two cardboard boxes, the remnants of the missing hunters case. They never officially close homicide investigations in the state police, but this one should have been about as dead as they get.

It was a big deal when it happened—"There's not a policeman in northern Michigan who didn't know about it or interview someone about it," he says. It was a case he'd had a special interest in at the time, being from up north, not far from where they'd gone missing, and having worked near the suburbs they came from, too.

No one ever told him not to work the case. It was officially still open. But no one would have been upset, by then, if nothing much more ever happened, either. They didn't expect anything to happen. They didn't expect him to bust his hump on it. But Bronco wasn't going to just sit there and have those boxes mocking him every time he opened the closet door and saw them sitting there on the floor.

"If it was someone in my family, I'd expect the cops to do everything they could, and to keep me involved," he says.

The first thing Bronco did was try to make sense out of all the reports and notes in the boxes. "I had two boxes of a mess." Nothing was organized. It had all just been dumped in there, which was all right if it was your case and you knew it backward and forward, the way Halleck did, and could keep it all in your head.

But inheriting the case? Starting it anew? It was one big headache. He went to his boss, Captain Dan Miller, who worked out of Saginaw, an hour to the south. He was the district commander, overseeing State Police posts in a twelve-county region.

Miller, nearing retirement, had worked big, complicated cases before. And gruesome ones. One case, they were digging up a body they'd been told about by a suspected killer. It had been buried ten years or so and as they were digging it out, groundwater seeped in, more pouring than seeping, filling the hole. The body was decomposed and began falling apart as they pulled on it. A forensic anthropologist working the scene reached into the hole, his arms deep into the water. He pulled the head up out of the water, and as he did so, the head tilted back and the scalp just slid off. Freaked everybody out.

Over the years, Miller lost track of how many times that scene—the hair sliding off the head—had replayed itself in his dreams, waking him with a heart-pounding start every time.

Miller was an unlikely state cop, an art education major at Northern Michigan University. Just out of school in 1972, he got a teaching job, funded by a federal grant for impoverished school districts, in a little Upper Peninsula town called Trenary, midway between Escanaba and Marquette. The mines had played out throughout the U.P., the land wasn't much good for farming, and tough times had been as much a fact of life as black flies in the summer and snow in the winter for as long as anyone except the oldest of Finns could remember.

After a year, the grant ran out "and teaching jobs were slim and none." Miller heard the state police were hiring, stopped by the police post at the old prison in Marquette, got an application and was hired.

Bronco was one of his favorites, a hard-working cop with no patience for the politics that often goes with rank. He didn't need his ass kissed and he wouldn't kiss ass, and that suited Miller just fine. Miller wasn't a nitpicker. He didn't micromanage. He believed in the kind of chain of command that had strong links. He expected his post commanders and their detectives to do their jobs. As far as he was concerned, no one did theirs better than Bronco.

"There's a tremendous amount of trust everyone puts in Bronco, from the local coppers and chiefs to victims," he would say later. "No one is more open and honest than Bronco. He'd just die before he'd betray a trust.

"He's got sensitivity and a lack of cynicism. So many of us seem to be so far the other way. But he can be hard when he needs to be."

Miller had a special interest in the missing-hunter case. In the early 1980s he'd been working the Detroit freeways, then got promoted to detective sergeant in the small town of Caro in 1982. Five years later, he was temporarily assigned to the case, as were many others, to help track down tips and leads. But soon after, he was promoted to assistant post commander in Flint.

Miller gave Bronco advice on how to organize an index and begin cross-referencing names. More important, in a department always being besieged by budget woes and under command by the brass in Lansing to cut costs, Miller assigned two troopers to help him sort things out—Douglas Gough out of West Branch and Jennifer Pintar out of Tawas. Pintar was pregnant and appreciative of the light-duty assignment. Coincidentally, Gough was a native Detroiter, a graduate of Osborn High who had gone to school with Tyll and Ognjan.

They started pulling out pieces of paper and putting names into an alphabetical list that grew to 820 names, people who had either been interviewed or associated with the case in one way or another. Tediously, timelines and connections took shape. Eventually they'd fill three big loose-leaf binders with reports and interview notes and an index that told on which of the 1,209 pages each name could be found.

Actually, they filled nine binders. One set of three was for Bronco. And, confident from the start, despite the odds, that one day he'd make an arrest, he made a copy for whoever would end up as prosecuting attorney, and a copy for the eventual defense attorney.

On October 27, 1998, Bronco wrote his first report, detailing in one page what he'd done since July 15, when he'd started reading and filing, which is what he'd spent most of his time on. The day before he wrote his first report, he got a call from Helen Ognjan, asking him if he'd be working on the case in Halleck's absence.

Boy, would he ever. Once they'd worked the files into shape, Bronco began working the case hard, often at night, on his own time, after working the regular day shift on his current caseload of recent crime.

It wasn't, thought Bronco, a classic who-done-it. It was a we-think-we-know-who-done-it-but-can't-prove-it. There were rumors and whispers, and had been for years. But if the Duvalls had, indeed, killed the hunters, and folks other than them knew about it, they were keeping remarkably buttoned up. It's hard to keep things quiet for a week when there are witnesses or others in the know, but for thirteen years? There had to be one heck of a motive to keep people quiet that long: Fear.

Time can hurt an investigation—leads go cold, witnesses die, memories go bad.

But time can help, too, thought Bronco. If fear was the reason people had kept their mouths shut, well, bad guys get old and maybe they get a little less scary and maybe there's not as much fear, anymore. Who knew, maybe even someone out there had a conscience that had been bothering him or her. Like a small sliver in a finger that slowly works its way out.

Bronco wanted to interview people, but there was more to it than that. "It wasn't the message," he says, "it's how it's delivered." He wanted to show people he was serious about the case, but not a hard guy. Someone who understood their fear. Someone who was on their side. Someone who would take on the bad guys.

Captain Miller's support remained steadfast. At one point, Bronco needed to go to West Virginia to interview someone, one of the Duvalls' former live-in girlfriend who'd been beaten once too often and fled there.

No problem, do what it takes, said Miller.

turned to the Duvall's

39
FIRST INTERVIEW

On November 2 Lesneski made the three-hour drive down
to the Detroit suburb of Roseville, to lie in wait for Connie
Sundberg, Coco's old girlfriend. Bronco had gotten a tip
four days earlier from her sister, Donna, that she knew more
than she'd let on in past interviews or grand jury testimony.
Connie'd recently told her, still angry that her testimony had
been leaked to the Duvalls, "Those cops are fucked. They
said they would provide me protection and didn't. Those
hunters weren't fed to the pigs, they're still in the woods under a couple piles of garbage."

Lesneski parked out in front of the address he had for
her and her boyfriend, Charlie Mellor, and a little later, just
after noon, Connie and Charlie walked up the street and
into the house.

Lesneski knocked on the door and Charlie let him in.
Connie was in the kitchen making lunch. She was nervous, a
bit displeased, but she calmed down—Bronco has a way of
putting people at ease—and said she'd do whatever she
could to help.

She told him about two incidents. One was during deer
season when J.R., Coco and Rex pulled up in Sherm Heilig's
truck. They were all shit-faced. Coco got out of the truck,
fell down and couldn't get up.

"Get that fucker out of here!" Connie yelled to J.R., but he just laughed and Heilig drove off, leaving Coco on the ground. He crawled on his hands and knees to the door and Connie helped him into bed. He passed out for a short while, then woke up and sat up, holding his head in his hands.

"We killed someone," he said.

"What! Who?"

Coco snapped out of it, like he'd been in a trance. He looked at her and snarled, "You shut the fuck up."

She said she brought it up once in a while, but whenever she did, he'd threaten to kill her if she didn't pipe down.

Around the same time, she and Coco were over at J.R.'s when a black Bronco pulled into the driveway. Randy was driving. J.R. met Randy at the door and told him, "Get rid of that fucking vehicle, you're going to get all of us in deep shit."

Connie's opinion was, all that talk about pigs was just the Duvalls showing off, running their mouths, acting tough. She thought they'd buried the bodies, instead. Said there was a place in the woods in Alcona County she and Coco and J.R. would go to steal firewood, an area they all referred to as Grizzly Adams' area for its being out in the middle of nowhere. Said she thought that's where they'd buried the bodies because all of a sudden, even though there was still all the hardwood in the world in there, the brothers stopped going there. Would avoid the area.

Not wanting to waste time—enough of it had gone by—Lesneski arranged for Connie and Charlie to meet him the next day, up north in Curtisville. From there they drove into the woods in a state police Jeep, going deep into the woods until the Jeep couldn't go any farther. But someone—a logging crew working under contract for the federal government—had recently clear-cut the area she had in mind, and a thicket of small trees and saplings had sprung up, making a detailed search impossible.

They drove to a second spot she remembered. You could see it had been used for camping for years. There was a two-track heading in and a lot of decaying plastic and metal litter, even an old refrigerator that had been dumped and was half buried. The Forest Service had taken efforts to make the area inaccessible, moving dirt with heavy equipment to form berms that made it impassable to four-wheeled vehicles.

The two-track, Lesneski noted, headed straight to Mio. It would have been a convenient, fast way to get a couple of bodies deep into the woods. There were several low swamps nearby. They searched till nightfall. Bronco made a note to come back when he had some time and do more looking.

Bronco began driving around the county with a shovel in the back of his State Police car. He'd occasionally visit the spots Connie had taken him to and start digging at likely spots, looking for body parts or Bronco parts.

40

REWORKING THE CASE

Time didn't really permit, not with his caseload and sheer size of his territory, but Bronco made time. He'd read all the reports from Schram and King and Maxwell and Halleck, and knew what everyone had to say, but he wanted to hear it himself. So, he began reinterviewing as many people as he could.

He tracked down Sharon Russeau in Florida in November. He spoke to Mrs. Tyll about getting some new flyers made up. In January of 1999 he talked to Mrs. Ognjan to nail down some detail about one of Brian's guns. In February he interviewed someone who thought he might have some information on the Bronco. A guy who'd been drinking heavily in Timbers Steak House said the Bronco had been hidden behind a nearby barn.

Lesneski drove over there, found out the farmhouse, barn and eighty acres had been sold. The new owner wasn't happy to see a cop come calling. Lesneski's summary of the meeting gives an insight into his techniques and personality:

> On 3-01-99 I traveled to the above residence and
> met with the property owner. He was not friendly
> and wasn't happy with my presence. I introduced
> myself to the man and offered to shake his hand
> and he refused. I asked the gentleman for his name

*and he declined to give it to me. The man stated,
"What the hell do you want? I'm a retired Detroit
cop and I don't like people bothering me."*

*I advised the man that I wasn't there to bother
him, I was simply following up on information that
could be pertinent to a crime. The man then went
off on his hatred for African Americans (he didn't
use the African American term, however, he did use
several vulgarities along with his racist comments).*

*I was immediately offended by this man, how-
ever I maintained my focus on the investigation and
did my very best to communicate with him. (The
man was very dirty, he smelled offensively and his
breath was strong of intoxicants.) I apologized to
him for the inconvenience I caused and advised him
that if he truly was a former police officer, he would
do the same thing in my shoes. The man again
started on his hatred remarks and advised me that
"If I didn't understand him, I didn't belong on the
State Police."*

*I then asked the man if we could set aside our
personal opinions and get to the reason for my visit.
I explained to the man that I had received information from a confidential source, that evidence from
a crime could possibly be on his property. I also explained to him that it was my understanding that he
was completely innocent of any wrong doing, and
based on what the informant had told me, you were
a pretty good guy who would be very happy to cooperate with the investigation.*

The truth was, the informant didn't know the property
had been sold or who it was who now owned it. But it
worked. The cranky racist asked Bronco what he was looking for, then said, "Let's go look." They went out behind the
barn, then the man insisted Bronco look in all the buildings
for parts or evidence, including his house. The search turned
up nothing.

On March 3, Lesneski called the Tylls and Mrs. Ognjan, explaining to them that this investigation was still open and very important to the state police and to him, personally. He took it very, very seriously, he said, and they should call him whenever they wanted.

Cathy Tyll was ecstatic. Something in his voice. Nothing against Alison King, but she hadn't inspired their confidence. It was an old case and she'd had other things to work on. They likely would have been shocked if they'd seen a log of the actual hours she'd put in on it. Bronco got them fired up. They hadn't felt like that since Schram's early days on the case.

"Great, we've got someone who's going to solve it," said Cathy Tyll to her husband when she hung it up. She told her kids the same thing later.

David Tyll's sister-in-law, Margene Tyll, had a tip she wanted passed on. She had been up in Lucerne the previous fall and met a woman named Ruth Fawcett, who was working at Ma Deeter's Bar. They started talking about the case—it was something the Tylls were never going to let go of—and Fawcett claimed she knew something.

Lesneski said he'd look into it. All the while, the investigation was still officially classified as inactive. The official status meant nothing to Bronco.

Bronco made it a point as he worked the case, to constantly keep in touch with Mrs. Ognjan—and the Tylls.

He'd even make the long drive down once in a while to meet with them, show them that he might not have much to report, but if he was willing to tell them in person, the case must be pretty important to him.

One trip he brought with him boxes of records he wanted to go through with them.

"I know who did it," he told the gathered Tyll clan. He told them about the Duvalls and showed them their photos. He also told them why they hadn't been able to do anything about it, despite what they knew, or thought they knew.

One of the Tyll boys said, "Let's go get 'em."

Michael, big at 6–4, looking just like Dave, said, "No, then we'd be like them."

Michael had been born the day after Dave's 17th birthday. Dave asked if he could be the baby's godfather. The Tylls had had someone else in mind, but how do you say no to that? You don't. Dave doted on the newest of the Tylls.

Early on, just after Dave's disappearance, Mike came home from school crying. A couple of kids, being the cruel creatures they can sometimes be, had taunted him on the playground, telling him they'd heard his brother was never coming home, that they heard he'd drowned.

The Tylls had a hard time later putting into words their affection for Bronco. "He was so good. He's family," said Cathy Tyll. "He must be the most devoted policeman in the world. He was the best guy to talk to. We'd call him and he was always happy to talk to us."

When Bronco hit those not-infrequent temporary dead ends, or something more pressing came up—like a 13-year-old filling his dad full of holes with two blasts from the family shotgun, or a couple of county commissioners getting trapped in a perjury prosecution after falsely charging a local pain in the ass with assault—he'd call them: "Listen, guys, I'm still with you, but something has come up," he'd say. "I gotta put you on a back burner. But I won't forget you."

As he explained later, "You work the hot one and jump back on the cold ones when you can."

Nonetheless, it pained him when he had to call and say things were on hold awhile. "I've really gotten close with them. They're like part of my family," he'd say of the Tylls.

41

A FAMILY TIP

On March 3, 1999, Bronco got a call back from a message he'd left for Ruth Fawcett. This is what she had to say:

She had a friend named Barb Klimmek, a one-time heavy drinker. During one of her binges, she'd confided to Fawcett that she knew more about the lost hunters than anyone would believe. Barb had told her she was in a bar called something like "Sky Ranch Lost Creek" when there was a confrontation between some locals and some hunters. Barb was sitting by the pay phone and heard the locals make two calls, one to Comins and the other to South Branch, for additional backup. A fight ensued and Barb was told to leave the bar and go home.

She went home and later heard some noises in the woods by her house. It sounded like fighting and arguing. Then, or soon after, a couple of guys showed up at her door and told her, "Keep your mouth shut. You didn't see anything. We know how to take care of you. Pigs need to eat, too."

Barb told Fawcett these were very bad characters, capable of killing at any time, and that she'd never cooperate with the police because of fear of retaliation.

Fawcett told Lesneski she thought Klimmek lived somewhere in the vicinity of M-72 and Mapes Road.

It was a tip like dozens of others. Word-of-mouth, friend-of-a-friend bar talk. They'd all led nowhere. This one would, too, most likely. Still, it gave Bronco something to do when he got off work, other than drive around with a shovel in the trunk of his car looking for places to dig.

But it was more than just working a lead. Something about it just registered true. It was a lot of details, more than you'd expect if it was all just horsehit. Bronco had a feeling about this one. The next night, after putting in a full day in West Branch, he headed over to Mio and started knocking on doors, asking if there was a Barb home. He'd been canvassing neighborhoods, like a salesman making cold calls, off and on in the months since he'd inherited the case. Introducing himself, asking if anyone knew anything. He had the drill down.

No. Next house. No. Next trailer. No. Tedious stuff. Eventually, time to call it a night.

"It was all I had," he said. "I did it the hard way. I banged on a lot of doors. I volunteered a lot of hours. If the department had been paying me all the hours I worked on this case, they'd have said, 'Get this guy off the case. We can get a bigger bang for the buck.' I was doing it on my own time. I'd get down. I'd think, I'd rather be out on a run, or walking in the woods. And then I'd think: What if it was my family?"

But there weren't that many houses near the intersection of M-72 and Mapes. He didn't have any luck the evening of the 4th. On Friday, March 5, he thought he'd put in some time on the case before he headed into West Branch. It was 8 a.m., light just coming into the sky, wind whipping as it funneled down the road between the woods. He pulled into a long driveway on Mapes Road, smoke pouring out a brick chimney that faced straight out at the yard from the middle of the front of the house.

A woman opened the door and peered out. He introduced himself, told her it was about the missing deer hunters. "Are you Barb Klimmek?"

The woman flinched. She started shaking uncontrollably, so strongly it seemed she might be having an epileptic fit.

"You're going to get me killed," she said, pushing the door shut.

42

A FOOT IN THE DOOR

It took just the tiniest slice of a moment, an internal double take, for it to register. *"You're going to get me killed."* Bingo! "I just about fell over," he said later. "I knew then, I absolutely knew I had something." For the first time in his career, he literally stuck his foot in a doorway, blocking the door just before it closed.

"Can I come in?"

"No. You're going to get me killed," she said, again.

"I'm not in uniform, I don't drive a marked car. No one will know you're talking to a cop," he said.

"I don't want any part of this."

It was snowing. It was cold. For some reason, a stroke of genius, Bronco said, "Do you heat with wood?"

She nodded.

"Can I . . . Can I come in? Let's keep the heat in."

Later she'd say he didn't knock her over or anything, there wasn't any brute force. One minute she wasn't letting him in and the next minute there he was, in.

"Can I sit down?"

"No." Said harshly, emphatically. "I was hostile to him," she'd say later.

He sat down.

"Will you sit down and talk with me, please?" he asked.

She was still shaking. She started crying. "You're going to get me killed."

"The last thing I want to do is cause you harm in any way," said Bronco. "You can understand, if you were the investigator, it'd be shame on you if you didn't pursue all the leads that surface."

He told her he had leads and just needed to know if he was on the right track. "I'm going to solve this if it takes the rest of my life," he said.

Her heart sank. "I knew I was screwed," is how she'd put it later. She could tell looking at his face, hearing his voice, he was dead serious. He *was* going to solve this if it took the rest of his life. If it took hers, too.

"I didn't like those deer hunters much," she said. "Those two deserved to get their asses kicked, but they didn't deserve to get killed."

She started crying, again. "Why bother me? I don't want to get involved."

Clearly she needed to get something off her chest, and just as clearly it was going to be mostly on her terms. Bronco was going to have to play this one by ear, and play it just right.

"Can I record you?" he asked.

"If you record me, I won't talk."

Lesneski knew from the way she said it to keep his notebook and his pen in his pocket. He could write it all down later, after he left. He needed her as relaxed as she could get under the circumstances, and the sight of pen and paper was likely to clam her up. Lesneski knew instinctively, too, not to speak of the Duvalls by name. If that's who she was afraid of, mentioning them by name would shut her up, too.

"Have you ever been interviewed about this before?" Lesneski asked, to keep her talking. He'd read the reports, he'd compiled the index, he knew nobody had talked to her.

Klimmek—her married name, she told him, the one she went by, now, was Boudro—said she hadn't been, officially, but she'd had an affair with an Iosco County deputy and, she claimed, told him what she knew. He just blew her off, she said, didn't take her seriously. Said she was just a drunk. A lot of people back then didn't take her seriously. She had been a hell of a drinker.

Eventually the deputy lost his job, but she was sure he hadn't done anything about her information when he'd had the chance, she said.

Bronco began pleading with her, politely but firmly, saying he needed her cooperation, that he desperately wanted to put some of this to rest for the sake of the families.

"Kim, you find Kim. If she'll talk, so will I." Kim had been a barmaid, or maybe with the band, at Linker's Lost Creek Lodge up the road, she said. There a lot, anyway. She knew stuff.

Barb wasn't school-smart, but she was savvy. She'd seen enough TV shows and movies to try to frame what she wanted to say in a way that just might keep her out of trouble. Maybe aim Bronco in a certain direction, so he could get stuff he could use. What did they call it? Hearsay? Yeah, hearsay. She was going to try to frame it all that way.

Lesneski asked her if she had any relationship with the killers.

She looked at him with disgust. "I knew who they were, but I never had any relationship with any of them."

Her anger at thinking he'd been hinting at some boyfriend–girlfriend sexual relationship seemed to dissipate her fear. She started telling the tale:

She'd been sitting in the bar when the two hunters had started some shit with the barmaid. They were drunk, acting like assholes. Two of the Duvalls—she mentioned them by name, without prodding; Lesneski's heart jumped—confronted them, it looked like there was going to be a fight, she threatened to call the cops, things died down.

Then one of the Duvalls made a call to a pig farmer in South Branch—Sherm Heilig, no doubt, thought Lesneski—and to someone in Comins.

A little later, friends of the Duvalls arrived. The brothers, or their friends, brought her over a six-pack, told her to "Leave, you didn't see anything and you don't know nothing."

She left and drove down Mapes Road to her home less than a mile away.

A little later, she heard screaming coming from the woods, between her house and the bar. Hollering and screaming.

Lesneski asked her how she could hear the noise with the doors and windows closed and with the trees in the way. She said it was so loud she could hear it right over her TV.

"I knew that the hunters were going to get their asses kicked and figured they deserved it, but I didn't know that they were going to be killed," she said.

A little while later, the noises stopped, and a little while after that, there was a knock at the door. It was the Duvalls.

" 'You didn't see anything and you don't know anything,' " she quoted them. " 'If you ever open up your mouth, you'll be killed. Pigs gotta eat, too.' "

Since then, every once in a while one of the Duvalls would stop by to remind her, "You didn't see anything, and you don't know anything, or else."

"I'm sure they'll be giving me a visit soon," she said. "Every time things heat up, they call me or stop by and threaten me. You have no idea what trouble I'm in. They will kill me and my grandchildren."

Lesneski said he'd keep their talk in confidence.

"They'll still find out and come looking for me."

"What will you tell them?"

"I'll tell them you were here asking questions, but I'll lie to them and tell them I didn't say anything." Boudro was upset, again, ready to cry, quaking.

Lesneski said he had to go. Call him if she had anything she wanted to tell him. He'd be back in touch if he could find Kim and see what she had to say.

43

BACK IN TOUCH

Boudro didn't wait long. At 11 a.m. the same day, Lesneski got a call from the Oscoda County Sheriff's Department. Boudro was there, all upset and wanting to talk to him.

The sheriff's deputy put her on the line.

"I'll tell you everything I know. Just let me spend the weekend with my granddaughters."

They agreed to talk, again, at 2 p.m. Monday.

On Monday, March 8, Boudro called Bronco at the post. She said she'd feel more comfortable talking at her girl-friend's house. Could he pick her up at 2 and drive her over there? Not a problem.

A problem. Boudro, scared, again, changed her mind. A second meeting was eventually held, but not until March 23. This time, Lesneski took Halleck, now a detective lieutenant and officially off the case, with him. He had worked the case so long and so hard and knew it so well, it might help to have him on hand.

They met Boudro at her friend's house in Luzerne. She was clearly nervous and said she didn't know anything more than what she'd already told him.

"You're the one who asked for a meeting," said Lesneski. He told her he knew that she was holding back out of fear. She countered by saying that days after their first meeting, someone had come to her door telling her not to talk or else. Word must have leaked out.

"I only told my post commander and Detective Lieutenant Halleck," said Lesneski. "Officer Halleck has forgot more about this case than I know. He's spent countless hours on it."

He asked her if she trusted the Oscoda County Sheriff's Department.

No. She didn't think much of them based on her former affair with that former deputy she'd told him about.

Well, then, maybe she ought not to go there and ask them to call him. Maybe it'd be better if she dealt with him directly and work out the details of future meetings just between the two of them.

She agreed. A big step forward, thought Lesneski. She was committing to more meetings. He was sure she had a lot more to add and just needed to have it cajoled out of her.

She started talking about the night at Linker's.

"One of them grabbed me on my ass when I was playing pool. I told them to knock off their shit." Lesneski showed her photos of the two. Which one had grabbed her? She pointed to Tyll's picture.

There had been almost instant tension once the Duvalls arrived, like they'd met earlier and already had bad blood brewing. She'd approached the Duvalls' table and said something about the hunters. One of the Duvalls said they were going to teach them a lesson.

She'd been there with a buddy, Ronnie Emery. It was a new name for Lesneski. Hadn't seen it in any reports.

An old friend of hers, dead, now. Kind of a suicide, she said. He'd supposedly gotten drunk and crawled out on the highway and gotten his head run over. Back in 1995, run over by a 1990 Chevy pickup. Though she was suspicious it might have been something else, a murder made to look like suicide, done to keep him quiet about what he'd seen.

Anyway, about Linker's. She'd been in there with Ron and there was talk about getting dope. The hunters were looking to score. The Duvalls were trying to line something up from a 50-year-old couple who lived down the road and sold pot. She thought the Duvalls might be trying to lure the hunters outside on the pretext of getting them dope, and then have at them.

The story followed its earlier telling. The Duvall party buying them a six-pack and telling them to leave. Men fighting in the open area down from her house. But there was an added detail: They'd heard pinging, the kind of pinging sound an aluminum bat makes when it hits a ball.

"I'll never forget that sound," she said.

While all that was going on, Ron had crawled out the bathroom window and taken off down the trail behind her house to see first-hand what was going on. A little later, Ron came back, said he'd seen several men beating the hunters, saying they were killing them. That they were lying on the ground, not moving and they were still beating them.

Then came the knocking at her door and the words of wisdom: Keep quiet, pigs gotta eat.

After a while, she and Ron went back down the trail and could see a lot of blood on the snow, blood everywhere.

She'd told all of this to two persons years before. To her deputy boyfriend, who she claimed had told her he'd been called to Linker's the night of the fight, but stopped off at a beer store on the way and never made it. And to her psychologist, who she was seeing because of depression.

The psychologist had suggested putting her under hypnosis because Boudro told him she suspected that she knew more about what had happened than she could remember, that maybe she was repressing things.

"I'm a former alcoholic," she told Bronco. "I don't always remember things exactly right."

But the psychologist never got around to hypnotizing her. He'd committed suicide first.

Bronco told her if anything else came to her, to write it down. And if anyone paid her any threatening visits, to write down a license plate if she could. He'd be happy to pay them a return visit.

Bronco left, convinced she still knew more. "Don't upset the apple cart," he told himself. She knew more than she was letting on. But he knew if he pressed too hard, he wouldn't get it out of her. She'd have to ease it out at her own pace.

As it was—if she was telling everything she knew—the one eyewitness they'd been searching for all these years had crawled out on a highway and lined his head up with an oncoming tire.

44

KILLED HIS WIFE . . .
OR DID HE?

Nelson Bolzman was 50 years old in 1995, when he was convicted of second-degree murder in the 1994 strangulation death of his wife, Eileen Bolzman, better known throughout northeastern Michigan as Eileen Seitz, J.R.'s longtime girlfriend.

Over the years any number of informants had told cops up north and cops in Monroe that if anyone knew the truth other than the Duvalls, it was Eileen Seitz. And if anyone was going to need to be permanently silenced to eliminate a possible threat of prosecution, it was Eileen.

One day, somebody did just that. Her body was found in the middle of a dirt road just down from a shack J.R. lived in on and off, a dirt-floor hovel surrounded by car parts, garbage and various forms of rot and rust. It was meant to look like she'd been run over, and she had, but what killed her, the medical examiner figured out right off the bat, was someone's hands squeezing her throat so tightly no air could get through. The jury said it had been Bolzman's hands.

Bolzman said it wasn't. He maintained his innocence before, during and long after the trial. He told anyone who'd listen to look at the Duvalls, not him.

Eileen had had a ten-year relationship with J.R. and was the mother of two of his children. Witnesses at Bolzman's trial testified they'd heard J.R. threaten her over the years if she didn't keep quiet about the missing deer hunters.

One of J.R.'s best friends was a Vietnam vet named Robert Provost. Though he wasn't charged with any crime, police determined that tire tracks swerving around where Eileen Bolzman's corpse was found in the middle of a muddy road had come from Provost's car.

Provost later died of a drug overdose.

In December of 1998, Bolzman typed a letter at the E. C. Brooks Correctional Facility in Muskegon Heights and mailed to Macomb County Prosecutor Carl Marlinga:

> *Hopefully, you could tell me if your office had held a grand jury investigation hearing into the deaths of missing hunters from your county. I am in prison on the charge of murder being blamed in the death of my wife. (She testified in a grand jury hearing concerning those hunters.) I wish to correspond with you on this because I have very important evidence of who was involved because my wife had testified concerning her boyfriend who was the real father of my stepdaughters and he just before her death threatened her over custody matters. (Such as she could give over custody of the girls either the easy way or the hard way.)*
>
> *If you have any kind of knowledge write me back. Or of any investigator in your county who knows of the missing hunters case. Please write me back soon. The vehicle driven by those hunters was in my yard in Cass City after their disappearance driven there from up north by the sister and brother of the prime suspect on their way down from up north heading to Monroe.*
>
> ********IMPORTANT********
>
> *Do not send just any investigator on this matter. These are all Green Beret/Vietnam-trained vets and have connections with police to learn of any kind of investigation into their doing, to include the ability to*

*make people disappear. They now own car and truck
crushers in the Monroe area.*

Marlinga sent the letter on to Lesneski, who had heard from
other sources, as well, that he ought to look into the suspicious circumstances behind Eileen's death.

What Bronco had heard from Boudro made Bolzman's
claims all the more credible. By then, Bolzman had been
transferred to the Thumb Correctional Facility in Lapeer
County, named for its location in the sparsely populated region that looks like—what else?—the thumb of a mitten
when you look at a map of the state.

Lesneski asked Detective Sergeant Joseph Juhasz to drive
down to speak to him, and on March 9 he did.

Bolzman told him he'd met Tyll and Ognjan the opening
weekend of 1985 deer season at a deer camp near Mio. The
night before the season began, both the hunters had gone
into South Branch to drink at Timbers.

While they were there, someone had broken into their vehicle and stolen their rifles. Later, back in camp, the enraged
hunters had told Bolzman they knew the Duvalls were the
thieves, but couldn't prove it. They'd headed home because
they didn't have anything to kill deer with, but said they'd be
back the next weekend.

The next weekend they'd gone missing. Maybe they'd
run into the Duvalls, had words about the missing guns, and
gotten themselves killed.

Maybe not. There was just one thing wrong with the
story. It was a stone certainty Tyll and Ognjan had stayed in
the Detroit area for the opening weekend. They'd planned to
go to White Cloud, but canceled at the last minute so Tyll
could go to a party with his wife. But a lot of witnesses over
the years had confused the weekend, or the days, they'd seen
the hunters. After all the years, who could be sure if a sighting in a bar had been on a Friday or a Saturday, or one weekend or the next?

According to Bolzman's trial transcripts, defense attorney Robert Betz had described the area where Eileen was

murdered as "the most dilapidated nasty mess in the world . . . and in the midst of what I would call a murderous corner of the world, Curtisville."

It was the Duvalls' corner of the world. In and near Curtisville, that's where they'd lived when the hunters had gone missing.

45
A CHAT WITH J.R.

On March 24, the day after his second talk with Boudro, Lesneski paid another courtesy call on J.R. Duvall, himself, at his house in Hale. "When you stir the pot, you never know what's going to surface," Bronco would say later. Knowing J.R. wasn't the early-to-rise type, Lesneski came knocking at 8 a.m.

Bronco told J.R. he had inherited the investigation from Halleck and had been working on it since October. He told him he had strong suspicions J.R. had been involved in the hunters' disappearance. That he was, in fact, a suspect.

This investigation is not going away, he said, adding that if J.R. at any point thought it might be in his best interest to cooperate, if he thought he might have any information that could be useful, to contact him. He'd be sure to make "the appropriate notation in my police report." In other words, it'd look good for J.R. to be helpful, might help mitigate things down the road.

J.R. was clearly nervous, but he struck Bronco as friendly, nonetheless. He wasn't belligerent or hostile, nothing you might expect from reading the reports. It was as if he expected Bronco to play his part and didn't hold it against him.

J.R. volunteered that he'd taken a polygraph years earlier

and had flunked it. He said it was inaccurate and he wasn't going to take one of the fool things again.

"They asked me about a very important lie," he said. "Hell, I've told several very important lies. Why don't they just ask me if I had anything to do with killing those hunters? I've never seen those guys. I don't know shit about those guys."

"We're not on a fishing expedition," said Lesneski. "I'd like to eliminate you from this investigation just as bad as you'd like me to. Short of you assisting, confessing or passing a polygraph, I will not leave anything to chance."

And until proven otherwise, J.R. would remain a very good suspect.

J.R. surprised Lesneski, then. He told Bronco that he'd arrested him a few years ago when he was still a deputy with the Iosco County Sheriff's Department.

Bronco had remembered—how could he forget, as crazy an arrest as that had been?—but he hadn't brought it up for fear of pissing off J.R.

It was back in the late 1970s, winter, a heavy snow falling. Bronco had been a deputy sheriff, driving an old Blazer that was good in the snow. Generally it was used in the summer to haul the county's marine-patrol boats. It was pretty beat up, no back seat, not your typical cop car.

And there was this old 1960s yellow Chrysler driving down the road in front of him, broken windshield, license plate dangling from a wire, other equipment violations he could spot through the snow. Bronco pulled it over. It was J.R. and some buddies, but you'd never know it from the names they gave him, figuring, Why tell the truth when a lie will do?

So they give him their fake names, borrowed from drinking buddies of theirs. Unfortunately for J.R. and two of the others—"the fiasco crescendoed," is how Bronco would describe it years later—three of the names they claimed as their own, when Lesneski ran them, came up as wanted on arrest warrants, one of them on a rape charge out of New York.

The Blazer had two bucket seats. One of them sat there. The others were handcuffed and taken to jail lying down on the floor in the back.

"This was the start of my relationship with the Duvall family," he'd say.

But even under the circumstances, Bronco treated J.R. courteously, with more respect than he usually got from the law, and J.R. seemed to appreciate it all those years later.

"I said I would never take another damn polygraph, but for you, I will—but you've got to go with me," said J.R. "I don't like that damned Halleck."

Lesneski said he'd talk to his commanding officer and gave J.R. a business card.

"Call me if you've got anything useful."

Another polygraph was unlikely. It was generally against policy. Having failed one, you're a failure. Period. Passing a second one on questions involving the same set of circumstances didn't prove anything. Maybe you're telling the truth this time, maybe you've just gotten better at telling the same lies. No way to tell. No point in asking the questions.

Bronco didn't have a case they could prosecute, not yet. He might never get one. Hell, he couldn't even prove he had a murder, much less who did it. You usually need bodies for that and all he had were two guys who'd gone missing and had never been seen again. He didn't have a weapon. He didn't have any blood evidence. All the breakthroughs in DNA technology in the world wouldn't help him a bit.

But he did have a couple of scumbags and they didn't scare him one bit. Bronco started stopping by J.R.'s house at odd hours. Where Halleck and others had always made it a point to come calling on the Duvalls with obvious, visible backup, Bronco made it a point to go alone.

"I wanted them to know I wasn't afraid of them," he said. And that he was coming for them, now and forever.

"I'd see a friend or a relative of theirs at the Subway and I'd say, 'How's J.R. and Coco? Tell 'em I said hi.' " Word kept getting back to the brothers, of course. Coco was down in Monroe a lot, he could slough it off. But J.R. was living there. How'd you like it? Brothers telling you they'd been getting a sub and that fucking cop had said to say hi? Looking out the window and never knowing when you'd see Bronco's unmarked SUV sitting there? Give you a wave, drive off.

It was Bronco's way of saying, "Fuck you, assholes." Saying it for David Tyll and Brian Ognjan. Saying it for their parents and siblings, for David's wife and Brian's girlfriend. Fuck you.

46
GROUND-PENETRATING RADAR

On April 5, Bronco got a call from Gerald Kroczaleski, who said he and his brother, Randy, wanted to meet with him about a good lead on the missing hunters. It was set up for the next afternoon.

The brothers said the source of the information was their brother, Steven, who had killed himself in Florida after a standoff with police a year earlier. He'd told them that he had first-hand knowledge of the Bronco's disappearance.

Steve had been living near Mio back in deer season of 1985, and was having an affair with a married woman whose husband was in a band of car thieves and chop-shop artists.

He'd been in bed with the husband's wife at her trailer in a remote corner of the woods, near the Rifle River. Her husband was supposed to be gone for the night. Suddenly they were awakened by the sound of vehicles driving onto the property. Steven, scared to death he was going to get caught, peeked out the window trying to decide whether to hide or flee.

But the vehicles kept on driving past the trailer and into the woods. One of them was a black Bronco. The cuckolded husband and his crew often cut up cars out back, selling off the good parts and burying the rest.

The brothers told Lesneski that several times his brother had called the Arenac County Sheriff's Department from Florida, where he'd fled to avoid domestic abuse charges. He'd called, hoping he could trade his information for some kind of plea deal.

"Arenac County's lack of response pissed my brother off, because every time he called from Florida, he was put on hold, and the long-distance phone charges were outrageous," said Gerald. "Even worse, they never returned his calls."

One of the chop-shop crew was Sherm Heilig, the Duvalls' old friend and a longtime suspect in the hunters' disappearance. That got Bronco's attention. The Duvalls, though, weren't part of the gang Steve saw.

On April 12, Lesneski visited the property in question and got permission to search it. The next day, he rented a metal detector and came back. The owner's son told him that when his dad had bought the property a few years earlier it was full of junked cars, snowmobiles, motorcycles and car parts. He'd hauled out three or four semis full of junk, and that was just taking out what was visible on the surface. They'd made no effort to get anything out of the ground.

Lesneski started to search. The detector kept going off every couple of feet. There was metal buried everywhere. Lesneski turned down the sensitivity level so they wouldn't be digging so much small crap, but the detector still kept sounding. The owner's son and a state police trooper helped with the digging. Using picks and shovels, they soon had one corner of the property pockmarked.

They were unearthing rocker arms, gears, head gaskets, nuts and bolts, all kinds of stuff. After several hours and just a tiny portion of property done, Lesneski called the dig off. He decided, he said, to "try a more technical, geographic approach."

He wasn't kidding. He tracked down a geophysicist, a backhoe operator and ground-penetrating radar and came back on May 12 to finish the job. Armed with the radar and the backhoe, they again dug up all kinds of stuff. They uncovered a trailer that was buried six to eight feet deep. They uncovered stoves, refrigerators, washers, dryers and parts of all descriptions for cars, snowmobiles and motorcycles.

They didn't find a Bronco.

47
MAKING FRIENDS

Bronco kept in touch with Boudro, stopped by from time to time. She'd let him in, never less fearful, but more and more at ease with him. They were chatting like old buddies, now. "Shooting the breeze" was how she described it. "He was my friend."

They talked about her dogs. About the garden. The hard-drinking, hard-partying good-time girl was a grandmother, now, who did her own canning. She liked to talk about that. They talked about life. They didn't focus on the hunters. Usually they got around to it, sometimes they didn't.

They were involved in a thing that just had to evolve at its own pace, Bronco knew that. So did she. So he'd come by and she'd let him in and they'd talk. One day she said, "Bronco, I'll tell you some things, but I'll never tell you all the things. Never."

The reward might as well have been a million dollars. It might as well have been ten cents. Big or little, it meant jack to her.

"These are bad, bad dudes," she said.

He'd stop by her mother's up the road, visit her. Barb'd find out later, hey, your detective was by. He'd stop by her brother's shop in Mio, Klimmek Sales & Service, which sold snowmobiles and four-wheelers. Shoot the breeze with him, too.

Bit by bit she let out more details of the night in question. Details that seemed too sharply remembered, too vividly expressed, to be words filtered through the eyes of a friend who was dead.

She never talked on the record, with him taping or even writing notes. She told him if anyone else in authority came to her asking about what she'd told him, she'd lie, say she'd never said any such thing.

She'd tell them, she let him know, that she'd lied as a way to get the reward, but that she didn't really know squat. Made it all up. Just an old ex-drunk telling stories.

One of the stories she told intrigued Bronco, and infuriated him. It was about her affair with the former Oscoda sheriff's deputy. Bronco didn't care who the officer had been sleeping with, or if he'd had a wife he was cheating on, but if it was true Boudro had told him about what she knew and he'd blown her off . . . or, if it was true he'd been called to Linker's and never bothered to show up because it had been late at night, the end of the shift and he'd pulled into the parking lot of a beer store to sit it out . . . Well, that was going to piss him off, big-time.

He had her go over the account on several visits.

During one, she said, "It happened right here in my living room. We were sitting on my couch. He told me to keep my mouth shut, that I didn't know what I was talking about." She was a known drunk then, people generally blew her off, didn't take stock in what she had to say.

The deputy's attitude had pissed her off. He knew she was mad, had started talking about the night, himself, showing her he was interested in what she had to say, after all. Confiding in her. According to Boudro, he'd been called to Linker's, called to the fight. But (she claimed), he'd stopped at the Camp 10 store, instead, just down from Linker's.

Eventually Bronco paid the former deputy, Richard Smith, a visit at his home in Mio. Typical for Bronco, he showed up at 8:25 a.m.—he liked to hit people with stuff early in the morning, catch them a bit unawares, not quite ready for the day.

Bronco identified himself, told Smith he was there about the missing hunters. Smith seemed reluctant to let him in, but did so. He told him he was surprised to hear they were still working that case. Bronco asked him what his interpretation of events had been, getting him to relax, let him think he was there plumbing the knowledge of a fellow crime-fighter.

"I believe they were killed, all right, but I don't think it can be proven that they were up in our area," he said.

Bronco doesn't suffer fools gladly, and wasn't going to suffer Smith. Quietly, but pointedly, he said they had eyewitness accounts to the contrary.

"That's only their word. It can't be proven," he said.

As Bronco later put it, "I then rattled off the names of people associated in the area, including Barb Boudro." Dropping her name on him. Seeing how he liked that.

Smith kept calm at the mention of her name. No reaction, like it meant nothing. But his wife, who had just entered the room, ruined the act, had a punchline of her own.

"Did he tell you he had an affair with Barb Boudro? I mean, back then it got so bad that Barb came to my house demanding she see my husband. She threatened to kill herself and everything!"

Bronco apologized for having brought Boudro's name up, and asked Smith if he remembered talking to Boudro about a fight at Linker's, or deciding to sit things out in the parking lot of the Camp 10 Store.

He didn't deny or confirm it, but he acknowledged being out on patrol that weekend of the 1985 deer season, didn't remember which day it was, but said he was out with one of the Department of Natural Resources conservation officers about 2 a.m. when they saw a black Bronco coming out of a ditch near the store.

Bronco asked him if he'd pulled the vehicle over to ask what was going on.

"I wish we would have. It was 2 a.m., cold outside, you know? I figured it was a drunk driver and I didn't want to be bothered with arresting a drunk driver," he said.

It might have been a drunk driver. It might have been

worse, a murderer, or an accomplice. Bronco felt like wringing Smith's damn neck, but politely thanked him for his time. Before he walked out, he asked Smith if there was anyone he'd suggest talking to. Alex McDowell, said Smith. Used to live next door to Linker's. Word was, used to sell pot to the Duvalls.

Bronco had heard the name before. Had heard that the hunters and the Duvalls, both, had been looking for pot that fateful night back in 1985.

Bronco wrote in his report:

> Note:
> The marijuana issue may have been used to lure
> the hunters out of the bar.

48
"NOBODY TO MESS WITH"

Lesneski tracked down the former DNR agent Smith said was working with him the night he saw the Bronco driving out of the ditch.

"That never happened, I guarantee it," the agent said. He said he usually worked with the sheriff, but once in a while got stuck with Smith, who was not someone he favored working with.

If he'd have seen a Bronco driving out of a ditch, he would have insisted on pulling it over, he said. Bronco didn't know whether to believe him or not. The agent had retired from the DNR and was working, now, in Smith's old job, as a sheriff's deputy in Oscoda County. Giving a drunk driver a free pass wasn't something he was likely to admit to.

Lesneski tracked McDowell down, too, at the Montmorency County Jail. He was a month away from getting sentenced for something or other and not at all what Lesneski might have been expecting had he not read up on him beforehand. One-time pot dealer of renown, one-time member of a local rock and roll band, party-hearty northwoods guy, McDowell was 75, grizzled and looking every bit of 85 when Bronco came calling.

McDowell confirmed that he'd lived just down the road from Linker's, said he'd been in the band that often played there and had known the Duvalls, though he wouldn't call them friends.

He said the Duvalls would come by his house and smoke some weed and drink some beer.

"They were really kind of scary. They would be having fun, partying, drinking and singing along. Then the next thing you know, something would piss them off and they would be ready to fight at the drop of a hat. They'd get real mean."

One time J.R. saw this guy sitting on one of the bar stools at Linker's. Minding his own business, it looked like. Maybe they'd had a past beef, who knows? But J.R. walks right up to the guy, pulls out a large knife and holds it to the guy's side. The guy, of course, is freaking out. And J.R. proceeds to walk the guy out of the bar, knife poking him in the kidney. A little while later, J.R. comes walking back in, calm as can be. The guy? Who knows what happened to him? Didn't come back.

"I knew right then the Duvalls weren't nobody to mess with. I always kept my distance after that."

Basically, though, McDowell had nothing to add. No independent information. Had heard all the pig rumors, but who hadn't?

49

"I KILLED THEM"

Months went by. Bronco worked his burgeoning caseload, not much to be done on this cold one, other than telling Duvalls to pass on his regards to J.R. and Coco and talking about canning with Boudro.

On March 3, 2000, Lesneski got a call from a Detroit attorney. He had a client who might be able to solve the deer-hunter case and wanted to know the details about getting the $100,000 reward.

His client was afraid and would like to maintain his anonymity as long as possible. Satisfied with the introductory talk, the attorney said he'd have his client, John, call.

The next day, the improbably named Johnny Force called.

"I know I'll have to testify, but I just want it to be kept a secret as long as possible for my own protection," he said. "Two guys are responsible for the hunters' deaths. One of the guys who did the shooting, he's the crazy one who worries me."

This was Force's story:

A few years earlier he'd been living in Lincoln Park with a guy named Tim Walz. Tim's girlfriend told Force that Tim had confessed to her that he and a buddy had killed the hunters and taken their vehicle, that they were buried in one spot and their Bronco dumped in a swamp.

Johnny told her Tim was full of bullshit and probably just high, and everything he said should be taken with a grain of salt.

Later, though, while applying for a permit to purchase a pistol, Force saw a flyer on the case and became suspicious. One day, Force and Tim were in the basement working on a project and Force decided to try to trick him. He said he'd heard from two different sources that Tim had been involved in the hunters' deaths.

"Tim looked at me and started to cry," said Force, then quoted him as saying, "Why did you have to bring that up? I'm trying to forget it."

Tim then said that he and a friend named Scott had been high on acid and out shining deer—illegally using lights at night to hunt—and accidentally shined the light on two men standing in the field. The men were pissed off that they were shining. Words were exchanged. Scott aimed his rifle at one of the men and shot him. Tim was in complete shock—that was the last thing he'd expected. Scott told the other man to get on his hands and knees. He'd started begging for his life, that he had a wife and family, and Scott shot him, too.

He then turned the rifle on Tim and said he had no choice, he was a witness, he'd have to kill him, too. Tim begged for his life, told Scott they'd been friends for years, that he wouldn't say a word. Scott told him if he did, he'd kill him, and then ordered him to help him get rid of the bodies.

They took off the hunters' boots and socks. They put the hunters' socks over their hands to avoid leaving fingerprints, loaded them up in their Bronco, drove deep into the woods and buried them. Then they drove over to Foley Swamp and drove the Bronco in.

Force told Bronco he'd be happy to take a polygraph.

I don't doubt you, Bronco told him, but what if this is just all a bunch of bullshit by Tim?

Force said he thought it might be bullshit at first, "but Tim was visibly upset. He's had a drinking problem ever since I've known him, and now I understand why."

Plus, he said, if you knew Scott, you'd know how crazy he

and his old man are. Completely looney tunes. Scott wouldn't think twice about shooting someone. One day Force and his cousin were riding around in a car and Scott just reached down and pulled out a sawed-off shotgun and aimed it at them for laughs. Scott's father was always bragging that he was so crazy, if he killed someone they wouldn't even put him in jail.

Lesneski ran a LEIN check. Walz had a lengthy driving record and several warrants out for his arrest, including one for violating probation out of the 82nd District Court in Ogemaw County.

On March 23, the Michigan State Police Fugitive Team arrested Walz at his home in Lincoln Park and took him to jail in Northville. Lesneski drove down and picked Walz up on the bench warrant out of West Branch and drove him north.

On the way, Lesneski read him his Miranda rights, something that doesn't usually happen to you for getting busted on a parole violation.

"I fucking knew there was more to this than those outstanding warrants," Walz told him.

Lesneski told him he was a suspect in the murder of the two missing deer hunters and that the information he already had could be used to get a warrant for murder.

"I don't know shit, I never said anything about killing anybody to anyone," he said.

Lesneski told him he had two persons who would testify otherwise, that he and Scott had shot them and disposed of their bodies and the Bronco.

Tim denied it vehemently. Bronco, not under oath, said one of the informants had already passed a polygraph test, so either Tim was lying now, or had lied to his friend about the murders.

"Do you want to trust your future to a jury of your peers?" asked Bronco as they sped up I-75. He told him that his fate, that their course of action, would depend on how truthful Tim was from this moment on.

Tim burst into tears. "I told my friends that we did it, but we really didn't. I was trying to look big and bad in front of my friends."

Talk is cheap, said Lesneski. I don't know if you're lying now, or not.

"I can't fucking believe I said that. I was fucked up. It was stupid. I wasn't thinking," said Walz.

Bronco told him he had one way out: a polygraph.

Walz was eager to take it. So Lesneski made a phone call and drove straight to the Midland post, which was just west of I-75, on the way north. Walz took the test and passed it. He hadn't participated in their disappearance and had no knowledge of it.

And then Bronco drove him to the Ogemaw County Jail, where he was lodged on the bench warrant.

50

E-MAIL AND "CRIME STOPPERS"

On October 25, 2000, Lesneski got a very hot tip by Internet. It was about Connie Sundberg, and was e-mailed to him by one of her former bosses. Some of it Lesneski had heard before, some of it was new, and all of it was good.

The boss had seen her crying at a copy machine and asked her if there was anything he could do to help. Perhaps someone at work was harassing her? She then told him it wasn't work related, that it was about some missing hunters, that she couldn't get it out of her mind.

He told her he was aware of the case, that every year when the anniversary rolled around, he would see the news coverage, and hope the killers would be brought to justice and the riddle solved.

That got her going. She told him she knew what had happened, that she'd played a part in it. She said she and another girl had been dancing with the hunters in a bar one night. Her boyfriend intervened and there had been words. The boyfriend and his friends had waited outside the bar to continue the argument.

The next day, her boyfriend was acting strange and told her they'd killed someone the night before, and if she ever told anyone, they'd kill her, too.

She told him that one of her boyfriend's brothers was so

stupid that he drove the Bronco around for a few days, until word got out in the media about them and their car. She told him her ex-boyfriend and his family deserve what they have coming, but that she was afraid for her life, that they would not hesitate for one minute to kill her.

~

As the Thanksgiving holiday and the fifteenth anniversary of the disappearance of Brian Ognjan and David Tyll approached, a series of TV spots began running around the state, as part of the Crime Stoppers Alliance, a program the state police started in 1999. It featured a toll-free tip line available twenty-four hours a day and offered a reward of $1,000 for tips that led to felony arrests.

They brought forth a slew of tips, most of them worthless, some interesting, a few good enough to spark genuine interest by Lesneski.

One tip cited the Duvalls by name. It said the whole thing had started at Timber's Steak House. Tyll and Ognjan had been playing pool with the Duvalls and refused to pay up when they lost. Later that night, the Duvalls had killed them.

Another came via phone call on January 17, 2001, from Sandra Lee James, who was a sister of Connie and Donna Sundberg. She, too, mentioned the Duvalls and she, too, said it had started with an argument over a game of pool.

"I know my sister Connie knows more than she's saying. She's afraid of them. They've beat her up and threatened her before," she said. "Hell, I'm scared just talking to you. Please don't tell anyone that I spoke with you. These guys are crazy. They'll kill me in a heartbeat."

And she asked him not to tell Connie that she had called.

51
THE PSYCHICS

There was something about missing hunters in a north-woods setting that brought out the best (or worst) in psychics and clairvoyants.

In 1986 and 1987, Chris Pilkus, who said he was a psychorientologist, a 1972 graduate of what he claimed was the Silva Forward Thinking Institute, wrote a series of letters to police in Troy, St. Clair Shores and Traverse City describing his visions.

In his letter to Troy Detective Philip Steele in March of 1986, Pilkus said the hunters had been shot with a bow and arrow by someone up in a tree stand, David first. What happened was, they were cruising down the road, David driving, tapping his fingers on the wheel in time to the music. It's night. David has his window down so he can look out and see the stars.

They pull over, David gets out to pee. Brian's waiting and waiting and finally hollers out, "Hey, man, shake it off, let's go."

Still no David. Brian gets out and goes looking for him and sees him on the ground, a crossbow arrow with black striping on the feathers through his neck.

Brian starts sobbing, tries to lift David up, and is shot in the lower back with the same crossbow.

"That'll teach the motherfuckers a lesson," says a big, heavyset guy in thigh-high black waders.

Pilkus added that the name Patton kept popping up in his visions.

And, "If I psychically detect anything further, will give you a call."

~

On December 2, 1988, Christy Hawley came into the Oscoda Sheriff's Department to talk to Sergeant Smith. She was a psychic, she said, and had recently seen in her dreams what had happened to the two missing hunters.

They were murdered, in a shallow grave. She didn't know the location, yet. They'd been shot with a pistol. Two persons were involved, a white male with light brown hair and a blue suit with blue and gray stripes, and a white woman with long blonde hair with a blue suit and red and white stripes.

She could see a black truck, too, with a dent in the front fender. The license plate had an 18 and either an RX or an RZ. And she could see something about a park off County Road 489, too.

I'll get back to you when I know more, she said.

Three days later, she did. The license plate was RC 4182.

Smith ran the plate. There was, indeed, such a plate. It was registered to a trucking company in Wyoming, a suburb of Grand Rapids on the far western side of the state.

The truck and the owner were cleared.

~

On February 22, 1991, Halleck got a letter from Mrs. Ognjan, who was in Florida for the winter. She wrote that her husband was in very ill health. (He died of cancer shortly thereafter.) She also sent a clipping of a newspaper story about a psychic who had helped police solve other cases around the United States.

No one would ever accuse Halleck of leaving any stones unturned. On March 4, he talked to psychic Noreen Renier by phone and she said she'd be willing to help on the case, without charge either to the state police or to the Tylls or the Ognjans.

She told Halleck she'd send him a list in the near future of what she'd need to get started.

The next Halleck heard was on September 18, when he got a letter from a program manager at the University of Delaware, asking if the state police would be interested in hosting a seminar on psychics' techniques in assisting criminal investigations.

The State Police had about zero interest, and Halleck's might have been even less. It was certainly less than Mrs. Ognjan's, and nothing came of it for nearly a decade. Renier wouldn't be the last psychic involved in the case, though.

~

On October 13, 1999, Maxine Burhams called the East Tawas post and left a message for Bronco to call her. They had a lengthy conversation six days later. She was, she said, a spiritualist and psychic who lived in the small northern town of Alanson. She had worked with law enforcement officials in the past and had been able to provide corroborative information for their investigations.

"I've been contacted by the lost hunters' spirits," she said. "They want to be found."

She'd gotten their message a while back but had been hesitant to call, not sure how receptive the detective would be.

Bronco told her he was, as he put it, "not a practitioner of psychic spiritual intervention," but that he'd be very happy to hear what she had to say.

Burhams told him she visualized the hunters as having been in a car accident in a remote area, probably on a two-track. Their Bronco had been run off the trail by a small white Toyota truck with a big, fully enclosed cube-style box on the back.

The Toyota had been speeding toward them, far too fast for conditions, forcing the Bronco to veer over. But it had veered too far to the right and toppled down a steep ravine.

Bronco, ever polite, told her the description put him in mind of the high banks of the AuSable River, but that there were other areas that could fit that description as well.

Burhams said she'd like to contact him in the event more spiritual information came her way. Bronco told her that would be nice.

~

Mrs. Ognjan didn't see what harm turning to psychics could do. It wasn't as if traditional police methods had done them any good.

Both Helen and Catherine Tyll talked to Lesneski on June 30, 2000. They wanted Noreen Renier to help them out, now that Halleck was off the case. If there was a cost involved, the families would share it. They were adamant.

Bronco wasn't exactly eager to pursue the occult, but if it made them feel better, that something was being accomplished, fine. At least he wouldn't oppose it.

He and Renier finally talked by phone on August 15. She said she'd send some information to him about her procedures, but in the meantime, he ought to talk to the families and see what personal belongings they still might have of Brian's and David's.

Helen told him she still had Brian's rosary and prayer book. If that wasn't spiritual, what was? Catherine wasn't sure they still had anything personal. She'd have to look and would get back to him.

A month later, he still hadn't heard. When he called to see if they'd found anything, he learned there had been a good, but sad, reason for the delay. One of her sons, Archie, had died unexpectedly, from an epileptic seizure.

On September 22, she called Lesneski to say she had found an old T-shirt. Would that be good enough? Bronco told her he'd check with Renier.

Renier said she'd need more than a prayer book and T-shirt, though. She'd need other personal items. The families sent Bronco some photos. Not good enough, Renier said, she'd need things like jewelry, a toothbrush, maybe a comb. Surely they must have something else.

They didn't, though. Renier said she couldn't proceed without more, and on November 13, the families agreed to cancel an upcoming meeting that had been scheduled with her.

Renier would later resurface in the murder of Laci Peterson. While she was still missing, her husband Scott's mother hired her to help find her stepdaughter. Scott mailed her a shoe and Renier later claimed she sensed from Scott's handwriting on the package that he might have been her killer.

That wasn't the end of it, though. Helen Ognjan called Lesneski on November 14 and said she had another psychic in mind, one from the Detroit area named Linda Edgar. Helen gave him Edgar's phone number and he promptly called her. She said she'd be happy to meet with him, but it would likely have to be early into the new year.

~

Detective Sergeant Alison King, like Maxwell and Schram and Halleck before her, had spent hundreds of hours tracking down hundreds of tips or interviewing and reinterviewing hundreds of persons, some of them suspects, some friends and relatives of suspects, some well intentioned, some off the wall, some who really did seem to know something about what had happened to David Tyll and Brian Ognjan.

Finally, there was nothing left to do except periodically write one line in a journal to show she hadn't stopped thinking about them:

> *11-8-99, no new info to report.*
> *12-8-99, no info to report.*
> *2-8-00, no new info, pends further investigation*
> *as time permits and/or recovery of the bodies.*

3-8-00, no new info to report.

4-10-00, no new info to report.

5-15-00, no new info to report.

6-13-00, no new info to report on the missing hunters.

7-8-00, no new info to report.

In all that time, with all those witnesses, the one thing she hadn't done was interview a psychic. That was about to change.

At 11:20 a.m. on February 20, 2001, after hearing about a psychic who'd attracted some publicity in Michigan recently, King called The Alhambra Institute, hoping to talk to a woman named Alexia. She wasn't in.

At 12:30 p.m. Alexia returned the call. She said she'd be happy to help, asked for the names of the victims and said she'd call back in a few days.

On the 27th, Alexia called to say that it was her feeling that both Brian Ognjan and David Tyll were dead, and that their bodies were located in Otsego County, in a location not yet known to her. She told King she was going to get a map of the county and would be in touch.

King then called Helen Ognjan, who had pushed Schram to get psychic help years earlier, to give her an update.

Alexia next called King on March 16. She said she had more information and wanted to have a face-to-face meeting to discuss it. Because of some court duties, King couldn't meet with her until the afternoon of the 26th, on the second floor of the Monroe post.

Alexia had a county map and pointed out a spot where the hunters could be found. And then she told this tale:

It wasn't all clear, just bits and pieces. The hunters had driven the Bronco off the road near a curve, and crashed down a ravine to a trickling stream. The truck would be found on its side in an area of dense trees and bushes.

Tyll had died first, but not until he was pulled across the stream by Ognjan. Tyll had died on his back and his bones were still sticking out of the debris and could be found.

Ognjan was badly injured and had broken bones, including ribs, and he'd either died of his injuries or committed suicide because he knew he was badly hurt and couldn't get out. His remains would be more difficult to find. Some of them were scattered, some remained where he'd died, leaning up against a tree.

Alexia could see camping equipment nearby and she was picking up the name of a woman whose first name started with an "S," possibly Sharon.

Who is she? asked King.

I don't know, said Alexia. "I only see two bodies."

She saw something else—airplanes flying overhead.

King looked at the map and noticed that the road just to the northwest of where Alexia was pointing was named Poquette. It gave King a jolt.

After not making any reports or doing any interviews from October 1999 till January 2001, a hot tip had come in through Lesneski up in West Branch, who'd gotten a call from a member of the Wayne County Sheriff's Department.

An informant had come in and told him that a guy he was doing construction with on a new terminal at Wayne County Airport said he knew all about the missing hunters. He'd once leased space in a building to two guys who had killed them, chopped up their bodies and fed them to pigs.

The old, familiar tale from a new source gave Lesneski a start. It gave King one, too, and the investigation was reopened on January 16.

The name of this construction worker who knew the killers: Poquette.

In April, King found out that Poquette had his information second-hand, but a very interesting second-hand—he'd once worked at the Bentley Nursery with the Duvalls, and someone else who worked there told him what he'd heard the brothers saying. The Duvalls, eh? When Lesneski found out their connection to the tip, he was convinced he'd still get them one day, one way.

On May 6, King and Alexia searched the area on the map. They didn't find any bodies. Alexia couldn't even find a ravine. Woods were rare, too, in a county full of them. The spot she'd chosen was well-populated farmland dotted with residential homes, numerous natural gas wells punctuating the landscape.

The case was returned, yet again, to inactive status.

52

MORE PSYCHIC VISIONS

King wouldn't have to wait long to talk to her second psychic. She got a call on May 24, 2002, from Vicky Ankley, who had just returned from her second recent trip north to Roscommon.

About two weeks earlier she had stopped at a rest area, seen a flyer on the hunters and started having visions of the two missing men.

She came home briefly, but the visions forced her to return to the Roscommon area to do some investigating. She now had a suspect in mind and detailed information she wished to share.

Money wasn't an issue, she said, she was just a clairvoyant wishing to help. She'd worked with the police in the past, she said, and helped solve a case involving a Ryan Getz.

King interviewed 32-year-old Ankley at the Richmond post just north of Detroit on June 3. Ankley told her the murderer was a 45-year-old with sandy hair, a hunter who had met Tyll and Ognjan at a rest stop along I-75 and decided on a random killing as a challenge.

The murderer was going to retire in November and may have been involved in inappropriate behavior with his stepdaughter.

She said the killer had used a Taser to stun the two

David Tyll. *(Cathy Tyll)*

Brian smiling. *(Helen Ognjan)*

A gathering of the Tyll clan and some of the first grandkids. David is standing at the back.
(Cathy Tyll)

Brian holding a fish just caught in Lake St. Clair, near where he lived.
(Helen Ognjan)

A beaming Brian.
(Helen Ogn

Brian's modest house in St. Clair Shores. He and David left from here for their weekend hunting trip.
(Helen Ognjan)

A shrine to David in the Tylls' backyard.
(Cathy Tyll)

David's Bronco.
(Cathy Tyll)

Brian at the wheel of his beloved boat. (*Helen Ognjan*)

Detective Sergeant Bronco Lesneski out of the East Tawas State Police Post. (*Tom Henderson*)

The home in Hale where J.R. Duvall was arrested by Det. Sgt. Lesneski. (*Tom Henderson*)

Timbers Steak House, a Duvall hangout, where J.R. used to bartend and serve as a bouncer. *(Tom Henderson)*

The house between South Branch and Curtisville, where Rex Duvall lived in 1985. Police suspected that the missing Bronco had been chopped into parts in the garage, which were sold, buried, or dumped into swamps. But no one was arrested in connection with the disappearance of the vehicle. *(Tom Henderson)*

Coco Duvall's house in 1985, much improved since. *(Tom Henderson)*

The site of J.R.'s residence that burned under mysterious circumstances. Police suspected it was arson, but no charges were ever filed. Later, they excavated the ground without success looking for human remains or car parts. *(Tom Henderson)*

Views of Alcona Pond, a large lake formed by the Alcona Dam. The levee the left has a steep slope where it was rumored the Bronco was rolled into the lake. The lake was searched by dive teams and later by a crew using a magnetometer, without success. *(Photos by Tom Henderson)*

Linker's Lost Creek Lodge. *(Tom Henderson)*

Barb Bourdo, outside her house near Luzerne. She climbed out a rear window the night she says she saw the hunters beat to death in a nearby clearing in the woods. *(Tom Henderson)*

Walker's bar and bowling alley, where the hunters drank one night and worked on their hangover the next afternoon. *(Tom Henderson)*

The view across Mapes Road, taken from where Bourdo would have stood the night the hunters died. *(Tom Henderson)*

Donna Pendergast.
(*Dan Stoudacher /
Bay City Times*)

Helen Ognjan
(*left*) and Cathy
Tyll embrace
after the verdict.
(*Dan Stoudacher
/ Bay City Times*)

The Duvalls
react to the
verdict. (*Dan
Stoudacher/Bay
City Times*)

hunters, then gotten into their truck and driven into a heavily wooded area. The two victims were put in a crate with metal bars. Four other men showed up and the two hunters were released so they could be chased through the woods at night like animals.

Tyll was the first to be caught. He'd eluded his pursuers until the next afternoon. Both were tortured before they were killed and burned. Their kidnapper kept one of Tyll's fingers as a souvenir and was using it to intimidate his wife and stepdaughter.

All of this came from her visions. Unable to get them to stop, she had driven back up north with her boyfriend to do her investigation. Her visions had included the kidnapper's name, and she knew he lived in a brown house off a dirt road. His wife was short with curly blond hair. His daughter was on Xanax and worked in a flower shop or beauty salon. She also could see where the man worked.

Ankley and her boyfriend were driving to his place of employment when she saw his car parked outside a building and saw him standing there. They stopped. She got out and approached him. "Are you Norman?"

"You're here to get me," he said.

She looked into his eyes and knew her visions were true. Terrified, she ran back to her car and they fled the scene.

Ankley said she knew from her visions where the bodies were buried and she agreed to take police officers there, provided they bring a K-9 dog from the Great Lakes Search and Rescue Company. The dog had helped on the Getz case.

After Ankley left, King did an Internet search. Some of Ankley's story checked out. King found that a Ryan Getz had been reported missing in East Lansing in December of 1997 and his body was found several months later by a K-9 unit, but details were sketchy.

Another search showed that there was, indeed, a Great Lakes Search and Rescue of Michigan, and it listed a phone number. King gave it a call.

On June 6, King talked to Detective Doug Wyonette of the Michigan State University Public Safety Department.

His version contradicted the Internet report. One of his officers had found the body. Death was ruled accidental. Intoxicated, Getz had fallen into the Red Cedar River on campus after leaving a New Year's Eve party, and the body was discovered in April.

53

A DEAD HORSE

On October 29, 2001, likely in response to a rerun of one of the syndicated or cable TV shows that had episodes about the missing hunters, Bronco got a message to call a Jerry Killian in Missouri when he got a chance.

After several tries, Bronco reached him on November 6.

Killian said he had once been close friends with the Duvalls and Sherm Heilig. They'd traveled the area together and, in his words, "violated a lot of deer."

They would often fish together off the beaten track, in secluded places that no one knew about. One spot was a particularly beautiful little lake deep in the woods. It was tiny, maybe 300 yards around, but deep for such a small lake, maybe forty feet. He couldn't be sure how to find it, again, after all these years, but it was ten to fifteen miles outside Curtisville.

There was a levee or a trestle they had to cross to get there. Back then, he'd been the only guy who had a 4×4, so he did the driving. It was a rough ride, with branches scraping the roof.

Anyway, said Killian, "We went there often. We caught a lot of fish from that lake." But spring of 1986 rolled around and they stopped going there. He brought it up one day, thought they ought to go there and fish. The Duvalls said no, without explanation.

The missing hunters were in the news, then. Whenever they'd be sitting around, drinking or playing cards, and someone brought the subject up, one of the Duvalls or Heilig would say, " 'Shut the fuck up!' And the conversation about the hunters would end," said Killian.

"Back then, the police were sniffing around a lot. I started asking questions once and they told me not to discuss it. Later on, I got more suspicious. We were drinking a lot one night and I was asking questions about the hunters and talking about how easy it would be to dump the vehicle in one of the many deep lakes around. I was threatened to keep my mouth shut or they would teach me a lesson.

"A few days later, I had to go someplace, and when I returned home, I found one of my horses had its throat slit. I knew then I had to get the fuck out of the area. I moved to Missouri and never went back."

54

A MESSAGE FROM J.R.

November 23, 2001, sixteen years to the day after Tyll and Ognjan had been drinking Budweiser up north in either Walker's or Linker's, Lesneski got a call at home about 6 p.m. from the Alcona County Sheriff's Department.

J.R. Duvall had been arrested at 3 p.m. for driving under the influence, and a computer check showed he was wanted on outstanding warrants out of Alcona, Tuscola and Monroe Counties, involving failure to pay child support in excess of $45,000. He'd just gotten out of the Gladwin County Jail after serving 45 days on one beef.

J.R. wanted word relayed to Lesneski that he was willing to talk. Lesneski drove over to Harrisville and met with J.R. in the jail.

"I want out of here," he said. "I'm due in court, again, and I know they're going to give me at least six to nine months. I want you to P.R. me out," he said, jail talk for having Bronco arrange for his release on personal recognizance. He wasn't able to post whatever bond there was.

Bronco asked him what information he had that might be worth a get-out-of-jail pass.

"I heard these two hunters were into drugs. I know some people who were also into drugs back then. I thought it was strange that the two hunters and those acquaintances of mine would both disappear at the same time."

"Are you saying these drug people had something to do with the demise of the missing hunters?"

"I'm just saying these drug people split the scene around the same time. Maybe they got involved with the hunters, maybe the hunters tried to fuck them over. Maybe the people I know had nothing to do with it."

Didn't seem like much to bargain with.

"You know," said Bronco, putting an edge into it, "you've been contacted several times by law enforcement officials, and you've adamantly denied having any knowledge about the missing hunters. You know—because I told you—that you are the number one suspect, and have been for years.

"Now, today you're telling me about this hypothetical situation under the guise that I get you released from incarceration? I'm sorry, but I don't buy it. Now, if you want to reconsider taking a polygraph, maybe I can get you some relief, but I'm not making you any promises."

Bronco told him to think it over, let him know before his court date on the 27th.

At 8:30 on the 27th, Bronco stopped by the jail to talk to J.R. again.

He'd talked to the Monroe County folks and J.R. was in arrears in that county, alone, to the tune of $44,000. Tuscola and Alcona needed bond of $2,500 combined. So P.R.ing him out wasn't going to happen.

But, he needed to know that Bronco had boxes of information supplied over the years by people who had hunches and theories and what they claimed was first-hand knowledge of various events. None of them, by the way, were incarcerated and looking to deal.

"In the event you want to take a polygraph, I'll do my best to accommodate you. If you truly want to help yourself, contact me and I'll set it up."

He didn't tell J.R. that his superiors had already said no

to another polygraph. At that point, he didn't care what policy was. What was the harm? Get him talking about events and you never knew where it was going to lead. If J.R. was willing to get wired up, by God, he'd get him wired up.

55
ANOTHER DEATH

Meanwhile, Lesneski had been calling around, asking if any law enforcement folks in northeast Michigan could help him locate the hidden lake Killian had told him about. The problem was, the area was so dense with woods and so thick with small lakes, that there were seemingly infinite possibilities. No one could recall any levees or trestles, but that didn't mean anything. There were so many trails and two-tracks and firebreaks that you could get to a lot of hidden lakes from a variety of directions; you might have been to the right lake and just never seen the levee.

On December 4, Lesneski contacted district headquarters. He told Detective Lieutenant Dan Bohnett that he wanted to go up by chopper and do an aerial surveillance. Lake levels were down in recent years, so a car once submerged might very well be visible. Plus, with all the foliage gone from the trees, you'd be able to spot small bodies of water much more easily.

Not waiting for approval, on December 7, he met with Warren MacNeill, a conservation officer assigned to the area. True to character, Lesneski had scouted him out ahead of time and written in italics in his reports:

> *"Note: Warren has the reputation in the DNR* [Department of Natural Resources] *as an excellent*

woodsman. He is also extremely familiar with the
secluded areas of interest to this investigation.

Lesneski and MacNeill came up with a list of likely lakes,
small enough, deep enough, secluded enough—Little Trout
Lake, Reid Lake, Wilbur Creek, Hughes Lake and Penoyer
Lake—and marked out their GPS coordinates.

The same day he called Jerry Killian in Missouri, to go
over his story and to run by the list of lakes. See if any of the
names rang a bell or if he had more to add since the last time
they talked.

Killian's wife, Glenda, answered the phone, with what
sounded like a note of apprehension to Lesneski. She immediately became distraught. Jerry had been killed in a traffic
accident two weeks earlier. A head-on with another truck.

Just to be on the safe side Lesneski called the Missouri
State Police. They confirmed that Killian was dead—it
wasn't just a cover-up for changing his mind about cooperating. Just to be on the safe side, Bronco asked them to send
him a copy of the accident report. Not that he was paranoid
or anything, but a lot of people related to this case had died
over the years, and reading the report was one way of making sure in his own mind it was an unrelated death.

On December 10, Bohnett told him the chopper flyover
had been approved. He told him to be at the Iosco County
Airport at 9 a.m. the next day.

Armed with the coordinates and a detailed map, Lesneski
and the pilot flew in a grid pattern for hours over a roughly
400-square-mile area of eastern Oscoda and western Alcona
Counties. His short list was only a tiny percentage of the lakes
you could see in all directions. The woods were bisected northwest to southeast by the AuSable River, designated a National
Scenic River, and in every direction by streams and tributaries
such as Blackhouse Creek and Hoppy Creek.

There was water glistening in every direction. There was
Vaughn Lake, Hoppy Lake, Grassy Lake, Stuart Lake,
Mitchell Lake, Guilford Lake, Chain o' Lake, Red Head
Lake, Catherine Lake, Marlbed Lake, Alice Lake, Jose Lake,

McGraw Lake, Perch Lake, Slab Lake—and those were just the lakes in the bottom one inch of a map that was twelve inches high.

Back and forth they flew, swooping low, peering into the water of all those lakes to see if they could see metal reflecting light beneath the surface.

Nothing.

When he got back to the post, Lesneski called the families to let them know.

56
CADAVER DOGS

Barb Boudro called Bronco on December 13. Somehow, nearly three years had gone by since he had put a foot in her doorway to keep her from shutting him out. He'd had such high hopes, then, that a breakthrough might be imminent.

She wanted to know if anything had developed. And she had some advice. If he hadn't already done so, he ought to talk to Steve Linker, the owner of the Lost Creek Lodge at the time, and an old friend of hers, Dickie Baker, who'd been drinking that night with her and Ronnie Emery. And he oughta check to see if he could find William Parrott. He'd been working dispatch for the Oscoda County Sheriff's Department back then and might have been on duty when someone called from the bar about a fight. Finally, there was her old boyfriend, Dick Smith. He was the one she claimed had been dispatched to the bar, but stopped along the way at a party store and never made it.

Bronco oughta check all of them out. And he oughta check out the area where the hunters were killed.

The call got Bronco motivated—not that he wasn't the self-motivating type. He drove on over to Mapes Road to scout around. He walked the property, then went over to the county courthouse to see who now owned it.

In the late afternoon, he called Sergeant Warren Miller,

commanding officer of the state police K-9 unit. They agreed to meet on December 18 and have the specially trained cadaver dogs have a go at it.

The dogs snuffled back and forth, working every square inch of the clearing down from Boudro's a quarter mile or so toward Linker's. They worked the woods, circling out in all directions.

As dogs who smell professionally will do, they got excited over any number of scents. Briefly. Just something that had caught their interest, but not the smell they'd been trained for, the one that got them their rewards.

They found nothing.

57

FREAKING OUT A TRAPPER

Bronco was a made-for-TV cop. Almost kind of a Dudley Do-Right kind of square-jawed, good-looking, deadly serious defender of good and battler of evil, what every cop's mother wished her son looked like.

They filmed a news segment on the case that was distributed around the state early in January of 2002. It ran on TV-12 in Flint and Saginaw on January 7. It ran on TV-9 and 10 in Cadillac and TV-4 and -2 in Detroit, as well as the 50,000-watt radio behemoth of the Midwest, Detroit's WJR-AM on January 8.

And Robert Verellen, a 55-year-old former trapper, called on January 9. He'd seen the news clip and said he felt the need to call and talk.

Bronco told him to come in at 9 the next morning. He was on time and told this tale:

Back in deer season of 1985—he remembered the year very clearly because he had just bought a brand-new Dodge pickup, back before any schmoe could lease a new car, and buying a new car or truck was one of those events you never forgot—he was working a trap line in a remote region of Alcona County, deep in the woods.

At the end of a trail he used to check his traps, he came to a parked dark blue or black Bronco. At first he thought it was an early-bird hunter who'd wanted to be in place for dawn, then realized it must have been there overnight, because it was covered in a light coating of snow.

Verellen had to come back the next day to the same area. This time, the Bronco was gone, and tire tracks headed off into the woods. He parked his Dodge and headed toward one of his traps, coincidentally following the tire tracks. Small trees were snapped off along the way.

"The area gave me the willies," he said.

The tracks led over an embankment, and down to a freshly dug mound of dirt. There, tracks led right up to the mound, which looked big enough to hold a Bronco.

Two days later, checking on some traps in the same area of the woods, he heard a vehicle coming down the trail. When he spotted it, it was at the base of a steep hill. "The driver had to use the creeper gear to get over the hill." It was an old, goldish Chevy pickup, with baby blue doors and tailgate, like it had been assembled from junkyard parts.

Verellen was heading that way. Two guys got out of the Chevy and started in his direction, but they hadn't seen him, yet.

"They were very dirty and messy, almost like they hadn't taken a bath in months. Their hair was long and messy," he said. They kept walking toward him, heads down. When they finally looked up and spotted him, "they gave me a look that burned right through me. I stood there for a second. My instincts told me something wasn't right. I backed up, turned away from them and headed in the other direction."

This from a trapper who made his living in the woods, on his way to a trap. Maybe it had a mink or a fox or a beaver waiting for him, but a pelt could wait.

One thing people always said about the Duvalls of the mid-1980s. They looked a mess. Photos always showed long, stringy, greasy hair. Verellen was, thought Bronco, *exactly* describing the Duvalls as they looked in the photos he'd seen.

That same day, Lesneski, conservation officer MacNeill and Verellen drove into the woods, Verellen leading them to the spot he'd talked about, as best as he could recollect events, though trails and two-tracks can change their look dramatically in fifteen years, as saplings grow into small trees, or berry thickets spring up where once there had been breaks of pasture.

There was snow on the ground and, as Bronco described it, "frost in the earth." They conducted a limited search of several areas, to no avail. Bronco suggested they return soon with a metal detector.

The Lincoln Outdoor Center had metal detectors, but only the run-of-the-mill ones you see wrinkled old folks using on Florida beaches in the wintertime to find rusting old ring-tops from beer cans. They made heavy-duty ones, the kinds you'd get a "ping" on from a car buried deep in the earth, but the owner said he'd have to special-order one.

Special-order, then, said Bronco.

On February 1, the detector was in and four days later, Lesneski and MacNeill searched the areas where Verellen had taken them. They also searched the area known as "Trees for Tomorrow," a Christmas tree farm and deer-camp where the Duvalls had spent the season of 1985.

Other than the usual bits and pieces of metallic junk, nothing.

58

WEST VIRGINIA BOUND

A while back, Donna Sunderg had called Lesneski to let him know that Connie was now living in West Virginia with her two children and their father, Greg Brown, an old boyfriend she'd gotten back together with.

He'd asked West Virginia State Police to make discreet inquiries without letting her know he was trying to find her, and to provide him an address and phone number if they could. They reported back that she was living in Coolridge, West Virginia.

Bronco didn't want to do it by phone. The department, always cash-strapped in its budget battles with state legislators, had already funded Halleck's trip to Virginia to talk to her when she was living there. But Bronco was Bronco and if he said he needed it, his bosses would work the budget out one way or another. No one would have blamed them if they'd said it was a sixteen-year-old case that had already cost a fortune and they had plenty of live ones to solve. Truth was, it rankled everyone up and down the chain of command north of Flint that they thought they knew who'd done it, and it was a couple of lowlifes no one had been able to figure out how to outsmart.

A few days after he got confirmation where Sundberg lived, word came down from command. The trip to West Virginia was approved.

On February 12, three and a half years after he had waited for her outside her home in Roseville, Michigan, Connie Sundberg was opening her door at 10 a.m. and inviting Bronco Lesneski into her home in Coolridge.

She was very cooperative, forthright, seemed almost happy to see Bronco, who wrote later that she seemed very honest in her answers.

Some of what she'd said about Coco before, she said again. But there was more.

"What I didn't tell you back then was: He tried to kill me the next morning. I told you he threatened me, but he actually tried to suffocate me," she said. "I started asking questions about what the hell he was talking about, killing people last night. The next thing I know he's beating the shit out of me. He tried to choke me. I ran outside and he chased me, tackled me to the ground and started pushing my face in the mud and snow.

"I couldn't breathe. I thought he was going to kill me. I fought for my life to get away from him. Finally, I ran away and went to my mother's house."

What about Linker's Lost Creek Lodge? Were the Duvalls regulars there?

"The guys would mostly go there and get sloppy drunk," she said. Not her. She'd go there and hang out, but she wasn't much of a drinker then. Smoked a lot of weed, that was her buzz of choice.

What about Barb Boudro? Would she recognize the brothers if she saw them? For sure, said Sundberg. Word was, Barb and a girlfriend had had a thing going with J.R., at least, and maybe one or two brothers. They'd drink together over to Mio.

What about Sharon Russeau? Everyone said Eileen Seitz, now dead, had known a lot more than she'd let on. Did Sharon? It was her and Rex's garage, after all, where it was believed the Bronco got "parted out."

"If Sharon knows anything, I don't believe she'll tell you. She's scared of Rex. He beat her so bad, he almost killed her. Eileen and I tried to get her to go to the hospital, but she wouldn't. She was beaten so badly, every part of her body was swollen, even her earlobes. We all believe Sharon suffered brain damage as a result of that beating; she's never been the same.

"We tried to get her to go to the hospital, but she was so scared she refused. Sharon told us, 'He'll kill me if I go to the doctor.'"

Sundberg said she'd run into J.R. occasionally when she'd returned to Michigan to visit relatives. One time he asked her, "Are you talking to the cops?"

She told him she had been, but she didn't know anything.

She finished by telling Bronco she'd do what she could to help the investigation. He left her his card, told her to keep in touch.

59

DNA SWABS AND
THREATS IN THE NIGHT

Bronco had been driving around northeast Michigan with a shovel in his trunk. He'd dug holes all over the woods. He'd used high-powered metal detectors and backhoes and pickaxes, and one day the gruesome reality struck: If he ever did find any human remains, he'd better damn well be able to identify them.

So, after coming back from West Virginia he drove down to the Detroit area and visited the Tylls and Mrs. Ognjan for an unpleasant but necessary task: He took cotton swabs and swiped them on the insides of their cheeks. It would prove, he told them, if the DNA in any bones or remains that turned up matched theirs.

The next day, coincidentally enough, Bronco talked to a sergeant with the Oscoda Township police. He was working on another cold case, a twenty-two-year-old homicide. A cadaver dog he'd been using had dug up several bones, but the bones turned out not to be relative to his case. The FBI had them and was providing the lab work, and when he learned more, he'd get back to him.

If they weren't his bones, maybe they were Bronco's.

Lesneski finished the month making a call on Rocky Harmon at his home in the western Michigan town of Hersey. Harmon had been married to one of the Duvalls' cousins and was the one who had told Detective Schram way back in 1989 about the family party at O'Shea's Tavern in Wixom, where Coco and J.R. had bragged about killing the hunters.

The first thing he told Bronco was that he was afraid of those two, and Rex. They were, he said, the family enforcers. If one of the family had a problem, those were the guys you called. They knew back then he'd been the one talking about O'Shea's.

Harmon recounted the night's events. Despite the passage of time, they didn't differ from what he'd told Schram. The brothers had bragged about the killings to some family members while others danced nearby. One of them said they'd submerged the Bronco in a lake and said, "If you go fishing on that lake, you might cast over the Bronco."

Rocky said he'd heard through another of the Duvalls' cousins that with all the heat Bronco was putting on everyone, Coco had said they were going to kill Harmon and whoever tried to stop them.

Later, another friend said Coco was in Reed City telling folks he was looking for Rocky.

Finally, just two weeks earlier his daughter had answered the phone in the middle of the night. The voice on the other end said he was with a police agency and was investigating the missing hunter case and wanted to know what the Harmons knew. She'd told the caller they didn't know anything and hung up. Clearly it wasn't the police calling. To this day, he said, he was still getting death threats.

Rocky's 20-year-old son, Gary, was there. He told Bronco it was common knowledge throughout the extended Duvall/McMullen family that J.R., Coco and Rex had killed the hunters. And he'd heard through his Aunt Debbie that Coco had been in town looking for Rocky and said he was going to kill him.

60

ONE-MAN SHOP

Oscoda County Prosecutor Barry Shantz basically ran a
one-man shop. Cabin break-ins, drunk driving, bar fights
and the like filled his time.

Murderers who busted heads like melons were a bit far
afield.

Over the years, the state police had asked him for warrants to search or arrest the Duvalls. Over the years he had
turned them down. In his defense, they had no bodies, they
had no eyewitnesses, they had a bunch of conflicting stories
about different fights in different years in different bars.
They had rumors and gossip and weird stories about pigs.

On April 1, 1999, Lesneski had paid Shantz a courtesy
call. He didn't think he had enough for warrants, yet, but
there was a chance he was getting close, if he could shake
the truth out of Boudro. *If* his hunch was correct that there
was a truth inside her and so far she was keeping it hidden.

But at the least there was some movement and Shantz
ought to know about it. Start getting him primed when it
came time. If Shantz turned Bronco down when and if he
came calling for warrants, well, there was always the attorney general down in Lansing.

Three years later, to Bronco's surprise, he was still updat-
ing Shantz, and still hoping against hope the prosecutor would

214   **Tom Henderson**

say that finally there was enough of an accumulation of circumstantial evidence to let a jury decide the Duvalls' fate.

On January 17, 2002, Lesneski met with Shantz again, bringing him up to date. He said he'd consider charges only in the event of more corroborative evidence.

Bronco thought they had enough to get warrants. Warrants might get one of the Duvalls talking. Their arrests might get others who knew something to talk, thinking the brothers were finally behind bars, were coming to justice and wouldn't be able to carry out acts of retribution.

Who knew? What he did know was, Shantz wasn't eager to move and Bronco was getting the feeling that might be a problem.

On March 18, Bronco talked by phone with Detective Schram, voicing his concerns. Schram pointed out an alternative, that they consider going over Shantz's head to the state attorney general's office. Schram had worked with Brian Zubel with the Oakland County Grand Jury and Zubel was now on the AG's staff. It was something to consider.

Two days later Schram e-mailed him. Mark Blumer, now head of the criminal division of the attorney general's office, was considering his own investigation. At the end of March, Blumer confirmed his office's formal involvement. He wanted to review their work, read their reports, decide what to do next.

61

A SHALLOW GRAVE

What Bronco did next was what he'd been doing since he inherited the case. He worked the list of names in his index hard. He'd reinterview all of them if he had to.

He'd become fixated by this case. "It'd piss off my wife if she knew," he'd say later, "but it was the last thing I thought of when I went to sleep, and the first thing I'd think of when I woke up.

"I know most seasoned detectives would think I was nuts. 'You gotta step back.' But I can't. I'd be going for a run or kayaking and it'd be, 'Shit, why didn't I think of that?' It'd be something I should have thought of."

On April 30, 2002, Bronco made the four-and-a-half-hour drive down to Monroe to have a ten-minute chat with Anne Payne at her house. She was a barmaid who had told Detective Sergeant Alison King four years earlier that, after hearing the song "Footprints in the Snow," the Duvalls had bragged about the footprints they'd followed in the snow the night they killed the hunters. She'd said, then, she'd never testify.

"I really don't know anything," she told Lesneski. "I don't think there is much I can help you with."

Bronco reminded her about what she'd said about the song.

"Look, I don't remember. Even if I did, I wouldn't say anything. You can subpoena me into court, but you can't control what I say. These are very dangerous people. I've known them twenty-five years."

And then Bronco got back in his car and drove four and a half hours north.

Back home, he heard about a cadaver-dog seminar that was scheduled for June in Alpena on Lake Huron, a fairly large city by northern Michigan standards. He found out who was organizing it and asked if he could use their dogs.

On May 11, handler Janette Groner and her star cadaver dog met with Bronco to go over four areas—the clearing and surrounding woods on Mapes Road down from Boudro's house where he thought the hunters had been killed; the Trees for Tomorrow hunting camp, where the Duvalls and their cronies set up camp each deer season; and Coco's and J.R.'s former residences.

At the Mapes Road site—a glacial outwash with sandy soils, jack pine mixed in with some deciduous hardwoods in the lower areas, red pine on higher ground—the dog hit on one specific area three times. They couldn't find anything, but when they crisscrossed it, the dog would strongly react again.

They cleared the next three sites without incident, except that the dog sliced a pad on one of its paws on a half-buried piece of glass at Coco's. Groner cleaned the wound and bandaged it. Later, they went back to the Mapes Road site to re-work it, but by that time the dog was limping badly and it was clear it would need stitches.

Groner told Bronco she'd be happy to bring the dog back when the paw healed.

Later that day, Bronco drove down to Big Rapids, where he met with Detective Lieutenant Schram, Detective Sergeant King and his boss, Detective Lieutenant Bohnett, to review what they had.

When they were done going over everything, Schram said it was time to make a formal presentation to the attorney general. He said his contacts at the AG's office had been encouraging. Bohnett told them to work the case one more month, try to shore up any gaps they could.

On May 14, Bronco talked to a member of the Central Intelligence Unit of the state police, which worked out of the AG's office on big cases, many of them politically charged, and considered too sensitive for local authorities. A meeting was set up at the CIU office in Lansing on May 30.

Bronco was buoyed but not satisfied. On May 15, he spoke to a U.S. Forest Service officer and asked him to think about arranging a meeting with the assistant U.S. federal attorney in Michigan. The Mapes Road site was on federal forest land. If the hunters had been killed there, it was a federal crime and he could go over both Shantz's head and the Michigan attorney general, if need be.

He then called Dallas Kunkle of the Bay City FBI office, suggesting the same thing, asking for help if need be to set up a meeting with the assistant U.S. federal attorney. Kunkle told him no problem, just let him know.

Bronco wrote a note to himself:

Benefits to federal intervention include wiretaps and the death penalty.

On May 31, Bronco paid a call on Frank Duvall's ex-wife, Emily. She told him Frank had quoted Coco as saying once, "Them stupid cops, when they find one body, they'll find the other, they're buried on top of one another."

And she said Frank had told her that Rex claimed he'd only transported the bodies, he hadn't killed anyone.

It was all hearsay, inadmissible in court, and nothing new, really, but interesting to hear, nonetheless.

J.R.'s been talking a lot about the case lately, she said. He kept mentioning Bronco by name, how much the detective was pissing him off. J.R.'d gotten worked up once, then started staring off into space. Emily asked him what was on his mind. "Killing you," he'd said.

"That's the second time he told me that he's thinking about killing me."

Emily said she took him seriously, that she was afraid for her safety and that she thought J.R. had had something to do with Eileen Seitz's murder, the one her husband got convicted for.

"Even though I'm divorced from Frank, no one can actually leave the family. They put a hold on you and you can never escape them."

~

Groner's dog healed and on June 8 they took it back into the field off Mapes Road. They began away from the spot where the dog had reacted the last time. As they approached the spot, the dog reacted again. It was close enough that maybe what had been at the first site had permeated the soil to the second site, but far enough away to leave Groner puzzled.

Groner suggested Bronco bring in another dog to work the site, see if it could get confirmation to what her dog was reacting to.

On June 18, Sally Santeford, another dog handler based in Houghton in Michigan's Upper Peninsula, met Bronco at the site.

Her dog hit on the same general area. The handler pushed brush and leaves aside and found a shallow grave. It held the remains of a fawn.

At 2 p.m., Bronco called Mrs. Ognjan and the Tylls and told them the cadaver-dog search had finally concluded, fruitlessly. But, he told them, he was waiting to hear from the state attorney general. He had high hopes. He'd keep them posted.

62

GETTING READY FOR THE A.G.

It took longer than they'd thought, but on August 21, Schram called Bronco with the good news: They were meeting in Lansing. The attorney general had agreed to take on the case.

Assistant AG Mark Blumer met with them as scheduled and confirmed that the department had taken the case and assigned it to him. He gave them a small shopping list of things to do, including scheduling four or five key witnesses to be subpoenaed.

Investigative subpoenas are fairly rare in Michigan and must be approved by a judge. They carry a heft that a less informal interview with a cop does not, with the threat of perjury hanging over those who lie. Bronco thought, too, that enough time had passed that perhaps the Duvalls had grown old enough and less fearsome enough that someone would talk, on the record, about *everything* he or she knew. That someone, he had a feeling, might be Barb Boudro.

Crack one, use his or her story to crack the others.

At 3:30 that afternoon, Bronco placed two happy calls to the Tylls and Mrs. Ognjan. Everyone was overjoyed.

Bronco had something on his to-do list that Blumer knew nothing about. Boudro was going to be a key witness before the AG's grand jury and, in the event of arrest warrants, at any subsequent trial. Any defense attorney reading Bronco's reports over the years could use Smith, her old lover and a former cop, to impeach her, to attack her credibility. He needed to nail down the inconsistencies between what Boudro had told him and what Smith had admitted to.

He was particularly interested in her account of a fight that Smith had been called to at Linker's. A loud and angry argument there would provide motive for what a prosecutor would try to prove happened later.

And he needed more on Smith, stuff a prosecutor could attack him with, if he ever ended up as a defense witness being used to try to tear holes in Boudro's testimony.

On September 10, Lesneski met with Oscoda County Sheriff Michael Larrison to see what he knew about the former deputy, and what he or others might know about Smith's affair with Boudro. He'd already talked to a former dispatcher, William Parrott, a friend of Smith's who had left the department by the time the hunters went missing. Smith had told Parrott of Boudro's pillow-talk admission about how the hunters had died, that Smith hadn't taken it seriously at the time, but later regretted not doing more about it.

Bronco hit the jackpot with Larrison. Larrison had been a detective when Smith was a road sergeant. One of Smith's perks was being able to take a patrol car home. Larrison said Smith was one to enjoy his authority and his perks.

Larrison kept hearing from other deputies that Smith was having an affair with Boudro. That was of little concern to Larrison. What bothered him were reports that Smith, who worked the midnight shift, would park his patrol car out behind Boudro's house much of the night and sleep there.

The reports Smith turned in claimed he spent many of his nights in remote corners of the county, working hard, going the extra mile, literally and metaphorically, to check on the many seasonal cabins and cottages that were frequent targets of local ne'er-do-wells.

One night Larrison had gotten a call at home. One of the deputies told him Smith's patrol car was parked out behind

Boudro's house. Larrison drove over and staked it out. A couple of hours later, sure enough, Smith walked out, got in his car and eased out of the driveway, the headlights off. A good ways down the road, he turned his lights on and continued on his way.

At the end of the shift a little while later, Larrison was waiting in the office when Smith walked in. Smith turned in his activity report for the day. According to Larrison, Smith lied in his report about where he'd been for much of the night.

Larrison called him into his office and asked him about his night. Smith started lying to him, but Larrison cut him off and told him he'd staked him out at Boudro's.

The sheriff demoted Smith, taking away his patrol car and assigning him permanently—to the end of his career, as it was put—to working the radio desk. A little while later, Smith quit.

"I wouldn't believe a single word Dick said," said Larrison.

It was good stuff. Stuff a prosecutor would eat up. The kind of stuff that destroys witnesses.

~

On September 12, 9 a.m.—another of his early morning rendezvous—Bronco was back knocking at Dick Smith's door in Mio. His wife said he was off in town, though, so Bronco went looking for him. He found him at Blair's Sunoco, just north of what passes for downtown.

Bronco told him they needed to talk, so they walked out of the garage and into the parking lot of the business next door.

Bronco told him he was worried about inconsistencies between what Boudro had told him and what Smith had told him. That there was a potential for this case to go to a jury someday and he was worried that Smith would be called to impeach her. That'd mean, he said with import, the state would have to call one of his friends to impeach him.

Bronco spelled it out for him. He'd talked to one of those friends, it wasn't just what-ifs. And the friend had told Bronco that Smith had talked about Boudro's pillow talk.

"I wouldn't believe a word Barb Boudro said. There isn't anyone from this county that would believe anything she said. Besides, I've personally taken her to Alpena before," Smith said, referring to a psychiatric hospital in that city, "for trying to commit suicide. She cut her wrists, probably looking for attention. I don't think she actually wanted to do it. But you're going to have big trouble trying to convince anyone she's credible."

Bronco asked him if it was possible that Barb had talked to him about a fight and he had concluded she didn't know what she was talking about, or that it was inconsequential.

"It's possible. Back then, bar fights were a common occurrence. People were always telling me about some bar fight or a fight between a couple of drunks."

And what of her claims that he had sat out the call to the bar in the parking lot of the Camp 10 store?

Smith did not recall it that way. But he did acknowledge that "Whenever I was dispatched to a fight, I'd take my time getting there. What in the hell do I want to get in the middle of a couple of drunks for? I figured to let them beat the hell out of each other. Most of the time, everyone was gone by the time I got there, anyway."

Especially, thought Lesneski, if you sat long enough in the parking lot down the road.

And what, again, about the relationship with Boudro?

"It wasn't really nothing much. I always figured she had information on the hunters' case. I was trying to get information out of her. She always had a rough crowd hanging around her place. I figured between her and Alex McDowell, they'd know what happened to the hunters."

How long did the relationship last?

"There wasn't much to it. It didn't last very long. I was using her for information."

Lesneski made a mental note: So Smith keeps telling me she's not credible, you can't believe a word she says, and practically with the same breath says he carried out an affair with her as a subterfuge to hear what she had to say. How'd he ever make road sergeant?

* * *

There was one piece of potentially dismaying news in Smith's account—that he'd taken Boudro to the local psychiatric hospital after she tried to kill herself. That was the kind of stuff defense attorneys prayed for. He'd need to know all he could about that, so he got back in his car at the Sunoco station and drove straight to Boudro's.

Boudro admitted the suicide attempt, said it had come after Smith broke off the relationship.

"We were going to get married," she said. "He told me he was going to divorce his wife and marry me. We even had our wedding invitations picked out."

She said they'd carried on their affair for about a year. It was serious enough that they'd exchanged Christmas presents. She fetched her photo albums and showed Bronco photos of a smiling Smith opening his presents.

There was some truth to Smith's claims that he thought Boudro could provide him information on Tyll and Ognjan. "He would ask me about the missing hunters. I told him what I knew. He always told me not to say anything to the state police detective in West Branch. I know he wanted to solve the case, because he told me so."

63
POLITICS

Michigan's office of attorney general is notorious for its political intrigues. It's an elected position and re-election campaigns generally begin just about the time the last ballots have been tallied.

In August, Lesneski had allowed himself the flush of optimism that things would start moving quickly now that the AG's staff had taken on the case. That flush gave way to frustration.

He called Blumer on October 10 to see what was up. Not much, said Blumer. Because of campaign considerations, there might not be any action until after the November elections.

On November 15, after the statewide elections for governor, secretary of state, treasurer and attorney general, Lesneski sent Blumer an e-mail, asking the assistant prosecutor to give him a call and tell him what the status of the case was.

Meanwhile Bronco did what he does, kept soldiering on, relentlessly. If this case was to eventually die without prosecution, at least he'd know he'd done everything conceivable.

There was an old, now-disused garage down the road from Boudro's house. She'd told Bronco she thought she'd heard sounds coming from it the night the hunters had gone missing.

He arranged to have technicians from the state police crime lab in Grayling test the concrete floor with luminol, a compound that fluoresces in the presence of blood. The results were inconclusive—hardly a surprise given the passage of time—but did indicate that there might be blood there. Further testing would be needed.

On November 25, crime lab technician Connie Swander returned to the garage. She chipped off areas of the floor, which were then crushed for DNA analysis. The analysis was negative. They also found a one-inch piece of what appeared to be human hair. It was sent for DNA analysis to the FBI lab in Quantico, Virginia.

The year 2002 ended the way all the years since 1985 had ended on this investigation, with a frustrating lack of progress. So much seemed to be known; so little seemed achievable to make those responsible pay. The year ended without word from the AG's office.

Bronco carried on, thinking now, though, in terms of what a prosecutor would need, both in terms of evidence and in terms of what might be needed to counter possible defense tactics.

An obvious defense question would be, how could Boudro hear anything in her house, with the TV on, from a clearing a quarter mile or so away, down a trail through the woods?

So, on January 25, Lesneski conducted a test with the help of Trooper Douglas Gough. Naturally it was done early, at 8:30 a.m.

Lesneski positioned himself inside Boudro's house. Gough went down the road to the clearing and starting hitting an aluminum baseball bat against a one-gallon milk jug filled with frozen water. He yelled and screamed the way you might if you were getting beaten to death and hoped to get someone to come to your rescue.

Gough drove back to the house. Lesneski told him he could hear both the pinging of the bat and the screams.

"That sounded almost the same as it did back then," said Boudro.

The successful test elevated Lesneski's spirits. It was something they'd be able to use at trial.

Two weeks later, he got other mood-altering news. He'd had a meeting with Blumer in Lansing on February 11. Blumer told him he'd gotten approval to issue investigative subpoenas. The new Michigan attorney general, Mike Cox, had used them to good effect during his recent days with the Wayne County Prosecutor's Office in Detroit, and was eager to use them now. Subpoenas for Barb Boudro, Connie Sundberg and Rocky Harmon would be ready by the end of the week.

Because of scheduling conflicts, Blumer told Lesneski to hold off serving them until the middle of March.

It was a happy drive back north. It was a happy day for the Tylls and Mrs. Ognjan, too, when Bronco called them.

64

HOLDING HER HAND

On March 21, Trooper Wally Tremonti drove to Rocky Harmon's house in Hersey to serve the first of the subpoenas. It was a coincidence bordering on irony that he had gone to school with Tyll and Ognjan and had been with them in the Boy Scouts.

Harmon wasn't there, but his ex-wife, Tammy Morris, née McMullen, one of the Duvalls' cousins, was. She told him Harmon had moved to Kentucky two weeks earlier. Had moved two states south because of death threats he'd gotten from Coco.

She said she knew what it was about, the long-ago conversation in O'Shea's Tavern in Wixom. She told Gough she'd been there, too, and had heard Coco talking about how they'd taken care of the hunters and the car. She had a telephone number for Harmon's Kentucky address.

Four days later, Gough reached Harmon by phone and told him about the subpoenas and that the assistant attorney general wanted to speak to him sometime in the next three weeks. Harmon told him he was worried who he might run into at the AG's office in Lansing. Gough told him not to worry. There were just two others being subpoenaed for now and he had nothing to worry about from the other two.

Gough told him he'd fly down and fetch him if he had to. Harmon told him that wouldn't be necessary. Give him a date and he'd drive up.

Boudro and Sundberg got their subpoenas without incident. They were nervous, but resigned to participating. On April 17, Harmon, Boudro and Sundberg would take turns before Blumer and Lesneski, under oath, telling what they knew.

Fear of the Duvalls had been palpable in everyone Lesneski had ever spoken to. He could see it in their faces. He could hear it in their voices.

"You mess with one of them, you mess with all of them," he said of the Duvalls. "I get a lot of calls from people wanting to remain anonymous."

Gough drove Boudro down to Blumer's office in Lansing. Bronco met them there.

She was the first to be sworn in and tell her tale. She framed it so it was all hearsay—what Ronnie had seen and told her. Blumer pressed, she told a bit more. He backed her up, had her go over some detail or other that didn't jibe. They went over it and over it and she kept telling it as if she'd heard it from Ronnie.

All of them were getting frustrated. It was clear she was holding something back. Blumer started to ask her something.

"You'll never get the truth out of me," she interrupted. "I could never tell you the truth."

Bronco interceded. He had them shut the tape recorder off, then he leaned forward, took her hand, put his face close to hers and looked her in the eye.

He asked her to tell them what she knew, that now was the time to finally tell it.

Something changed in her eyes or her face, something subliminal, some small hint of acceptance.

"Bronco, you know I saw it, don't you?"

Blumer and Lesneski felt the same jolt, Lesneski's all the harder for what the case had come to mean, personally.

"Yes, I know," he said.

"You know that I know."

"Yes."

"You know that I saw those deer hunters killed."

"Yes, but I need to hear it from you."

She turned to Blumer. "I'm a dead woman," she said.

She'd been there in the woods. She'd seen Tyll and Ognjan beaten to death. It wasn't a dead man's tale. It was hers. They had their eyewitness.

65

PING-PING! AND A LIGHT IN THE CLEARING

This is what Barb Boudro saw. This is her tale.

~

It was either Saturday, November 23, or Sunday, November 24, that part wasn't clear. The rest of it is as clear as it gets. Ronnie Emery, her best bud, has been out hunting and gotten himself a nice buck. Wants to go out and celebrate, take her to Linker's. Barb and Ronnie are very tight, but not in the way most people think. Like brother and sister is how Barb looks at it.

Ronnie shows up at her door about dusk, maybe 5:30, all excited. "I got a buck," he says. His first buck. Well, not exactly. His first buck during deer season, legal, Ronnie having done the unusual thing for him of paying for a hunting license. Like a lot of north-woods characters, like the Duvalls, Ronnie was a poacher, shot deer in all seasons. Shot them in the glare of headlights, shot them whenever and wherever he could if he didn't think anyone was around to see. But this is his first legal buck and it has a nice rack with a lot of points and he feels a need to celebrate.

Though Barb lives just down the road from Linker's, she's only been there a few times, started going there once in a while after Steve Linker bought it a few months earlier. Her usual party place is the Mio Saloon and that's where she wants to go. But Ronnie doesn't want to drive the five miles over to Mio, he has buck fever and needs a drink, so Linker's it is.

She and Ronnie start playing pool and drinking. She's a heavy drinker then, will be right up until 1994 when she stops cold after her last drunk-driving arrest.

Half an hour later, these two deer hunters come in, one of them real tall, both of them loud and obnoxious. Kinda par for the course, really, hunters in bars at night being loud, some worse than others.

She's walking over to the pool table. The shorter one, Brian Ognjan, reaches over and grabs her ass. "Keep your fucking hands to yourself," she says. He backs off and they put the quarters in the slot, rack their balls and start playing. She's bending over the table, about to take a shot. She prides herself on being something of a looker with a pretty good body in those days, fifty pounds and a lot of years from the woman telling her story to Blumer and Bronco.

Anyways, she's bending over the shot and the tall one wants to do more than look, he passes behind her and slows and rubs his pelvis up against her rear.

"Shove it up your ass!" she says loudly, spinning around. The hunters, not to be deterred, ask if Ronnie and her want to play pool for money. She tells them no, that they just play for fun. The hunters put some quarters up on the table, claiming next game, anyway, so Barb and Ronnie give up the table once their game is over.

"Those guys need to get their asses kicked," she says.

Just about then, three of the Duvall brothers show up— Coco, J.R. and Rex—and a fourth person she doesn't know, and they hone right in on the deer hunters. Looks to Barb like they recognize them, see 'em playing pool, perk up like a goal has been met and move right over to sit by them. Gonna be trouble, she thinks.

Barb's sorta surprised the Duvalls are there. They usually hang out at some of the rougher places around, like the

Mio Saloon, or the Wild Turkey, or the Knothole, or over in South Branch at Timbers Steak House or the Curtisville Trading Post.

The hunters are pestering women. Barb sees one of them grab someone's butt, the other saying something that gets a quick, angry response.

Barb is getting pretty well plowed, mixing Bloody Marys and Salty Dogs, maybe eight or nine in all. And as she gets more looped, she gets more and more agitated. She's watching the hunters, watching them make the rounds of the tables, seems to be pissing her off more than it is anyone else. Obnoxious, that's the word. That's what they are. She's bitching to Ronnie.

The hunters have some loud words with the Duvall table, well short of fisticuffs but loud enough and threatening enough. All cross words with the Duvalls are serious. The tall hunter probably thinks he's tough, maybe he is tough back where he comes from. The Duvalls are tough.

She's been at a few parties over the years with the Duvalls and she's seen them cause all kinds of trouble. In fact, she didn't think she'd ever been at a party with them where a fight didn't break out. One time, she showed up at Sherm (the Worm) Heilig's to buy some pot. Party was going on, she sits down with Rex Duvall to have a drink.

Next thing you know J.R. and Coco are duking it out. Coco pops his brother on the nose, breaks that fucker, blood pumping out, J.R. calls time-out. Only one thing to do, reschedule this fight till noon tomorrow. She wasn't there the next day, but heard they'd met as scheduled. "One rule," says J.R., way it was reported to her, "you can't hit me on the nose."

And Coco promptly pops him right on the nose, out comes the blood, damn fight's over just like that.

She tells Ronnie, "This is getting out of hand. I'm going to call the police."

Someone tells her someone else already has. Word that the cops have been called quiets things down, but there's still a feeling in the air. The cops never come.

"There's going to be trouble," she repeats to Ronnie.

They're sitting at a table by the door. There's a pay phone on the wall near where they're sitting. Coco walks past them and makes a call.

"We could use your help," is the part of the call Barb remembers.

Maybe forty-five minutes later, in walk two guys, go straight to the Duvalls' table and sit down. A minute later, someone from that table comes over to Barb, asks her if she knows where they can get some marijuana. She does, and tells them. They leave, return a little bit later.

She's still bitching to Ronnie about those guys, louder than she intends. Someone comes over, says Don't worry about it, we'll take care of it. He sets a six-pack of Michelob Light on their table, says Why don't you go home?

She's more than happy to go. Ronnie's reluctant, sure there's going to be a fight and he doesn't want to miss out on it. She and Ronnie get up. Dick Baker, another drinking buddy, he's in there and Barb asks him if he wants to come, too, over to her place to party. They go outside, she spots a black Bronco parked kinda funny. The other cars are pulled in straight and the Bronco is parked at an angle, hogging two spaces. There are people on both sides of it.

Ronnie, Dick and her drive down the road to her house, she's driving her car and Dick's driving his. She pulls in the garage, he parks in the driveway. They turn on the TV, the news ain't on yet, so it's gotta be like 10:30. Baker's pretty fried and not hardly in for the long haul and leaves after one beer. The news is coming on. She likes the news, wants to watch it. She's got one of the first VCRs in the north woods, and Ronnie wants to put Scarface on, has a thing about Scarface, the Al Pacino flick about Cuban drug lords. A thing is putting it mildly. She's seen it with him what seems like 200 times. Miracle the tape still works. She got her way about leaving the bar, lets Ronnie have his way about what to watch.

Al Pacino plays a gangster named Tony. Coincidentally, Barb's got a Sheltie named Antonio, who they call Tony. The movie's playing and Tony's running in and out of the kitchen.

Maybe he thinks they're calling him every time someone's talking to Pacino.

No, that's not it. She knows every noise in the movie by heart and there's some noise that shouldn't be there, almost subliminal. She gets up and follows Tony into the kitchen. There's voices. And a ping-pinging.

She opens up the kitchen window. She can hear guys yelling back and forth at each other. Arguing, but what they're saying isn't clear. Just loud anger coming through the woods. Then, louder, clear: "You are dead, you rotten motherfucker!"

And ping-ping.

She goes back to Ronnie.

"The hunters are getting their asses beat," she says.

"I want to see it," he says and they go out the front door. There's a pickup in her driveway wasn't there when they got home from the bar. It's not Dick Baker's. She can't tell if anyone's in it, doesn't know if it's someone on lookout, but she's afraid to keep going. They go back in the house.

Ronnie, he still wants to see the fight, so they go to the back of the one-story ranch and climb out a rear bedroom window. Ronnie goes first, goes to her wooden storage shed, gets out a stepladder and brings it back. She climbs down the ladder. "Ping," they hear, like the sound of a well-struck ball heading on a line toward the outfield. And "Ping."

It's a snowy night, pretty light out in the woods out back, and they head down the trail behind her property that runs parallel to Mapes Road.

Ronnie's a woodsman. It's a trail he made through the woods, a little zig-zaggy, but clear. Clear enough and smooth enough they run down the trail toward the noises, running north, the same direction as Linker's.

"Somebody please help us!" they hear someone yelling as they run.

They come to the clearing, on the other side of Mapes. Everything is happening on the other side of the road. There's a Bronco and a pickup in the field, their headlights illuminating the clearing. Ronnie always wears black, Barb's in a dark robe and dark nightgown, so they blend in at the end of the woods, watching.

J.R's there, and Coco. Three others who had been sitting with them at Linker's. There, clear as can be in the headlights, the tall hunter is on the ground, struggling to get to his knees. "Please, God, someone help us!" he hollers out.

Coco pulls the bat, or pipe, back one last time and uncorks one. This time it doesn't ping. Nothing so metallic. It makes kind of a plooshing sound, like a ripe pumpkin might make if you hurled it onto concrete, and with the sound, the hunter's head explodes. That what it looks like to her. An explosion of blood and bone and viscera. All the while J.R.'s kicking and punching away.

"Did you see that?" says one of the Duvall crew, not like he's upset. Like you might at one of the local small-town Fourth of July fireworks shows when a good one goes off. A couple of others are laughing.

They're holding the other hunter. They haven't lit in on him, yet, but he knows it's coming. It's not like they can exactly leave a witness. He suddenly breaks free and takes off, but they tackle him and bring him back into the lights, and he just sort of collapses in on himself.

"Look at that: He pissed himself," someone says, and they all start laughing. And then they start in on him, too, Coco and J.R. punching and kicking and they keep it up for what seems like forever, the others just standing there watching. A trick of time. They kick him and punch him, keep at it well after he's stopped moving, after he's stopped screaming, or even moaning, until it's like he's frozen in place. Dead for sure and they keep kicking.

Barb's seen more than enough. She heads back up the trail. Ronnie stays there. He wants to see what comes next.

Boudro climbs back up the ladder and into the house. Scarface is still playing. Pacino's just a short Italian guy, now. A few minutes later, Ronnie climbs in through the window. Moments later there's a knock at the door. It's Coco. J.R.'s behind him. "*You know we know you. We know your family. You heard nothing. Pigs gotta eat, too,*" says Coco.

Pigs? Barb thinks maybe he's talking about cops. Doesn't matter. He could be sitting there, his head spinning in 360s shouting out in Latin and she wouldn't be any more freaked out.

She closes the door, waits a minute, peeks out through the curtains. The pickup in her driveway had been backed in. It pulls out. It, the pickup from the clearing and the Bronco head off down the road.

Ronnie's pumped up by it all, sobered up and pulsing on adrenaline. "Let's go see where they bury the bodies," he says.

They head off after the caravan, a good distance behind. Barb is terrified, Ronnie's all geeked up. She's pissed off, too, madder than hell Ronnie's got her off doing this. They're so far back they can barely see taillights and that's way too close for her. They go south on Mapes, turn onto M-72 into downtown Mio, turn south on 33 to Curtisville Road. They see them stop at a trailer, then stop at another house. And then they lose them. They can't see any taillights, they don't know where they are, they end up in a little town called Glennie and that gives them their bearings to get home.

The next morning, they go back down to the clearing, not that they doubt what they saw, but just making sure, nonetheless. Barb won't go into the clearing, proper. Ronnie does. Even from the edge, she can see dark pools of red and black blood against the snow.

~

It was amazing stuff, made more powerful because finally, after more than seventeen years, they had an on-the-record eyewitness to the murders of Brian Ognjan and David Tyll. They had more than enough, now, for arrest warrants.

Harmon's testimony and Sundberg's testimony were necessary, but certainly anticlimactic.

Harmon told them what he'd said before, that he'd heard J.R. and Coco bragging at O'Shea's Tavern in Wixom about their fighting skills, and out of the blue J.R. saying they'd killed the two hunters and gotten rid of their car.

Sundberg told about visiting Eileen Seitz and J.R. one night when Randy Duvall had pulled into the driveway in a black Bronco. J.R. yelled at Randy to, in her words, "Get rid of that thing before he got their asses cooked."

About two weeks later, Coco came home drunk and told Connie they'd killed someone. When she asked him, "What! What did you say?" he beat her up. The next morning she brought it up, again, and he started choking her and pushing her face into the snowy ground. She thought he was trying to kill her. She broke free and ran to her mother's house.

66

BACK TO LANSING

Bronco didn't take the subpoenaed testimony as an excuse to slow down. If anything, it got him more energized. He wouldn't say who'd said what to Blumer, but he'd be able to use their testimony, now, as a pry bar to open up others.

Once word got out about what had been said on the record, Bronco thought some others were likely to be more forthcoming than they had been over the years. In the coming weeks, that is, in fact, what happened. A fuller picture began to emerge of how the Duvalls had kept the lid on, how they'd ruled with a fear so unyielding that they had been able to enforce silence for nearly two decades.

Not everyone was cooperative. Connie Coffey, née McMullen, married to David Yonkin at the time of the incident at O'Shea's Tavern—it was her birthday they were celebrating—told Bronco during a meeting at Tammy Morris' house the morning of April 23, "Listen, I called Coco the other night and asked him what the fuck is going on. We all went through this shit twenty years ago. Rocky's telling people that we're all going to jail for five years for not cooperating with police. I don't know shit!"

She said she had a son in jail in Florida facing prison time and was worried about him coming to harm because of all this starting up, again. She said she hadn't heard anything at

O'Shea's and doubted Harmon's story. "Lloyd was scared shitless of the Duvall boys. He'd heard all about their reputations and he didn't dare move from that table all night. Everyone else was dancing and having a great time."

Connie then left, saying she had worked all night and needed to get to sleep.

After she left, Tammy Morris sat down at the kitchen table. "I'll tell you what happened if the boys don't find out," she said. There were rumors going around and she didn't want her name attached to any of them.

She'd first been asked about it by Detective Sergeant Schram back in December of 1989. Then, she'd told Schram she'd spent most of the night dancing and didn't hear anything about any hunters.

Recently she'd told Gough she heard talk at O'Shea's that they'd "taken care" of the hunters, but wouldn't elaborate. Now, though, she told Bronco she'd heard it all as clear as could be, and it was just like Rocky had told it.

Bronco called Blumer down in Lansing and briefed him on what the sisters had said. Blumer told him to bring Tammy Morris down to Lansing on April 25.

At her deposition, Tammy said she'd heard J.R. and Coco telling her father, Charles McMullen, that they'd killed the two hunters, cut up their bodies and fed them to their pigs.

Near the end, Tammy told them to stop the recorder. She leaned forward. "Are J.R. and Coco going to find out about me testifying?" she asked. "I'm scared to death. Once the boys find out who gives any statement, they might as well kiss their asses goodbye, it's as simple as that. The boys will hurt them, family or not."

Her own dad would turn against her to protect the Duvalls, she said, "because they're his drinking buddies."

From the day Boudro testified, Bronco waited anxiously for arrest warrants to be issued. So did Alison King. On the 18th they were told the warrants would be issued within a week. On April 22, Lesneski made sure J.R. was still at his house near Hale. The next day King went by Coco's in Monroe to eyeball him. They kept checking in with the

AG's office: warrants still pending, sitting on Cox's desk, awaiting his decision, any day, they were told repeatedly.

On May 8, Bronco talked on the phone to King. They're coming down later today, he said. That afternoon, he called her back. Cox still hadn't signed them, didn't know why not, maybe tomorrow.

May 12, King and Bronco traded e-mails. Warrants pending, said the AG's office. But this time there was movement. They were awaiting coordination between the AG's office and the state police's Violent Crimes Task Force. Timing was crucial. The timing of the arrests on one end, the timing of press releases and press conferences on the other.

67
ARRAIGNED

Almost three weeks after Boudro's dramatic testimony, on May 13, 2003—a day that state police had been aiming toward for more than seventeen years, which perhaps everyone but Bronco Lesneski had despaired of ever seeing, which families had stopped daring to dream about—warrants were issued for the arrests of Raymond Wilbur Duvall Jr., 52, and Donald Dean Duvall, 51, for the murders of David Tyll and Brian Ognjan.

At 3:20 p.m. Bronco got his instructions. The arrests would be made simultaneously in Hale and Monroe at 5 a.m. on the 14th. King and Lesneski would take part, as would members of the State Police Fugitive Team, which was trained in the quick surprise arrest of dangerous fugitives.

Two hours later, Bronco called Lansing. He'd had one of J.R.'s neighbors in a heavily wooded area keeping watch on him. The neighbor had called. It looked like J.R. was getting ready to flee. He and his girlfriend were loading stuff into the trunk of his car. The police needed to move today, ASAP, not tomorrow.

King was told to sit surveillance at Coco's until the Fugitive Team arrived. Lesneski was told to move in on J.R. He did so within minutes.

Bronco pulled into the driveway, blocking J.R.'s car. Two other troopers had gone in a second car. They'd left their car in the street, hidden from the house, and had each staked out positions on opposite sides of the lot, hidden by trees.

The front door to the house was open. Bronco had set it all up in advance, not realizing it would happen this soon. He'd put the word out through the Duvall grapevine that he wanted to talk to J.R. about a matter involving Consumers Power. J.R. had wired his house into the power line and was draining off free electricity. Let him think it was the utility beef Bronco was interested in.

J.R. met him at the doorway.

"Hey, J.R."

"Hey, Bronco."

"You're under arrest for the murders of Brian Ognjan and David Tyll."

"Bullshit."

J.R. didn't put up a fuss. Bronco handcuffed him without incident and took him to the West Branch post to be finger-printed and photographed.

At 7:20, Coco was arrested without incident in the garage of his house.

That evening, at a hastily convened press conference in Detroit, Attorney General Mike Cox told the gathered media, "Our job is to convict them now that we got them."

At his side were Cathy and Arthur Tyll and Helen Ognjan.

"It's been a long time, but now we face the beginning of the end of our tragic experience," said Cathy Tyll.

Jan Payne, Ognjan's girlfriend when he went missing, had since married, had a daughter and was living in a Detroit suburb. When reached by a *Detroit News* reporter, she said that for years after their disappearance, "I always hoped that they'd come back."

The two-count warrants described the claims of Tammy Morris and her ex-husband, Rocky, about that night in O'Sheas, when the Duvalls had talked about killing the two hunters, dismembering them and feeding them to pigs, details guaranteed to spark big headlines the next day and urgent updates on the area's radio stations.

Tammy, freaking out that evening at the news of the arrest, had the courtesy to find Rocky, who was still in town. The boys—that's what everyone called them, all these years later, both of them in their 50s—have been arrested, she said, you gotta get out of here. She didn't think they, or their friends, would do anything to her. Rocky? Oh, they'd do stuff to him, given half a chance.

Rocky got his ass to Kentucky, posthaste.

The next day, the brothers were arraigned on two counts each of first-degree murder in the Oscoda County district courtroom.

Bronco, more sparsely than usual, perhaps bending over backward to rein in his glee, wrote prose pared to the bone in his report on May 14.

It started:

> Warrants from the AG's office were faxed to the post. Warrants were subsequently authorized by Judge Yenior of 81st District Court. 2-Count Murder Warrant for each defendant Raymond Wilber [sic] Duvall "JR" and Donald Dean Duvall "Coco."
>
> Both brothers were arrested without incident. JR was arrested at his residence, 6179 Cooper St., Hale, MI 48739.
>
> Coco was arrested @ his home; 318 Eastchester, Monroe, MI 48161.
>
> Both were printed and photographed at the post. Both temporarily lodged in Iosco County Jail pending their arraignment.

68

TALKING TO THE BOYS

Early the evening of J.R.'s arrest, Bronco had him brought into his office at the post and read him his Miranda rights. J.R. said he understood them and was willing to talk.

He reminded Bronco that around the previous Thanksgiving he'd gotten hold of Lesneski from jail, where he was being held on three warrants for failing to pay child support and had offered to make a deal. He'd had a hunch then who'd done in the hunters, he said, but Bronco had spurned his offer.

Bronco reminded him he'd mentioned a couple of nameless drug dealers who'd left town about the time the hunters went missing, but it was hardly worth making a deal to spring J.R. from jail.

"I don't know their last name.... We used to play darts with these people for a couple of different years in a dart league.

"They lived out on Heath Road. They was into doing a lot of drugs. I knew this. Somebody was saying, 'Hey, they have a free van if somebody wants it, they can have it, go get it.' Then the word 'Bronco' come up. But I heard right after that, the people adios'ed. I ain't never seen or heard from them since."

Bronco asked him about hanging out in bars in the Mio area—Ma Deeter's, Walker's, Linkers, the Mio Saloon. J.R. said he never drank in any of those places.

Well, he sold a lot of firewood to a guy lived across from the Mio Saloon. Other than that, well, let's see. He was in Mio once for the fireworks. Went there another time for the Lumberjack Festival. Once he went there for a horseshoe tournament.

"And the only other place I used to go to was a lodge. I think it was the Moose Lodge. Eagles, Moose, or something. We was in a horseshoe league. That's the only time I ever been to Mio." Hard to imagine, since he'd spent most of his adult life just a few miles up the road, and Mio was the only thing that passed for a city for many miles.

Bronco asked him he'd ever been in possession of a Bronco or Bronco part.

"I deal in a junkyard."

"Have you ever stolen a Bronco? Be honest with me here."

"I'm trying to think. I never stole a Bronco, but I did get rid of a Bronco . . . The guy couldn't afford his payments and he wanted his insurance to pay for it."

He said they'd kept what was working good, got rid of the rest.

"So the police would never find it, what would you do? Put it through a shredder? Bury it?"

"Actually, just bury it. I can take you where it's at. It was right there, in my garden. But that was only a one-time thing."

Why did Rex reportedly say, "I didn't kill anybody, all I did was transport the body"?

"I have no idea. I'm telling you I don't know nothing about this other than what I read in the paper. Other than being a detective, trying to figure out what the fuck's going on. Other than that, that's all the fuck, I don't know nothing."

"Being a detective, tell me what you think." Bronco, being ironic, giving himself an inner chuckle.

J.R. said it had to be the drug-dealing couple. "Why would they just up and disappear? They was always in the Timbers bar. They was in a dart league. I would go to their house and have a beer with them."

Why had his brother been spitting on flyers about the

hunters throughout the South Branch and Curtisville area and saying they'd deserved it?

"I haven't seen Coco in a couple of years." They'd had a falling-out over money J.R. owed him.

"That's not my question."

"I don't know why he would do that. I have no idea. Probably fed up with the bullshit because of all the aggravation. Every time, we're always getting blamed for it. We have been, right from day one, or accused of it."

How about bar fights? Ever been in any of those?

"Yes, just when I was bartending at the Timbers . . . It was just kind of breaking things up, telling people to get out, you gotta leave, go, whatever. I mean, never had a bar brawl or anything like that. Maybe from workin' and breakin' shit up."

"Have you ever been in a fight where you got your butt whipped at a bar?" Bronco asked.

"No, I'm not a violent person. I probably only been in fifteen–twenty fights in my life, most of them was in school." Saying it with a straight face, matter-of-fact, like fifteen–twenty fights was a good number to pick if you wanted the cop across the table to think you were a pacifist.

"You're telling me you've never been in a bar fight or anything associated with a bar fight?"

"I've been in a lot of arguments in a bar and what-have-you. There's been some push-come-to-shove shit, but never nothing drastic."

"Have you ever been jumped by anybody, gotten beat up by anybody?"

"Just when I was a bartender at the Timbers. [A couple] started a big fight in the bar. I went over there to break it up, and the old lady hit me over the head with a fucking bat. We all went to court for that over in West Branch."

Bronco asked him why there were so many people over the years who'd told a variety of cops about how the Duvalls had fed the hunters to their pigs, people who "are not out-laws who are on the fringes of going to jail, so they can sing out something and give us a bone to get the attention away from them."

"If I did something like that, fuck, I'd be in another county some-fucking-where. I have never hid from you. I've never broke and run from you. I used to break my fucking neck to get back with Detective Halleck and ask, 'Hey, what do you want?' I called you, didn't I? I mean, that's gotta tell you something. I didn't break and run from nobody. I don't know nothing about this."

69

TALKING TO COCO

Coco was driven north to the Iosco County Jail the night of his arrest. Bronco picked him up early in the morning and drove him over to the West Branch post and started his interview at 7 a.m. by reading him his Miranda rights.

Coco was a fount of denial. Didn't know the hunters. Wasn't much of a fighter. Got slugged on the chin once by a neighbor, but that was about it. Never had gone to the bars up north much. Had no idea where Linker's was. Wouldn't be able to find Walker's. Mighta been to Ma Deeter's once.

Had heard people had started rumors about his pigs. "I thought to myself, 'Man, what the hell's the matter with these people?'"

What about all that talk about him and his brothers running stolen cars up north from Monroe?

"The only place I took stuff to was Pennsylvania."

"Why would you take it to Pennsylvania? I don't understand. There are junkyards all over Michigan."

"Kenny and Randy have been dealing with those guys for years. If your last name was Duvall, you got more than if you took a car in. If you took a car in, you'd get twenty-five dollars a ton and I'd get thirty-five dollars."

And none of them stolen, neither.

"You know, like with the tow truck, you just go around and stop in the county where a lot of blacks live. Every one of them had ten–fifteen cars in their driveway. Sometimes you'd give them twenty bucks for them and sometimes they'd just give them to ya. Then you'd drive it over to Pennsylvania, give them the title and junk it."

Did the boys ever take a chainsaw to a pig or a cow for one of their roasts?

Nope. Never happened. Butcher shop over in Hale would cut up one of their pigs for $25 and wrap it if they were going to have a party.

Parties, he admitted to. Big ones, 200 people.

"Coco, is it safe to say you hung with a pretty rough crowd back then?"

"No, them were all pretty decent people . . . They use to come up on their bikes, but they weren't mean people. All they did was like to sit around and drink and look at their motorcycles. Up there, we had highly respected friends, including Norm, who used to own the bar."

Was there anything he cared to add?

"This Rocky character, you know? I probably only seen him twice in my life. That's all he ever does is just go around saying shit about people, you know? Trying to get them in trouble to get his self out of trouble and all this and that. He married my cousin Tammy and I ain't seen her in, shit, I couldn't tell you. I wouldn't know her on the street if I seen her.

"But then I heard they got divorced. Debbie called me and said they got divorced . . . I wouldn't know him if I seen him on the street. Stinky? He's the same way. They get theirself in trouble and . . ."

"Who's Stinky?" Bronco interrupted.

"Uh, what the fuck is his real name? That's my first cousin, too. Stinky. That's Charles McMullen. That's on my dad's side of the family. I don't talk to them because I don't get along with them."

When did he first meet Rocky?

"I think I was coon hunting down at Suzy and David's house."

The same day they all ended up at O'Shea's Tavern, J.R. and Coco drinking, Tommy out in the car with the coon dogs.

Did he remember talking at the bar about being in a fight?

"No. Why would I want to talk about being in a fight?"

Did he ever say anything about the missing hunters?

"No."

If someone said he had, it was a lie?

"Yes."

They were done.

70

TIME TO TALK

Word spread quickly in certain circles that J.R. and Coco had been arrested. It was a liberating event for some who'd lived, silently, in fear for years.

Alison King called Lesneski at home Friday night, the 23rd of May. A Katherine Sliwinski had stopped by the Monroe post, said she had some information they might find pertinent.

Saturday morning, operating on Bronco time, he called her at 8:35 a.m. Sliwinski, who'd had her 28th birthday four days earlier, said she was a former girlfriend of one of J.R.'s sons, Tommy. They'd lived together off and on for two and a half years and had a child together.

It was a rocky relationship, she said. "If you're a Duvall woman, you get beat up a lot. That's the way all the boys treated their women." Once, he'd hit her several times, then grabbed her by the throat and started strangling her, saying he was going to kill her. " 'We've done it before and we'll do it again,' " she quoted him as saying.

Later, he was full of remorse, sorry he'd hit her, saying it'd never happen again. Of course, it did.

Summer of 1997, they were visiting J.R. at the same house in Hale where he later was arrested. She and Tommy got in an argument and he threatened to kill her in front of

J.R. "We've killed before and we'll kill again," he said. "Tell her, Dad."

So J.R. told her. They'd met these guys in a bar one day. Later that night, they ran into them in another bar and beat them to death. J.R. told her they'd split their heads open like melons, then chopped them up and fed them to the pigs. And if you ever cross the Duvalls, we'll do it to you, too, the grandfather of her kids told her.

She apologized to Bronco for not having come forward earlier. "I know I should have, but you have no idea the kind of fear they can cause. I'm still very scared, but I know it's the right thing to do. After they were arrested, I figured someone would be looking to talk to me. I decided to let the police know where I'm at."

Like a melon. Crucial, crucial corroboration to what Boudro had said. And she was a witness who was going to need all the corroboration they could muster.

~

The same morning, Bronco got a call from David Henry Johnson. He wanted to let him know that Sherm Heilig had been in on the killings, which police had long suspected.

"Sherm bragged to me about them missing motherfuckers from Detroit and feeding them to pigs. He talked about being able to feed people to pigs and no one would ever find a trace."

One time Johnson's wife, Kimberly, was in a store and Heilig came up, pushed her up against the wall right there in public, put his hands on her and said if he wanted to rape her, there was nothing she could do about it.

Johnson found out and "I was livid. When I confronted him, he told me he'd feed me to the pigs like those missing motherfuckers."

Kim said she and her husband had some black friends, a rarity for that corner of northern Michigan, and Sherm and his friends kicked in the Johnsons' door one time, calling them "motherfucking nigger lovers."

The Johnsons put their house on the market and sold it in a hurry, at a big loss. They were worried that if they didn't get the hell out, they were going to be pig food, too.

~

Lesneski and King got anonymous calls telling them about the Duvalls' pigs. They got calls telling them about the Bronco. They got calls about buried Bronco parts here, there and nearly everywhere—you'd have thought every swamp in northern Michigan was a dumping ground; unfortunately, a lot of them were. They got calls about old bones and deer hunters hearing small-caliber gunfire in 1985—or was it 1987? And they got more calls from friends and relatives wanting to get secrets off their chests.

May 20, Bronco got a call from Florida. Charles McMullen—Stinky—one of the Duvalls' first cousins, said he'd moved to Florida after getting death threats over interviews he'd had with cops over the years. Said Bronco ought to come talk to him.

Bronco told him he'd make arrangements, and two weeks later, on June 4, Blumer and Bronco flew down.

McMullen told them it was 1990, maybe 1991. He'd been painting cars at the time and struck a deal with Coco to paint his boat. So McMullen's painting away in the garage, air compressor chugging away, and Coco at some point walks up, leans over and out of the blue says loud enough to be heard over the compressor, "The guy's head split like a melon," then walks away, snickering.

Like a melon.

McMullen said he knew Coco was talking about the hunters, based on family rumors that had been going around for years. The same rumors said the Bronco had been crushed at Uncle Mike's scrapyard in Monroe.

He was still getting threats, he said, even with J.R. and Coco in jail, or maybe *because* they were in jail, trying to keep witnesses to a minimum at any coming trial.

He'd been a witness to the Duvalls' propensity for fighting starting at age 15. He'd been having trouble with another kid, then, and his mom called Coco. "The whole family come up and took care of the guy," he said.

~

Thomas Yates was in jail in Monroe facing assault charges. His attorney contacted King and told her his client had been buddies with the Duvalls and was looking to trade what he knew about the murders for some leniency.

King said she couldn't make any promises, but something might be arranged if Yates had good information and testified in court. They later met in an interview room at the Monroe post.

Yates told her he'd met the brothers back in 1993–94. He'd been in a bar fight in Monroe and taken on six cops who'd been dispatched to the scene. The Duvalls were impressed by his fighting ability and soon they were all tight.

He said he saw a lot of their fights and "If a guy's too big for you, they'll use hammers." He said Coco would get drunk and talk about killing people and feeding them to pigs, but until he heard about the actual arrests, he thought it was just all hot air. Same as the rumors about them feeding the bodies into a wood chipper before they fed the pigs. "I mean, you hear a story like that, you're not believing it."

As for the Bronco, he said, "The guys have junked all their lives. It's so easy to get rid of vehicles. It's unbelievable how fast it can be done, and scattered all over Michigan. Twenty different vehicles and it's all the same vehicle. I've seen it done. I've seen the VIN numbers and everything go changing. I mean, all of it. They're looking for a vehicle that doesn't exist."

He'd done everything with the Duvalls, he said, hunted with them, poached salmon with them, been to J.R.'s, "the dirt-floored house, yep." And, "the one that got took over by the bank, and Coco's old house . . . I've butchered things with these guys and everything, they know their way around any type of animal that's ever lived."

Yates said the Duvalls had always traveled in rough circles. Three years ago, some of their biker buddies had thrown a buddy of his named Wes out of a limousine speeding down I-275 over a bad coke debt. "I mean, these guys are nothing to be messing around with, man."

Then there was one of their biker buds from years ago, you'd see him up north at their bonfires and pig roasts. He was named Bob.

"He's a hammer fighter. I heard an old story about Bob. He carried two bodies around in the trunk of his car until they really started stinking and he had to get rid of them. It was a big joke."

King asked him if he'd ever attended one of their parties where J.R. chainsawed a cow and, covered in blood, threw it in the fire pit.

"You ain't bullshitting. It never bothered us. I mean, as I told you, they're wizards. That's where I got taught a lot of my good ideals."

71

MAKING A BREAK

Lesneski got a call the morning of June 6th telling him to hurry over to the Montmorency County Jail, where the Duvalls were being housed in a small maximum-security area. It looked as if there'd been an attempted jailbreak.

Bronco got in his car and drove there at his usual high rate of speed. The undersheriff, David Benac, told him there were a pair of two-man cells in maximum security, and they opened out onto a common area. The Duvalls shared one cell, Chad Traub and Stafford Nolen shared the other. One of those two had tipped jailers to the attempted breakout, which was a work in progress.

A brick had been removed near the ceiling, along with a piece of conduit and some wire. The Duvalls denied any knowledge, of course.

Bronco interviewed Traub first. He said he thought the brothers were planning to assault one of the night-shift officers. He said the brothers had been given copies of police reports by the attorneys in preparation for upcoming hearings, and that they'd let him read some of them.

Traub said Coco had told him, "We didn't have a shredder. It was a crusher. They'll never find that fucking Bronco."

He'd also told him "that girl from Mio, her uncle did it. They're digging up the bodies in a couple of weeks."

Nolen told him some of the officers were women, and he'd heard Coco saying he was going to beat one of them over the head during her nightly watch. Coco had said, "On the nineteenth, one way or another, we're getting out of here."

"There is no way in hell I'd let anything happen to these ladies in jail," Nolen told Bronco. "They've been good to me and I wouldn't let anyone hurt them to escape."

72

JUST A BUNCH OF RUMORS

On June 19, 81st District Court Judge Allen Yenior held a preliminary exam in Mio to determine if there was enough evidence to bind Coco and J.R. over for trial in Circuit Court.

Townsfolk were tight-lipped. They wanted their names kept out of it, but off the record some would say they feared the Duvalls, others that they feared the police and thought they were railroading the most likely scapegoats.

Up the road from the trial, in Curtisville, longtime home to the Duvalls, the extraordinarily named Orf Flockhart told Hugh McDiarmid Jr. of the *Detroit Free Press* that he'd lived with J.R. for a couple of winters and another couple of years with another of the Duvalls, Rex. He didn't know Coco much, "but J.R. was a nice guy. I don't believe he did it. He was a guy that, if he cut a load of wood for you, he was fair about it."

J.R. wasn't a violent man, said Orf, though he acknowledged he liked to drink "and sure could handle his fighting. They had their fun," he said of the brothers. "Once they tied up Kenny [the youngest Duvall] with ropes and hoisted him up a tree and left him there. But it was just for fun."

Security was tight at the small Mio courthouse. Rumors were rife following the attempted jailbreak that the Duvalls were going to make a run for it with the help of their friends and family, and Coco's overheard claim that they were going to get sprung on the 19th, one way or another.

It was just a bunch of rumors, said Coco's attorney, Seymour Schwartz, rumors about escape, and rumors about the killings. The brothers' reputation for violence was overblown. They were brawlers, he acknowledged, but the good old-fashioned kind. "It was old-time rough-and-tumble, always fistfights, never weapons," he told McDiarmid. "These days, everybody brings their guns, their knives and their lawyers."

The last was an odd way to finish, considering that he was the lawyer Coco had brought.

Barb Boudro told the judge the same tale she'd told after being subpoenaed. She'd climbed out of her house the night of the killings, snuck down the trail and watched as "he swung a bat and his head sounded like when you drop a squash or a pumpkin. They just kept kicking them."

She told the judge she'd kept quiet over the years because "I knew enough about the Duvall brothers that . . . they would have killed me."

Tammy Morris repeated what she'd told investigators about the overheard conversation at the Wixom bar. But she also made an acknowledgment that helped the defense: "Everybody was making jokes that they was put in a tree shredder and fed to the pigs," she said. "It became a joke because actually nobody believed them."

"Our brothers are innocent," Randy Duvall told the gathered press after the preliminary exam. "They would not hurt you in any way, form or fashion."

They weren't the type, he said. Moreover, they didn't own a vehicle at the time of the murder that would have even made it the twenty miles from where they lived in Curtisville to Mio.

"I understand the victims' families want to put an end to this, but they've got the wrong guys," said J.R.'s attorney, Scott Williams.

It was a perfunctory hearing, just a formality. District courts don't hear felony cases in Michigan. They rarely dismiss cases, either. Yenior ruled there was enough probable cause to move the case over to circuit court.

On July 10, the brothers were arraigned before Ogemaw County Circuit Judge Ronald Bergeron, who granted up to $7,500 to help court-appointed attorney Scott Williams prepare J.R.'s case. The money would go, said the attorney, to an investigator to track down witnesses and leads contained in the bulging files assembled by police over nearly two decades.

Bergeron granted no money to Donald's defense. For some reason, the Duvall family was paying for his attorney and not for J.R.'s. J.R. was on his own.

73

ON THE CASE

It was one of the cases you live for as a prosecutor, that help justify in your mind why you work long hours for a fraction of what you could make as a defense attorney. Something horrible had happened to a couple of young men, and their families had been held in limbo since. Now, justice could be served, their families could finally—not for certain but maybe, and maybe was a big step forward—move on with their lives. And the bad guys could be put away forever.

It was a big case. It would draw a lot of attention. And it was Mark Blumer's. Or so he thought.

Michigan Attorney General Mike Cox hired Donna Pendergast in August, after the arraignment and prelim in district court and the arraignment in circuit court, and promptly pulled Blumer off the case and gave it to her at the end of the month.

Cox had been her boss when he was head of the homicide unit in the Wayne County Prosecutor's Office. When he'd recruited her to Lansing, he told people she was the best prosecutor in the state. And this was a case, he thought, that was going to need the best. No body, no forensics, no new technology riding to the rescue to interpret old blood clues.

Pendergast had developed a reputation for cold-case slayings—"Justice is a concept that never gets cold," she says—and this was one of the coldest of all.

Pendergast was, in the words of the headline of a *Detroit Free Press* profile, "Born to prosecute."

She was 45 when she got the case. She appeared ten years younger, not your typical prosecutor by looks. She's tall, blonde, with eyes a shade of aquamarine you can get lost looking into. If you saw her playing the star prosecutor in a TV drama, you'd likely mutter "I'm sure," or, "Yeah, right," like any prosecutor would ever look like that. She has one of those success rates you only see in TV or movies, too—she was 88–2 in her first ninety murder cases.

As Joe Swickard wrote in the *Free Press*: "Defendants can hear a cell door's cold clank when she enters a courtroom."

If Blumer wasn't happy to hand the case off, she wasn't happy to get it, either. Not at first. She was leaving September 23 for a three-week vacation in Greece with her husband, *Free Press* columnist Brian Dickerson, who, the story went, had seen her in court once and said, struck dumb, "Who is *she*?" They were taking his mother as an early Christmas present.

They were coming back October 13. The trial started on October 20. Hardly perfect timing. Couldn't Blumer keep it? No.

"Thank God for those indexes," she thought as she looked at the cross-referencing Bronco had done. If it was going to be possible to cram for this trial in the time she'd have, it was only because of the way Bronco had organized eighteen years of reports.

If Blumer was disappointed, and she was dismayed, Bronco was beside himself. Blumer had gotten him his legislative subpoenas. He'd gotten him his warrants. He'd gotten them all through the preliminary hearings without a hitch.

Suddenly, it's getting close to trial and Blumer's not returning Bronco's calls. He's told he's not available. He's ducking him, that's clear. But why? Makes no sense, not now. Weeks go by. Bronco's getting more and more steamed. And perplexed. It doesn't feel right. He leaves a message. He knows where Blumer lives and if he doesn't call him like right now, Bronco is going to come down there banging on doors.

Soon, he comes in and sees the red light flashing on his phone, and it's a message from Blumer telling him he's been removed from the case and this Donna character is on it. Frickin' politicians. Attorney frickin' general politician. Pulled his guy off the case and appointed one of his favorites to suck up the glory.

There's another message. It's from Donna, call me ASAP, it says. And it goes on to say she's on the case, but she has this vacation planned, she's going to Greece, she'll be back a week before trial. Bye.

Bronco tells the secretary he's gotta go for a run. And he heads out into the woods, running his ass off, burning off steam, getting his anger down to a manageable level. "I was pissed," he said later. "I was pissed off! She's going to Greece? I'm like, 'Holy shit!' I don't mind telling you, I was scared about the case."

~

Like the Tylls, Pendergast grew up in Copper Canyon, the east-side Detroit neighborhood that was filled with cops and firemen living as close to the suburbs as they could get.

Donna's father, Bill, was a cop who survived both twenty years on the streets and another twenty years at headquarters downtown, where Byzantine politics could make street life seem like punk's play. He'd retired with the rank of detective sergeant.

He was a tough guy, and recognized early on his daughter was, too. "She'd stand up and back me down, so I figured she'd either be a prizefighter or a lawyer," he said in the *Free Press* profile.

In high school, Donna worked as a lifeguard on Belle Isle, the big island that sits in the middle of the Detroit River. During law school at Detroit's Wayne State University, she tended bar in Greektown, just around the corner from police headquarters and just a couple of stone throws from the Frank Murphy Hall of Justice where she would later work.

Pendergast studied labor relations as an undergrad at the University of Michigan, planning on a career in labor law. But a course in advocacy in law school changed her mind. "A prosecutor—that's what I wanted to be," she says.

She landed her first job with the prosecutor's office in Oakland County in 1987, handling grunt work like signing arrest warrants and prosecuting drunk drivers and speeders in the county's numerous district courts. Misdemeanors and traffic offenses were handled in the district courts in each city. Felonies got kicked up to the more prestigious circuit court, where, in those days, just two women on a staff of fifty-seven were allowed to work.

She soon made it three. At first, the cops and sheriffs who frequented circuit court regarded her with skepticism or disdain, reacting perhaps to her looks. If they thought they could intimidate her, it wasn't a thought they entertained for long. The daughter of a cop, she could speak like a cop. She soon was accepted as one of the best, and one of the toughest.

She got her first murder conviction in 1989. Others soon followed. By the time she was recruited to be his star prosecutor by Wayne County Prosecutor Michael Duggan in 2000, she had won some fifty murder convictions.

Among them were several that made the national news and were played up big on the various cable court shows.

One was the conviction of Jonathan Schmitz. While on *The Jenny Jones* show for an episode on secret crushes, a man named Scott Amedure proclaimed a crush for Schmitz. After they flew back to Michigan from the taping, Schmitz went to Amedure's house and shotgunned him. It was during that case that Dickerson showed up looking for column material and found a wife.

Another was the murder case that became a true-crime book for St. Martin's in 1997, *The Coed Call Girl Murder*, by Fannie Weinstein and Melinda Wilson, about an Oakland, Michigan, University student named Tina Biggar whose secret life as a call girl named Crystal ended in her murder.

A trial in 2002—one that continues to haunt her—was of a couple of young psychopaths named Aaron Stinchcombe and Russell Oescher. They lured a pair of 12-year-old girls from a slumber party and then killed them. While chanting "wind-up toy, wind-up toy," they twisted the head of one of the dead girls.

Pendergast was met with hostility and resentment by many of her colleagues and by many of the judges, too, when she joined the Wayne County staff. The defendants in Wayne County circuit court are mostly black. So are a preponderance of the employees. The color of Pendergast's skin and her hair didn't help. Neither did the fact that she was coming in from Oakland County. She was regarded as some white interloper grown spoiled by the pace of the suburbs who would be chewed up and spit out by the caseload and the lack of budget in the big city. Too refined, too pretty, too privileged.

She was making too much money to suit her colleagues, too. It had been a practice in the office for years that all new hires—no matter how much experience—started out at level one on the pay scale. Duggan, new to the office and vowing to shake things up, wanted her on his homicide team. He knew he couldn't get a star to come in from Oakland County at a cut in pay, so she started at level four. Her colleagues filed a grievance with the National Labor Relations Board.

They would, slowly and grudgingly, learn what her predecessors had in Oakland County. She put in the best preparation, she formed relationships and friendships with victims' families, her direct and cross-examinations were organized, concise and relentless without coming across as mean-spirited, and she could connect with juries, even black ones.

As Cheryl Matthews, now an Oakland County Circuit Judge, told Joe Swickard of the *Detroit Free Press*, "She was a senior prosecutor and I was just a lowly district court misdemeanor prosecutor" when they became friends. "All the junior prosecutors saw her as very smart, good and prepared . . . She was absolutely prepared for every witness. Her opening and closing statements and questioning of expert witnesses were the best.

"Of course I snuck up to watch her work. It's important to steal from people who know what they are doing."

In Wayne County, Pendergast proved she could handle a docket that seemed nearly infinite. While some judges there have reputations for short days and four-day weeks, prosecutors work at hyperpace. Often, they have to get subordinates to pick their juries because they're arguing other cases right up until the next case starts.

What no one in Oakland County or Wayne County knew, though, was the toll that cases could take. Pendergast took them personally. They meant clenched teeth, knotted stomach and, before and during the trial, insomnia, her nights filled with bits of sleep and bouts of studying and rehearsing and more studying.

Pendergast made good money as a prosecutor. She could have tripled or quadrupled her pay as a defense attorney. Cashing out as a defense attorney is a time-honored part of the career path for many who start out as underpaid assistant DAs.

Not Pendergast. "The thought doesn't appeal to me. I like wearing the white hat. I know everyone needs a defense, but . . ."

She studied Bronco's three binders and wrote out a rough draft of her opening arguments before she left.

When they got back, her mother-in-law came to Detroit with them to spend the weekend celebrating her grandson's birthday. While they were celebrating, Pendergast left her home and checked into the Westin hotel in Southfield for four days. She put her hair up in a ponytail, put on a set of comfortable sweats and studied from 5 a.m. to midnight each day. She ordered her meals from room service.

Bronco had been pissed off big-time when Pendergast got put on the case. When they finally got together just before trial, she mentioned something about the case, some detail that caught Bronco by surprise. He asked her how she knew that.

"I've got it memorized," she said. "It" being the three thick books of reports.

"She knew all the names, all the relationships, how they all fit together," said Bronco. He was no longer cursing Cox for putting her on the case.

PART 4
JUDGMENT

74

A ONE-EYEWITNESS TRIAL

It would be a one-eyewitness trial, and the eyewitness was hardly a prosecutor's dream.

Barb Boudro was one of the most impeachable witnesses you'd ever come across, an admitted hard-partyer who'd rarely missed a night at the bar throughout the 1980s, who'd had at least nine drinks the night she saw what she claimed to have seen. A drunk, who was drunk at night, who was drunk in the woods, who was drunk at a distance. A drunk who had told who-knows-how-many contradictory versions of events over the years before finally settling on this one just a few months ago, nearly eighteen years after the fact.

It was testimony that a kid out of law school would have little trouble impeaching.

The first time Pendergast met Boudro, she dressed down for the occasion. Didn't want to come in wearing the navy power suit and put her on edge.

Pendergast liked Boudro right off the bat. Maybe working her way through college as a barmaid had tempered her opinion of drinkers. Maybe it was Boudro's unassuming lack of pretension. Pendergast found it charming hearing her talking about her grandkids or canning vegetables after reading about her party ways in the reports gathered over the years.

Just before trial they went out to lunch at a nearby McDonald's. Pendergast had given her a little charm for good luck. They ate lunch, walked out, got in the cop car and Barb realized she'd left her charm on the tray she'd dumped into the garbage. Not a good sign. The trooper went back in, rifled through the garbage and retrieved it.

It helped that she liked her witness and her witness could sense it. She needed Boudro to bond with her. She needed to form ties that would counteract her fear of the Duvalls. There were no guarantees Boudro would testify, there was always the thought that at the last minute, fear would get the best of her and she'd back out. Or get on the stand and get amnesia.

And even if she did take the stand and was forthright, there was the issue of her credibility, or lack thereof. Pendergast made a decision: to call far more witnesses than normal. At the risk of boring the jury, she needed to add every little bit of corroboration she could.

She needed to have the jurors see and hear as much about the Duvalls as possible, not just of the night in question but of *them*, their *lives*, their penchant for violence and invoking fear over the years, with friends, family and loved ones. Hell, with each other.

75

OPENING ARGUMENTS

"No bodies. No truck. No guns. No DNA. No finger-prints. No blood. No hairs. Nothing."
—Defense attorney Scott Williams, summing up the
case against the Duvalls in the Detroit Free Press,
which hit the newsstands just hours before
the trial began

*"They weren't there, and they didn't do anything, and
they're angry because they think they're being worked
by the cops."*
—Defense attorney Seymour Schwartz, saying there
was a good reason for all those no's

"I've never had a case of this magnitude with no phys-ical evidence."
—Bronco Lesneski

Monday, October 20, 2003. The outside world had come to
Standish. Big-city reporters from Detroit way to the south,
TV crews and photographers setting up inside the courtroom, mobile units out front, their extendable transmission
towers rising up from the tops of their trucks.

The trial had been moved from Mio in Oscoda County to

the 23rd Circuit Court in Arenac County, fifty miles south, for fear of pre-trial publicity. Not to mention—nobody had, but it was on everyone's mind—fear of the Duvalls.

It was a sensational case, to be sure. According to one local reporter, the last sensational case to come to Standish had been back in 1999. Made big headlines then, too. The Duvall case would make some of the cable TV true-crime shows. So far, that previous case has not. Locally, they called it "the cussing canoeist" case, where a jury convicted 24-year-old Timothy Boomer of violating the state's 105-year-old law against swearing in public when a family on a nearby river heard him using foul language over a canoeing mishap. (The conviction was later overturned.)

Williams could have added a single "one" after his string of *no*'s, but didn't: The prosecution had one eyewitness.

Williams had access to all the police reports over the years. He'd gone over what Boudro had said with a fine-tooth comb. He'd read what she'd told Lesneski on April 4, 2002, when he'd asked her about reports she'd been lovers with the Duvall brothers, her and a girlfriend.

It could be true, she told him. "I can't deny it. I spent time with a lot of people when I partied. Oftentimes people would tell me that they were with me and I didn't have the foggiest."

An impeachable witness? One who said her memory was so bad she couldn't say if the Duvalls were former lovers or not? Williams must have been salivating at the chance to have at her in court as he spoke to the reporter.

Witnesses didn't get any more impeachable than this. If the jury didn't believe her, game over.

Pendergast had had stronger cases. On paper, it'd be harder to imagine a weaker one.

~

The Duvalls entered the courtroom, J.R. still lanky at 52, Coco shorter and squat. Coco sat down, caught Pendergast's eye and gave her his best tough-guy look, a sneer that had scared plenty of north-woods and Monroe folks over the years.

"You don't stare me down," she sneered loudly at him, giving him her best evil eye. The deputies in the court laughed out loud. Coco turned away.

Early on, Kevin Tyll walked into the courtroom. He had a beard like his brother Dave's, and a strong family resemblance. Cathy Tyll had been waiting to see how the Duvalls would react if they saw Kevin when he came in. She observed them as they noticed him, then looked quickly at each other.

"That was it for me. I knew they did it," she would say later.

It took four hours to select a jury, eight men and six women, two more than would be needed for deliberations. By lots, if all of them made it through the trial, two of them would be sent home without having to cast a vote for guilty or not.

They were from a wide variety of backgrounds. Several were retired. Some said they had heard about the case over the years, but could render an impartial judgment. There was a nurse, a former store owner, even—a surprise the defense didn't cast a peremptory challenge—an employee at the nearby Standish Maximum Correctional Facility.

Pendergast, speaking without notes, her pen and legal pad back at her table, began her opening argument poetically, facing the jury:

"Screams bottled up in boxes and binders, sitting on a shelf. Boxes and binders that would get bigger by the year as they sat waiting, waiting for the day when someone, despite threats and intimidation, would have the courage to speak out about an act of brutality so savage, so ruthless, so horrific that it would make your skin crawl.

"What you're about to hear in this courtroom will terrify you, will horrify you, will haunt your dreams for a long time to come, maybe the rest of your lives. It's got all the elements of a grade B horror movie—terror, torture, two men begging for their lives in a dark field. Unfortunately, it's no horror movie, but real life.

"This trial will tell that eighteen-year-old story, not only a story, but the final chapter in the life of two twenty-seven-year-old men who would die alone with their murderers, terrified in a pool of blood, and in an agonizing manner . . . Plain and simple, it was an execution."

She recounted the timing of the last day Tyll and Ognjan were seen by their friends. Of debating in front of Brian's girlfriend whether they should go hunting or not. Of finally heading out, but north, not west.

She told the jury what police had been able to piece together. That the two had been seen drinking in a bowling alley in Mio. That they'd had words with a waitress at the Linker's Lost Creek Lodge near Luzerne. That they'd had more words with the two defendants, who had gone to a phone and made a call.

"Several individuals came up to that bar, reinforcements, if you will," said Pendergast.

She told them of Boudro having words with the hunters, too, then leaving for home, starting a movie, having it interrupted by sounds of distress—pinging noises and cries for help.

"Barb told Ronald, 'Those hunters are getting their asses kicked,' Ronald Emery wanting to view this because he had never seen a good whooping before," said Pendergast. "Ronald Emery wanted to go watch, but Barb Boudro was terrified."

They went anyway, and when they got to the clearing down the path from her house, they watched the Duvalls and three others beat the lifelong friends from Detroit to death. "They lured them outside into the woods and beat them until their heads exploded like melons," said Pendergast.

And she told jury members they would soon hear from witnesses that the Duvalls had bragged over the years about the killings, about feeding the bodies into a wood chipper and then to their pigs. About threatening friends and family who got word of their deed. About J.R.'s carnivorous pigs, who had grown up on deer guts and anything else thrown to them.

"Ladies and gentlemen of the jury, there is an old statement, or saying, that 'Dead men tell no tales,' but may I suggest to you that in this courtroom, two dead men will speak to you through the evidence, the evidence that will scream out to you, even though David and Brian's cries and screams have been silenced forever, the evidence that will say: 'J.R. and Coco Duvall, it's been a long time coming, but the law doesn't forget and justice is a concept that never gets old.' "

76

A DOOZY!

Coco's attorney, Seymour Schwartz, told the judge he'd reserve his opening statement.

J.R.'s attorney, Scott Williams, rose. "I've got to use notes. I'm not as organized as Ms. Pendergast," he said, pausing and turning to the jury.

"Wow! What a story! She's told you a doozy. Unfortunately for Ms. Pendergast's version of the story, there is no scientific, physical evidence to back up one single bit of it," he said.

"No bodies were ever located. No vehicle was ever found. No vehicle parts were ever found. No body parts, bones, teeth were ever found. No guns were ever found, what they were supposedly hunting with. No alleged murder weapon was ever found. No gear or clothing or anything belonging to the hunters was ever found. No DNA, no fingerprints of the hunters were ever found, no blood, no hairs, no other scientific evidence whatsoever."

Williams hammered away, as expected, at Barb Boudro. He told the jury of her drug and alcohol use, and of the various accounts of events she'd told over the years.

Not only was she an ex-drunk and an ex–drug user who kept changing her tale, Williams said, but he was going to call witnesses who would refute nearly every one of her claims about what had happened in Linker's the night the two hunters supposedly crossed paths with the Duvalls.

"The only one who says what Ms. Boudro saw is Ms. Boudro. No one else is going to verify a single thing to what she's saying."

Claims that the jurors would later hear in trial about various Duvall confessions over the years were nothing more than "misunderstood and misinterpreted bar talk" by "ex-girlfriends or others with an ax to grind."

"This case is like a big urban legend. It just kept growing and growing . . . Every time it gets told it gets elevated, and that's what we have here."

Williams said there were numerous tips over the years of sightings of the missing hunters during the three days in question back in 1985, tips that came in from towns in counties all over northern Michigan, far too many sightings for all of them—or even most of them—to be real. There was, he said, one crucial *non-sighting*. Before Tyll and Ognjan left Brian's St. Clair Shores home they talked about possibly going to see an old friend named Dennis Gallop. And where did Dennis Gallop live? Oscoda County. And who was absolutely clear that he never saw Tyll or Ognjan during their trip? Dennis Gallop. If they had talked about going up to see him, and then in fact had driven three hours to the vicinity of his house, way across the state from their original destination, wouldn't they have at least called on him once?

"There is absolutely no physical evidence, number one, that the hunters are dead and, number two, that they were anywhere near Oscoda County in Mio, Michigan," said Williams.

"Can we assume they're dead? I don't know. They may be. They may be off living in Hawaii, I don't know. But the fact is, no one knows for sure. No one knows beyond a reasonable doubt."

77
THE FAMILY SPEAKS

After a recess, Pendergast called her first witness at 3:28 p.m. It was Denise Dudley, David Tyll's wife, who had since remarried. She had been married to David for seven years when he disappeared. She said there was no dissension in the marriage before he'd left to go hunting.

Though she'd filed for divorce in August of 1986 and remarried soon after, the pain of her loss was evident as she talked about their marriage and their last day together: how they'd had lunch at McDonald's on November 22, 1985; that he was due back Sunday night.

When he didn't show up by 10 p.m., she was worried. "From that day, everything started escalating. This was out of their character. They were both due back to work on Monday," said Denise. David had always been punctual, always responsible.

She spent the next few months searching for her husband and asking the news media and police for help. But, "I knew within the first week he had to be dead," she said.

He never accessed his bank account, never used his credit card, never used his health insurance.

Catherine Tyll, David's mother, took the stand late in the

day. She choked up when Pendergast asked her to identify a picture of her son.

She and her son were close, she said. He had called her just before he left with Brian. It was the last time she'd heard his voice.

78

WILL SHE OR WON'T SHE?

Tuesday, October 21.

Barb Boudro's testimony was expected to be the highlight of the trial. Or at least Pendergast hoped it would be. Up until Boudro took the stand and began talking, Pendergast wouldn't be able to breathe easily. She couldn't be sure there would be any Boudro testimony until it was over and done with.

If Pendergast was on edge over whether or not Boudro would come through, it was an edge she'd have to balance on for four and a half hours while a stream of other prosecution witnesses testified before her, laying the foundation for what she would have to say.

Matt Tyll came first. The judge ran a punctual courtroom. The jurors were seated and Tyll sworn in by 9:05. He told of waiting in White Cloud for his brother and Brian to show, heading out to the bar with his buddies and leaving a note for David before they left. Of his brother never showing up, and of going back the next week to ask around the local bars and hire a pilot to search from the air.

Then came Janice, formerly Payne, now Hooper, Brian Ognjan's old girlfriend. She told of the frugal hardworking mechanic who owned his own home, was saving for a bigger one, had a boat he loved, went deer hunting every year, but wouldn't aim the gun even when a buck walked right by his blind.

Of the neatnik she was hoping to marry, who wouldn't call if he was running late because he hated to waste the money on a long-distance call, who just left one Friday and never came back.

Dennis Gallop was called. On cross-examination by Schwartz he shaded the picture of Brian Ognjan that had been painted, of a frugal, hardworking nice guy. There could be a darker side to Brian.

One time, about 1979, Gallop and Brian had gotten into a fistfight inside a car. They were drinking beer, on their way to a local park when Brian shook up his beer and sprayed it on Gallop.

Schwartz asked if Brian had had a habit of causing trouble back in the late '70s, early '80s.

"Well, sometimes he would act tough towards other people, because he had his friends with him."

"When he was drinking he did that?"

"Correct."

Pendergast must have been happy at the line of questioning. If her theory of the crime was that Brian and David had been mouthing off to the wrong guys in the wrong bar and had been beaten to death as a result, so much the better that the defense attorney was getting it on the record that Brian had a habit of acting the tough guy when he was drinking.

Gallop also told the court about a shotgun Brian owned, had a hair-trigger, went off way too easily. Schwartz seemed to have something in mind when he began that line of questioning, but it ended quickly.

Williams picked up on it. Gallop told him that when he'd gone hunting with Brian, he'd walked behind him because he was worried about the shotgun going off.

There was just one problem with the theory, if that's what was being developed. Gallop had only hunted with Brian during bird season, when you used shotguns. You used rifles during deer season, and nothing was mentioned about any rifles with hair-triggers.

Another odd line of questioning followed, from a tactical viewpoint. Williams asked Gallop about a map Daniel Jacob had drawn for Brian and Dave before they'd left to go hunting back in 1985. Jacob had prided himself on his memory and his map-making and, since Gallop didn't have a phone, would have been crucial for the two to find him on their weekend north.

Gallop testified that the map was in error, nearly totally wrong, that it didn't have M-33 on it, the main north–south highway through northeastern Michigan and what you'd have to follow to get to Gallop's.

What was odd about the questioning was that it played right into Pendergast's needs. If the defense was trying to argue that the missing hunters certainly would have contacted Gallop had they been in the area, and since he never saw them, they must not have been there and therefore not subject to any beating by the Duvalls—well, there was Williams, doing Pendergast's work for her. If they had a bad map to his house, and he didn't have a phone, how in the world could they have contacted him once they got near Mio? They could have been there a week and he might not have known.

~

David Welch was the construction worker back in 1985 who said he'd seen Tyll and Ognjan at the bowling alley in Mio, the one who claimed Tyll had said he wanted to disappear to the Bahamas, but he recommended Alaska, instead.

Though he'd told the tale to reporters, who had written about it, oddly, their talk of running off never came up. Pendergast certainly wasn't going to bring it up, and neither Schwartz nor Williams must have read the accounts.

Welch told the court he was at the bowling alley seven days a week. He spoke slowly, agonizingly, the result of a metal plate implanted in his head after a crane had fallen on him.

Pendergast got Welch to recount meeting the hunters in Walker's Bar in Mio, chatting and drinking with them, then telling him about how they'd ended up there instead of White Cloud. And that Ognjan had left for the Northwood, but returned later.

The testimony about White Cloud was a cincher for putting the two in the right place at the wrong time. There was no doubt it was Ognjan and Tyll in the northeast woods that weekend.

"Mr. Welch, you were a regular at Walker's Bar, right?" asked Schwartz.

"Yes," said Welch.

"Were you there all the time?"

"Not all the time."

"But a pretty fair amount, right?"

"Every day, approximately."

Schwartz asked him to recount how the police had come to learn about his hanging out with the deer hunters one night at Walker's just before they'd gone missing.

"When you were interviewed by the police, had you been drinking?" Schwartz asked.

"It's really hard to say, because sometimes I drank from daylight to dark."

Schwartz asked about a second interview he'd had with the police, after a TV show on the case was broadcast on *Unsolved Mysteries.*

"They asked you if there was anything else you remembered, right?"

"Yeah, I think just about every time that I was questioned, there was always more that I remembered, you know? My memory came back."

"Had they been drinking a lot in your judgment?"

"Well, since I've quit drinking, my theory of drinking is, two drinks is too much. They had well over two drinks apiece."

Those who'd read about the hunters telling him about wanting to flee to Alaska were shocked when the defense attorneys told him they had no further questions. Maybe they didn't know how to Google.

♦ ♦ ♦

Cindy Steinhurst, known then as Cindy Socia, took the stand after the lunch recess. Her testimony gave the defense its first few good moments.

She was the waitress who'd been working in Linker's Lodge the night the deer hunters came in. She was the one Brian had offended when he told her he'd kick her ass if she took David's money for their first round of drinks.

On cross-examination, she said she knew Barb Boudro, but didn't remember her being there that night. She said she didn't know the Duvalls, but had seen their photos and didn't recall their having been in. And she said that the bar was a big, open, one-room place where it was easy to keep an eye on people and that she hadn't seen either Tyll or Ognjan have words with anyone other than her while they were there.

At 1:27 p.m., finally, the big moment everyone was anticipating was here. Pendergast said, "Your Honor, at this time, the people would like to call Barbara Boudro to the stand."

79
LIKE A PUMPKIN EXPLODING

The drama started before Boudro could be sworn in. She got three steps into the packed courtroom—a TV camera aiming at her, the rapid-fire clicking of the print photographers' cameras a loud staccato reverberating off the hardwood railings and chairs and wood paneling—when she looked at Coco, said, "I can't do this," burst into tears and ran back out into the hallway.

Bronco ran out after her. He caught up to her, led her to a bench in the hall. He kneeled down in front of her, took hold of her hands.

"You have to do this," he said, looking into her eyes. "It's for your own safety. You can't let them off, now."

"Okay, I can do this," she said, after a long pause.

Later, she'd say she was sure Coco had been about to come over the railing at her, was going to try to kill her right then and there. Her 14-year-old granddaughter, Ashleigh, was in court and saw it all, and during a recess later told her grandma that the look on Coco's face had said, "You are sliced and diced, bitch."

Meanwhile, the judge called a recess and invited the attorneys into his chambers.

"I think you guys shot her a look," said Bergeron to Schwartz.

Pendergast accused Coco Duvall of saying or doing something.

They all went back into the courtroom. "Are we ready to proceed?" asked Bergeron.

"The people are ready," said Pendergast. "Your Honor, the people call Barb Boudro to the stand."

Bronco walked with her past the defendants and their attorneys right up to the witness chair, where she was sworn in. She was alternately feisty, weepy, shaking—repeatedly telling the room she was scared for her life—as she told of drinking at Linker's (rechristened by the time of the trial as the Lost Creek Sky Ranch), of smelling trouble when the Duvalls walked in, of how the hunters had rubbed up against her at the pool table and grabbed someone by her rear end and made fools of themselves, of how the Duvalls had come in and seemed to hone in on the two.

"If you ever been in a bar, you can tell when there's going to be trouble," she said. "I told Ronnie [Emery] 'There's going to be trouble, now.'"

At one point, Pendergast asked her if she was nervous.

"Very."

"In the last week, have you been nervous about this appearance?"

"I've been terrified since Bronco showed up at my door."

Bronco, sitting next to her, was nervous, too. He'd been wired for sound all through the trial, but during her testimony his foot kept bouncing up and down, his knee rising and falling so fast Donna kept reaching under the table to hold it, to settle it, and him, down.

Pendergast got her back to that night in Linker's. The Duvalls and the hunters had had some words, and Coco had gone to the phone near where Barb and Ronnie were sitting and made a call.

"You indicated that you overheard something from the table?" asked Pendergast.

"I'm really scared to answer anything," she said.

The judge asked her if she wanted to take a break. She

did. They recessed at 2:00. Twelve minutes later, they resumed. Boudro was visibly calmer.

Pendergast led her through the rest of her narrative of the night at Linker's and its aftermath, of her and Ronnie settling in to watch *Scarface*, only to be interrupted by voices arguing out in the woods, and a pinging sound. She told Ronnie there was a fight going on. They started to go out the front door, saw a pickup parked in her driveway, decided to climb out through a rear bedroom window.

The voices and the pinging sounds were louder. "I said, 'Someone's getting their ass kicked,'" Boudro told the courtroom.

"Did you say, 'Somebody's getting their ass kicked,' or 'The hunters are getting their ass kicked'?" asked Pendergast.

"I said, 'Somebody's getting their ass kicked.' I figured it was the hunters, but it could have been vice versa."

Boudro and Emery had run down the trail to the clearing lit in the headlights of the Bronco and a pickup, and had seen seven men, two of them the hunters, the tall one prone, trying to get to his knees, begging for help.

"He was begging and they swung the bat, and it sounded like . . . like if you drop a pumpkin, and there was just blood," she said, everyone in the court staring at her, transfixed, with the exception of the Duvalls, whose eyes were looking down.

Coco had swung the bat, she said, and while he was swinging, J.R. was kicking and punching David Tyll.

"What was Brian Ognjan doing?" asked Pendergast.

"Two other people were holding him. He broke away and ran, and they pulled him back, and he says, 'My God, you're killing my friend.'"

"What happened next?"

"He kind of collapsed, and then they started laughing, because he peed himself."

Time seemed to stop for an instant in the court. The image was so vivid, so powerful, so utterly frightening that it demanded digestion, rumination. What was worse? A man's head exploding like some kind of rupturing squash? Or his friend, seeing it, collapsing in on himself as his muscles gave way out of sheer fear, the muscles in his legs and the muscles of his bladder and his tormentors erupting in laughter at the sight of his wet pants?

This, *this*, thought Pendergast, this is the trial. This moment. Who can doubt this woman speaks the truth?

"My God, they were killing them," said Boudro. "No one deserves to die that way."

80

A BOMBSHELL

Pendergast, having started with the dramatic, switched to the tactical, anticipating that the defense would claim Boudro was just seeking the big reward, and would hammer away at her as a liar. So, time to defuse both.

Pendergast asked Boudro why she hadn't come forward in all the years before Bronco came knocking.

"Scared to death . . . I was threatened."

"Did you see rewards posters over the years?"

"Oh, yeah. Everywhere. They were in bars, they were at the Post Office, every Glen's. They just stayed there, especially in the sheriff's department. It never came down."

"And did you ever try to collect the reward?"

"No. Be crazy to."

Pendergast finished up by taking Boudro through her history with Bronco, how she tried not to let him in, that she'd fed him bits and pieces, always careful to frame it as hearsay, the words of a dead man. How Bronco had come back over and over, gotten more and more out of her, how she told him she'd deny everything, that if anyone in authority other than Bronco asked her about the things she'd been talking to him about, she'd say she'd made it all up, it was a pack of lies to try to get the reward.

Yes, this woman lied, Pendergast was saying. And for a

good reason. And when she told the truth, she had lies ready about that, too. So many lies, because she'd had so much fear. Who wouldn't, seeing what she'd seen?

Pendergast finished brilliantly. She asked Boudro about the investigative subpoena, got her to tell of Bronco holding her hand and, finally, after all the hours of chat that had passed between them, her saying, "You know I saw it, don't you?"

Pendergast asked her what she'd said to assistant prosecutor Mark Blumer about her feelings at coming clean at long last. Boudro's last words of the direct examination were:

"I'm a dead woman."

81

KNOCKING ON WOOD

The defense attorneys had plenty of ammunition to impeach Boudro's testimony, but before they could have at her, more drama ensued. Schwartz began his cross-examination by saying, "Good afternoon, Ms. Boudro." And then, "Can I pull this over here, Judge?" as he dragged his podium ten feet over, next to Coco.

Pendergast jumped to her feet. "Your Honor!" she shouted. "He's bringing it directly next to his client so that Ms. Boudro is forced to look directly there."

Schwartz said he was just trying to get a better angle at the witness than the one he had.

The judge called another recess, invited the attorneys back into his chambers.

Boudro, and the rest of the room, could hear someone yelling, "You're an asshole!" Didn't take much of a detective to figure out it was the judge yelling.

Boudro leaned over toward the court reporter, Wendy DeMatio. "I can hear what he's saying," she said, a smile on her face.

"Well, you better plug your ears, then, you're not supposed to."

They came back, Schwartz moved his podium back near where it had been and they resumed.

He hit hard at Boudro, as expected. What wasn't expected was how well she held up. The harder he hit at her, the better she came off.

As for her shifting testimony, inconsistencies and contradictions in numerous conversations with investigators over the years, she readily admitted it: "I didn't want to be involved. I was scared to death . . . I feared for my life. I don't want to be on that list of deceased witnesses."

And as for the reward, $100,000, it hadn't—and didn't—tempt her, she said. She said she was well aware of it had been from the beginning, when it was $5,000, and she had watched it climb over the years—to $10,000, $25,000, $50,000, then, finally, $100,000, without any interest in it or what it could buy her.

"I wouldn't live to get to spend it, so, I'm not going to talk, no," she said.

Wasn't she a self-described "hard partyer" who'd hit the bars nearly every night of the 1980s? "A regular at the Mio Saloon?"

"Yes."

"And you'd go there two, three times a week?"

"Oh, probably more than that."

"Okay. Four, five times a week?"

"Probably more than that." No sense being on the defensive about your habits.

Later: "And while you were in there drinking, whoever was working that night used to come over and just refill your glass with vodka, gin or whatever it is that you were drinking, didn't they?"

"No, they'd bring me a new glass. You don't refill a mixed drink."

"They didn't just put more booze in your glass, right?"

"No, you can't do that in a bar."

"Well, really?"

"You've never been in a bar?"

Snickers could be heard in the courtroom.

"I've been to a lot of bars," said Schwartz, testy. "They used to refill my glass."

The judge about had a stroke. "Wait a minute! Wait a minute!"

"I'm sorry," said the attorney.

More snickering.

Schwartz learned the hard way about the axiom they teach you in law school: If you don't know the answer to the question ahead of time, don't ask it. Trying to downplay her testimony about her fear of the Duvalls, noting that eighteen years had come and gone, he asked, "The whole time you've been telling us that you're terrified, but you're sitting here today, are you not?"

"Knock on wood," said Boudro. And then she balled up her right fist, reached out and rapped her knuckles for good luck on the wooden railing.

"Oh my God," thought Pendergast, doing all she could to keep from busting a gut.

82
INCONSISTENCIES

Schwartz had his moments, too. He scored points by pointing out several conflicts in Boudro's statements over the years, to Bronco, to Mark Blumer, in preliminary hearings and now at trial.

She'd said once that it had to have been a Saturday the hunters were killed, because she'd gone to the bar after work at her brother's place in Mio, Klimmek's Sales & Service, and she didn't work Sundays. But another time she said it could have been Sunday if that's the day Ronnie got the deer.

Sunday fit the prosecution time-line much better, because Bev Pasternak was unshakably sure she'd served the hunters Cokes and Buds Sunday morning at her place, Walker's Bar.

Boudro had told of seeing the hunters harass other women. She'd also said she'd only heard about it. She said she and her friends had been given a case of beer and told to leave Linker's. She'd previously said it was a six-pack. She'd said the Duvalls had given her the beer. She said a barmaid brought it over. She'd said she told the Duvalls that someone ought to kick the hunters' asses. She'd said she had said it, but not to the Duvalls. She'd said one person had come to her door the night of the beatings in the clearing and told her to keep quiet. She'd said it was two persons, Coco and J.R.

Hadn't she said once there was a lot of snow on the ground on the night in question? About a foot? Hadn't she also said it was only two or three inches?

"To be human is to err," she replied.

One thing that had remained consistent over the years, anytime anyone asked, and often when they didn't, was that she'd said she feared for her life. Schwartz kept coming back to that, but lost points whenever he did. Her fear was palpable.

Schwartz: "The day before the preliminary exam, you were outside all by yourself working on your garden, were you not?"

"How did you know that?"

"Well, were you or weren't you?"

"Well, yes."

"Has your car been run off the road?"

"No."

"Has a toaster gone in your bathtub while you're taking a bath?" he asked, aiming for snide, hitting inane, points being lost. "Has anything unusual happened to you that caused you to die or to possibly die?"

"No. I'm just lucky I'm under police protection."

"Right," said Schwartz sarcastically.

"Yes, I fear for my life. And, yes, I don't want to be on that list of deceased witnesses."

Schwartz tried to hammer away at her account of climbing down the ladder from her house and running through the woods to the clearing. Wouldn't they have been running over leaves and sticks and noisy stuff?

"It's all pines there. It's all pines," she said. Most of the jurors in that county knew how quiet you can be on a trail covered in pine needles.

"So there was nothing that could have made any noise at all that could have alerted anybody, right? Is that what you're telling us?"

"I guess if they could get over the screams of the guys."

"Okay. So now you're up there looking through the woods over the bushes or wherever you were looking. And how far were you from Mapes Road?"

"Your investigator measured it. How far was it?"

"You could see Coco Duvall and J. R. Duvall, right?"

"Yes."

"What was Coco Duvall wearing?"

"Clothes."

"Describe his jacket."

"I don't know what he was wearing."

"Was he wearing a hat?"

"I don't know . . . I can tell you how David Tyll's face looked. It was all bloody."

"I didn't ask you that question."

And, a few questions later: "Now, you'd been drinking and probably not using drugs, but maybe, correct?"

"I hadn't lost my vision."

"You claim to see this beating, right?"

"I *saw* a beating, don't 'claim.' "

Schwartz was done. And done in, according to most court observers. Barb Boudro, uneducated, unsophisticated, had kicked his ass, no doubt about it.

Pendergast didn't think things could have gone any better. She knew she couldn't have scripted it this well.

~

Williams seemed shaken, too. It was his turn to cross-examine her. But he wanted the night to regroup. They needed to get to her and with something a lot stronger than jabs.

"Your Honor, this might be a good place to break."

"For?"

"Until tomorrow morning."

"I don't think so," said the judge. "Go ahead."

At first, Williams tried to discredit Bronco. He asked if Bronco had shown Boudro a lot of photos of bushy-haired men and asked her to pick out which faces she recognized

from the bar or the field. No, he'd just shown her the Duvalls' pictures and asked her if she knew who they were.

"Did you get the impression from Bronco that this is the
guy he wanted you to identify?"

"No."

"But these are the only pictures he showed you, right?"

"He just asked me. He didn't put it that they were even
there. He said, 'Do you know these two guys?' And I said,
'Yes, that's Coco and J.R.'"

Bewilderingly, he, too, hammered away at the quantity of
beer she claimed had been delivered to her and Ronnie before
they left Linker's. Hadn't she once said it was a six-pack?
Hadn't she once said it was a case? Was that all he could come
up with? If she was wrong about the quantity of free beer,
maybe she was wrong about seeing guys beaten to death?

Was it a man or a woman who'd given her the beer?

Was it two guys or one who'd come to her door after the
beatings she claimed to have seen?

Why had one of Bronco's reports of an interview with
her said she'd seen "deep blood" in the clearing and another
time she'd talked about "dark blood"?

And of course he had to hit on her drinking habits.

"Are you a former alcoholic?"

"I wouldn't say I'm an alcoholic. I just like to party
hearty."

"I believe you said at the preliminary exam that you
weren't feeling any pain that night, right?"

"I wasn't hugging the ceramic god," she said, referring to
the posture of a drinker in the midst of vomiting into the toi-
let. Some in the crowd chuckled audibly and members of the
jury smiled.

"Do you remember how many mixed drinks you had that
night?"

"Seven, eight, nine. I could drink back then."

"You might have had up to nine of them?"

"I could have had more."

No wonder Williams had wanted to wait a day. She was
kicking his ass, too.

"Do you want to stop here or keep going?" he asked the judge, clearly hoping for reprieve.

The judge called it a day at 4:50 p.m., told them to be back in court at 9 a.m.

83

KILLING HER DOGS

Wednesday, October 22, 9:03 a.m., Boudro was reminded by Judge Bergeron that she was still under oath, and Williams resumed his cross-examination.

It was more of the same, hitting away at what he could hit at, little stuff mostly. During one interrogation, she said she didn't remember which of the Duvall group had asked her where they could get some pot. Another time she said it was Coco.

If the pay phone was outside Linker's, and there was a band playing, how could she hear that he was asking for reinforcements? She said she'd heard "parts of it, because of the music, they had to kind of talk loud."

Again, for what seemed like the fifteenth time, was it a case of beer, twenty-four, that were brought to her table? Or six?

Why did she say she'd gotten home at midnight one time and in court say it had to be before 11? Why did she say a foot of snow one time, three inches another?

The judge finally had to tell him to quit asking her about the snow.

"I won't cover the depth of the snow anymore, Ms. Boudro," said Williams.

Near the end of his cross-examination, Williams asked her why she kept mentioning her fear during the trial. A little earlier she had said, "I've lived in fear for eighteen years. I've tried to kill myself."

He should have left well enough alone.

"Has anything ever happened in the last eighteen years to you?"

"Antonio was killed."

"Antonio?"

"My dog. Shot." Antonio was the sheltie who'd started barking while they were watching *Scarface*.

"How was he killed?"

"He was shot, shot through the head."

"Okay."

"And then, and then my other dog was run over."

"Okay, and you have a belief . . ."

"They said that they knew my granddaughters. I had pretty granddaughters . . ."

"Hold on, Ms. Boudro," said Williams, jumping on her line. It was all going downhill fast.

The judge broke in to admonish Williams. "We have questions, and then we have answers," he told the attorney. "As long as it appears that there is an answer that's somewhat responsive to the question, I don't want another question. You see what I'm saying? Repeat the question."

"Over the last eighteen years has anything happened to you personally? I'm not talking about— I'm sorry your dog got run over, but anything happen to you personally in the last eighteen years?"

"Somebody broke into my home."

"Okay, did they steal anything?"

"No."

"Okay. As a matter of fact, you've lived in the same place ever since this happened? Again, right?"

"Yes."

And then he said to the judge, "Nothing further."

Hardly a cross-examination to put on his résumé. One that was about to get worse.

Pendergast stood up for redirect. "You indicated two of your dogs, one was shot through the head and the other dog was run over. Was there something unusual about the circumstances with that dog being run over?" she asked.

"She was in my yard."

"What do you mean, she was in your yard?"

"She was in my yard when she was run over."

Boudro was done. And she'd come through. Pendergast was proud of her. Bronco felt like giving her a big hug.

The court recessed at 10:40 and reconvened twenty minutes later.

84

LAUGHING ABOUT
THE SHREDDER

The rest of the third day of trial was a time for ex-friends and former lovers of the Duvalls to tell what they knew, or had heard, or thought about the defendants.

Ed Lavere had known the brothers for more than twenty years. He'd first met them about 1981, when he had a class in night school with Rex Duvall's girlfriend. In the late 1990s he'd lived with Coco in Monroe. He was close enough he figured he was family. Close enough that he didn't say he'd lived *with* them, but that "I lived in the family for five years." Close enough he had Coco as the beneficiary on his life insurance policy.

One night, Ed got a call from his ex-wife, who was still up north, just as they were getting ready to go out bowling, a big pastime in the Detroit area.

She called to tell him his oldest boy, Brandon, had choked on something and they might have to take him to the emergency room. A few minutes later she called back to say they were on the way to the hospital. And a little while later he got a third call, that Brandon was being examined and might have to have surgery to remove whatever it was that was stuck in his throat.

Coco and his wife, Terri Lynn, insisted on heading out bowling. Terri told Ed he could stay there, if he wanted, and not come, but that he was not allowed to use the phone to call the hospital. If his ex-wife called him, that was one thing, but he was not to make any calls himself.

Ed went upstairs, Coco followed.

"I'll never call her my friend again," said Ed about Terri.

That ticked Coco off and started their friendship foundering.

Not long after, Ed bought the house the three of them had been living in. He told the Duvalls they could stay, but now that he owned the place, he'd like to move into the bigger front bedroom.

Coco told him he couldn't have it, and Ed told him that when he got back from work the next morning, he was taking the bedroom one way or another, even if he had to kick the door in.

The next morning, Coco called the police, who were waiting for Ed when he got home. They told him that since the Duvalls were already living there, he wouldn't be allowed to enter, he'd have to go to court and go through a formal eviction hearing.

He couldn't have his house, but maybe he'd be able to have a parking space. He asked Coco to move his truck from the alley out back so Ed could park his own vehicle there.

Lavere told the courtroom that Coco had responded, "You know what we did to those guys up north? I'll do the same to you. Me and my brothers have a plan for you. I'll kill you and your family . . . Wait until we get you up north."

That didn't stop Lavere at this point. He went down to the courthouse, filled out the paperwork, had Coco and his wife served and out they moved. And that's when the trouble began.

Coco attacked him one time, but Lavere, no shrinking violet, pulled Coco's coat over his head and held him down to the ground. "Immediately after that, I had trouble with pretty much everybody in the block and the neighborhood, assaults on myself by friends of his on my property."

"So he didn't kill you? He didn't hurt you, did he?" asked Schwartz on cross-exam.

"No, he did not."

"He didn't feed you to any pigs or anything, did he?"

"Am I sitting here in front of you?"

Schwartz got Lavere to acknowledge, though, that for all he knew, the guys up north Coco referred to could have been other guys they'd fought with over the years and not necessarily the deer hunters.

"You can't say they killed anybody, can you?"

"No, I cannot."

Tammy Morris, née McMullen and a first cousin of the Duvalls, took the stand next. Coco and J.R. were her mom's brother's boys and her dad's sister's boys.

She told the jury about the night in October of 1987 at O'Shea's Tavern in Wixom, celebrating the birthday of her sister and brother, who were twins. They were sitting around a table—the twins, Connie and Lonnie; Connie's husband, David Yonkin; another sister, Susan, and her husband, Tommy Yonkin; Tammy's dad, Charles McMullen; her husband, Lloyd Harmon, better known as Rocky; her stepmom; her stepbrother and his date; Coco and J.R.; maybe some others.

Various of them would be up and dancing at any given time, and the music was pretty loud, but Charles and the Duvall brothers ended up at one point in a sustained conversation. Tammy heard snatches of it.

"I heard bits and pieces of where they took care of the hunters, and that they were fed through a shredder and then fed to the pigs."

"Fed through a shredder. A tree shredder?" asked Pendergast, saying it with incredulity, as if she didn't know beforehand what Tammy was going to say.

"Yeah . . . Everyone was highly intoxicated, I mean highly, and they was joking and laughing about everything that night."

At 12:10 p.m., the court broke for lunch.

85

MORE ON THOSE PIGS

Rocky Harmon took the stand after lunch. He'd been married to Tammy for nineteen years and had met Coco and J.R. right after they'd gotten together, 1982, 1983. Rocky and Tammy were at his father-in-law's house and up pulled the Duvalls, driving some kind of rig for spraying grass seed and lawns. The Duvalls may not have been forty-hour-a-week types, but they'd had any number of ways over the years to make a buck.

Rocky had a clear recollection of the night at O'Shea's, since he'd been the designated driver.

J.R. and Coco had been talking to David Yonkin and Tammy's dad and Rocky'd had no trouble hearing their conversation over the sound of the band.

"They were talking about some deer hunters that they had beaten up and killed," he said. "Up north somewhere, they didn't mention a specific place."

The brothers had gotten into a fight at a bar with some deer hunters, he said, and they had killed them out in the woods and fed them to pigs.

"Fed them to pigs?" said Pendergast.

"That's exactly what I said."

Harmon said he'd moved to Kentucky after he'd heard from someone that the Duvalls were going to kill him. And that just three days before he testified in court, he'd gotten a call from one of the Duvalls' cousins that he took as a threat.

~

Donna Schultz had lived with J.R. from February of 1988 to September of 1989. They had a child together.

She was in court to share some pillow talk that had transpired between them.

"One day we were lying in bed, and I was joking with him about it," she told the court. "I said, 'J.R., where'd you put the skulls? You know pigs don't eat bone.'"

He told her to shut her trap or "'I'll cut you and feed you to the pigs,'" she recounted.

Another time, J.R. had come home from fishing and was talking to a friend about the cops' growing interest in him and Coco. "He said, 'There's a snake in the woodpile and we've got to find it,'" she told the court.

~

Schultz's sister, Connie Sundberg, had managed nine years with Coco, starting at age 16, and lasting till she ran off with a construction worker from the telephone company in 1989. She told about being at J.R.'s house in South Branch one day in November of 1985, right after the hunters had gone missing. She was helping make dinner when another of the Duvall brothers, Randy, pulled up in a black Ford Bronco with wagon-wheel rims.

"J.R. was pissed. He told Raymond to get the Bronco out of there 'before we all get in trouble,'" she quoted him as saying.

Another time, Coco had come home drunk. He dropped his head forward into his hands and said, "We killed someone." Then, realizing what he'd done, he swore at her, told her she'd "better shut the fuck up, bitch," and then slapped her around.

Williams did the best he could on cross-examination. He

got Connie to acknowledge that the Bronco wasn't necessarily the one everyone was looking for. Maybe the Bronco she'd seen was just another stolen car. Maybe the trouble they were worried about was getting caught with hot property, and had nothing to do with any murders.

86
FOOTPRINTS IN THE SNOW

Annie Payne finished things off for the day. She was a very reluctant witness. Her family had told her she'd be crazy to go up there. She told herself she'd be crazy to go up there. And she wouldn't have gone up there, except that Bronco had made sure a trooper stopped by to offer her a polite escort and she couldn't figure out a way to get out of it.

She'd long owned Annie's Bar on Third Street in Monroe, a favorite hangout for the Duvalls and many others in town. Not Randy Duvall, though. She'd booted his ass out and banished him.

One night, she told the court, 1991–1992, she and a bunch that included her ex-husband, Rex, and Coco were drinking pretty good and a song came on, "Footprints in the Snow," released by Bill Monroe in 1946.

> I traced her little footprints in the snow.
> I found her little footprints in the snow.
> I bless that happy day
> That Nellie lost her way.
> For I found her when the snow was on the ground. . . .
> I found her little footprints and I traced them in the snow.
> I found her when the snow was on the ground."

After it had come on, Coco said he didn't like the song and wanted it changed.

"I told him I couldn't change it," Payne recounted.

So Coco had given whoever had played it a buck to not play it again.

And then what happened? asked Pendergast.

"I don't remember right off," said the reluctant Annie.

Pendergast refreshed her memory. "Did you tell Alison King that when this song came on the jukebox, that J.R. and Coco began talking about the missing hunters running in the sand and how they were begging . . ."

"Your Honor, I'm going to object. These are all leading questions."

"Well, I am allowed to lay a foundation."

"All right, lay a foundation," said the judge.

Pendergast got Payne to admit that when police had first come knocking on her door, she wouldn't open it.

"I very seldom opened the door, because people were always there to borrow something."

"Did you tell Alison King you didn't open the door because you didn't want to talk to her about this?"

"I might have put it that way."

"Did you give Alison King some information and then say you would never testify to it if you were brought into court?"

"I didn't want to."

"And if you were called to testify, you would say that you forgot?"

"I probably did."

"And did you tell her that they can put you on the witness stand, but they can't control what you say?"

She didn't give the yes people were expecting.

Instead, she said, "Just that they were running through the woods and the hunters was begging for their lives."

"And they started talking about that after the 'Footprints in the Snow' came on?"

"Uh-huh."

"You specifically remember them talking about the missing hunters?"

"Yes."

"Do you remember telling Sergeant Alison King that they said that their strides, when they were running, got larger and larger as they tried to get away?"

"Your Honor, they are just leading questions," protested Schwartz. "Let her ask her what did she say instead of telling her what to testify to."

"Why don't you try that?" said the judge.

"What did they say besides that they were begging for their lives and they were running through the woods?" said Pendergast.

"They shot them."

"What did you tell Sergeant King, if you recall, that you were afraid of?"

"Just what would happen to me for talking."

"Did you tell Sergeant King, 'These are very dangerous people'?"

"Yes."

87

PART OF THE FAMILY

Thursday, October 23. 9:04 a.m.

Donna Fern Heilig was the first witness, a cousin of the infamous and now-dead Sherm Heilig, long suspected of having been there the night Tyll and Ognjan died, and of helping dispose of their bodies, at the least.

Heilig told the court she'd once had a relationship with J.R.

"We went out, I would say over a period of two, three months. We would go out with each other and have fun. It was really no commitment. We dated, we had fun, you know? Not serious, you know, like, 'We are getting married' or 'Let's move in together'. Just a good friend that I dated and had fun with."

J.R. was at her house one night in the winter of 1990 when police showed up to ask her about the missing hunters and what she knew.

"Can you tell the members of the jury, after the officers left, how J.R. was acting?"

"He got very nervous. It was very important that he get ahold of his brother Kenny to come and get him, and it was all a shock to me what these officers had told me, because I hadn't lived up there when all this went down, and I had heard nothing about it."

"Did he do anything after the officers left?"

"Yes. He called his brother in Monroe, and told him to come up and get him right away, and when he got off the phone I said, 'What do you got to do, get your lies straight?'

"And he says, 'Yeah,' and then he just kept pacing the floor. And finally someone picked him up and they left."

"Did you receive any threats from J. R. Duvall in this matter, pertaining to this case?" asked Pendergast. She was leading the witness, but neither defense attorney objected.

"Yes. Probably a week after. 'People that talk too much don't stick around too long.'"

Williams' cross-examination was devastating, but hardly in a way he'd intended. Asking questions you don't know the answers to is the attorney's version of walking across a Manhattan street wearing a blindfold and earplugs.

"Did the police ask J.R. any questions, if you know?"

"No. He was hiding in the bedroom."

"Did J.R. ever express any anger to you about being accused of this crime?"

"He just made the statement that 'They will never find anything, we have covered our tracks well . . .' He made the statement that they wouldn't find anything because they took care of everything."

Williams tried to salvage things.

"When the police were at your house questioning you, do you remember, were you drinking at that time?"

"I don't drink."

"Were you using any kind of drugs or medications?"

"I was high on drugs."

"Nothing further, Your Honor."

Maybe she'd imagined it all in a pot stupor.

88
WHO CAN REMEMBER?

Frank and Ken Duvall had insisted on their brothers' innocence before a grand jury in 1990, and Pendergast had subpoenaed them to discuss that testimony and whether it was perjured.

Frank came first. Pendergast asked him if he had lied to the grand jury.

"I don't recall."

"Isn't it true that you went into the Oakland County Citizens' Grand Jury and said you didn't know anything about this investigation?"

"That I don't recall."

"You don't recall what you said?"

"Not all of it."

"Do you recall subsequent to your testimony before the grand jury meeting with Sergeant Schram, now Lieutenant Schram, and you told him you had lied at the grand jury?"

"No, I sure don't remember that."

Pendergast asked him if he remembered testifying before the grand jury twice, on March 28 and April 12, 1990.

"I only recall going through the grand jury one time."

She recounted details and dates for him from transcripts. He'd told the grand jury the first time that he knew nothing. On April 6 he'd told Schram he'd lied. On April 12 he was back in the grand jury, where he'd testified, under threat of being charged with perjury, that he'd been in Coco's trailer and heard him say, "If they find one body, they will find the other underneath it."

"I don't remember none of that."

"You understand Lieutenant Schram is out there?" asked Pendergast, gesturing to the back pews.

"I don't— Doesn't matter to me."

Under prodding he acknowledged that he had been in Coco's trailer and heard a voice talking about the bodies, but he hadn't seen Coco say it and couldn't swear it was him saying it.

"I took it upon myself that it sounded like his voice, so I said it was Coco."

"When did you decide that you didn't see him say it, but that it just sounded like his voice?"

"I don't recall."

Pendergast asked him if he'd testified before the grand jury that one time Coco saw a WANTED poster about the missing hunters and said they'd deserved it.

"I don't recall."

She had Frank read that page in the grand jury transcript. "Do you recall that question and answer now?"

"No, I don't."

~

Ken Duvall came next. If you were writing a screenplay, you couldn't come up with more inadvertently funny dialogue. As the cliché goes, you can't make this stuff up.

"Now, Mr. Duvall, you are one of how many Duvall brothers?" asked Pendergast, easing him into it.

"Six or seven, I don't know."

"You have six brothers and yourself?"

"Yeah."

"Who is Tammy Harmon? Tammy Morris?"

"I don't know. Some people."

"Pardon?"

"What was it?"

"Tammy Morris. Tammy Harmon."

"I don't know."

"Tammy McMullen?"

"Cousin, I think it is. I ain't associatin' with them people."

"Were you subpoenaed in front of an Oakland County Citizens' Grand Jury on March twenty-eighth of 1990?"

"I don't know what day it was or what year it was."

"Pontiac, Michigan?"

"Yeah, I remember going there."

After some prodding, Pendergast got him to admit remembering he had told the grand jury he didn't know anything about the missing hunters.

She asked him, then, if he remembered a statement he'd given Detective Schram on September 8, 1993.

"I don't remember. I really don't."

"I will give you a minute to refresh your memory," she said, picking up a transcript to hand him.

"I can't read."

"You can't read?"

"No, I can't. I swear to God I can't."

She asked him if he remembered getting arrested for domestic violence at the time.

"I had a stroke back then. It's hard to remember."

"When did you have your stroke?"

"In the early 1990s."

"When?"

"I believe it was 1992. I have to ask my wife."

Pendergast asked him if he ran a business, a junkyard. He said it was his wife's.

Did he remember telling Schram he had lied to the grand jury?

"I don't remember lying."

Pendergast was ready for his obfuscations. Had planned for them.

"Do you remember being taped?" she asked, about his interview with Schram.

"No."

Whereupon, she pulled out a cassette recorder, set it on the witness stand and hit the PLAY button. It was Ken, telling Schram that he'd lied to the grand jury because "I was scared."

The courtroom listened raptly as he also told Schram that the missing Ford Bronco had been cut in half, and that he'd helped load salvaged parts—the transmission, the steering box, axles—and driven them south to Saginaw, where they were sold for $400.

"Your Honor, that's hearsay," objected Schwartz.

"Don't interrupt," snapped the judge.

At each parry from Pendergast about admissions on the tape, Duvall either said "No" or "I can't remember" or "That's what the tape says."

Or, "I don't remember, Your Honor . . . I had a crack problem. I was on crack back then. I was on crack, you know. I do not recall any of this."

Pendergast asked him if he remembered telling Schram he'd been in Timbers Steak House once with Coco, and his brother had spit on a WANTED poster of the hunters, saying they'd deserved it.

"No, because, I cannot, I got Alzheimer's disease, and you can check with Mental Health if you would like."

Schram was called to the stand to corroborate what the jury had heard on the tape. On cross-examination he admitted that diving and dredging operations based on Ken Duvall's statements had found nothing.

Williams asked if it was possible the information was wrong.

"That could be," Schram said.

89

"SPLIT LIKE A MELON"

Charles McMullen Jr., one of the Duvalls' many cousins, took the stand, and told the court about visiting his sister, Susan Yonkin, at her house in South Lyon, west of Detroit, one night in the late fall of 1985.

Coco had been pacing, he said, saying to J.R. that they had to get rid of it. J.R. had told him to relax.

McMullen left for a while and when he returned, the Bronco was gone.

He told of later, in better weather, painting a boat for Coco during a fish fry at his house in Monroe, everyone else partying and him painting. He was down on his knees in the garage, the boat up on jackstands, sanding some patchwork, when Coco had walked over, leaned down and said, out of the blue, no context to it, "His head split open like a melon."

Pendergast asked McMullen if he'd expressed during an interview with state police back in 1997 that he feared his cousins.

"I said if they knew that I was talking, they would kill me."

"Did you tell the police, 'If they find out I am talking, they will kill me, I guarantee it'?"

"Yes, I did."

Schwartz pointed out that it had been years since

MMullen first told police about the boat and Coco's comments, and got him to admit it had become common knowledge in the family that McMullen had talked to police, hoping to get consideration on a charge of possession of stolen property.

"And yet you are sitting here, are you not?" he asked.

"Yes."

"All right. Nobody has taken a shot at you with a gun, have they?"

"No."

"Nobody has blown up your car, burned your house, or done anything?"

"No."

"All right. Your cousins know where you live, too, do they not?"

"No, they don't."

~

Katherine Sliwinski testified that she'd lived with J.R.'s son, Tom, for three years. It was three years that would never loosen their grip on her. As she talked about them she shook visibly.

What seemed to scare her most was the Duvalls' concept of family.

After struggling to the stand with the help of a cane, she told of living with Tom from 1994–1997. One night, winter of 1996, she and Tom had been arguing at J.R.'s house in Hale, where they lived. It was a common occurrence for them, arguing. They were yelling back and forth and Tom had shoved her. Not real hard, but enough to make up her mind. She said she was through, she'd wanted to leave him. He'd heard it before. During the day, when he'd leave the house, he'd take her keys with him, so she had no way to go anywhere. So she couldn't decide to drive home to her mother's house in Monroe.

"I'd had it and I wanted to end it. At that point, Tom and I were sitting in the kitchen with J.R. Tommy did not want me to leave. He turned to his father and said, 'Dad, tell her what happened to the hunters.' "

"J.R. looked at me and explained how they'd gotten in an argument with another set of hunters over a deer. Later on that evening they ran into the same hunters in a bar and continued arguing."

"What happened next?"

"The argument continued outside, and they ended up beating them. J.R. specifically said that their heads smashed like melons. He didn't say with what, but that they were fighting and smashed their heads like melons.

"Then they chopped up the bodies and fed it to the pigs and got rid of what was left."

At that point, said Sliwinski, she turned around and looked at the back window into the woods behind the cabin. "J.R. looked at me and said not to worry, I wouldn't find anything around there."

The grandfather of her 3-year-old daughter and infant son had kept her gaze and then "he said if I turned against them or left the family, that the same thing would happen to me."

How had police come to hear what she'd had to say?

"I read an article in the paper that they had arrested them, and once I read the article, I felt that I needed to come forward with what I knew. I didn't know if it would help or not, but I had to do it. I felt it was the right thing to do . . . . to give the family of the hunters closure."

Schwartz worked his same material on her.

"You left the family, did you not?"

"Yes, I did."

"Nothing happened to you, did it?"

"I was threatened."

"Are you sitting here today?"

"Yes, I am."

"Was your car blown up?"

"No."

"Was your house burned down?"

"No."

"Was there a toaster in your bathtub when you took a bath?"

Schwartz asked her why no harm had come to the various witnesses despite the repeated claims that everyone feared the Duvalls. Didn't she maybe think the threats were of the idle variety?

"Not when I had bruises, I didn't," she countered, not missing a beat.

She had come forward, she said, but not without fear and not without precautions. She'd installed a video camera outside her home to ward off those with bad intentions. Or, rather, she'd mentioned her fears to Bronco, she told the court, and he'd installed it.

It was a morning packed with action. Not many in the audience had lost interest or had to fight drowsiness. And it promised to be a lively afternoon, too.

90

HIS EMOTIONS ON HIS SLEEVE

Schwartz had worked her over pretty good, or tried to. She'd held up well, but in her mind it had been a disaster. She felt like he'd made her look dumb. It hadn't gone how she'd pictured it.

She walked toward the low swinging door that allowed people in and out of the spectator section. Bronco leaned over to open it for her. She looked at him. "I'm sorry, Bronco," she said, her voice quivering.

"No, you did a great job," whispered Bronco. Later he'd say, "It broke my heart hearing her say that. She'd been so brave to come forward. They talk about men being brave. Well, I'll tell you, when it came to this case, it was the women who had the guts. I wanted to follow her out and give her some support."

And then he heard Donna calling his name as the next witness. He'd momentarily forgotten he was on deck, scheduled to be the last witness of the day.

Pendergast had been extremely nervous about putting Bronco on the stand. The case had become personal for him. Jurors distrust cops who seem emotionally involved, like they have an ax to grind. Bronco *was* emotionally involved. He *did* have an ax to grind. And he hadn't been sleeping, working the case over in his mind all night long, worried they weren't going to be able to sell the circumstantial evidence.

"This case just ripped him apart, what the families went through," Donna would put it later. And everyone who knew him knew that Bronco wore his emotions on his sleeve.

Her fear throughout had been a good fear, like the fear a fighter has just before the bell, or a kick returner waiting for the kicker at the other end of the field to start his trot to the ball, everyone else on the field frozen.

Bronco walked through the door he'd just opened, took the stand and was sworn in. He looked at Pendergast. And then, as he said later, "it just hit me. I'd worked on it for so long, for so many hours. It had just consumed me. Oh, my gosh, it just hit me. I looked at Mrs. Tyll and I looked at Mrs. Ognjan and I thought, I hope I don't let them down. It was more than I could digest."

Donna looked at him and her good fear turned to near-panic. There were tears in his eyes. He was close to freaking out right in front of her and the judge and the jury.

Pendergast asked him his name.

"Robert John Lesneski."

And what was his occupation?

Bronco surprised them all, his voice cracking, reacting instinctively in the smartest way possible. "Can I have just a couple of minutes? Can we take a break for just a second?" he asked the judge, fighting to keep his voice normal.

He had waited for this day for so long, for the chance to sit there and stare at those scumbags and tell the world what he knew and put their asses in jail for the rest of their lives, and he had grown so close to their families and so close to Brian and David, too, that by God, bulldog or not, tough guy or not, triathlete and weightlifter and hiker of deserts and rider of Harleys—Robert John Lesneski was about to start crying and there was nothing to be done about it but ask for a recess as quick as he could and get the hell out of the courtroom and calm his ass down.

"Sure," said the judge, who had no idea what was going on. "Let's take ten minutes." It was 2:10 p.m.

They all stood, the judge left the room, Bronco hurried out, Pendergast chased after him. She needed to constructively chew his ass out and get him to get his shit together. She did, and he did, or so she hoped.

During the recess, Cathy Tyll found herself in the bathroom with Sliwinski. "I hope you get 'em," she said.

Court reconvened at 2:23, but only briefly.

Williams had gotten word that his elderly grandmother had died earlier in the day. The judge called an early halt to the week's proceedings. Friday was set aside for other court business, so they'd all have a long weekend off.

It was bad news for Williams and worse news for his grandmother, but good news for Pendergast. Bronco'd have three days to get ready emotionally.

91

THE PROSECUTION RESTS

Monday, October 27, the fifth day of the trial.

Bronco was calm and reasoned. He outlined his efforts in the case, how he'd looked into scores of tips—credible or not—from thirty Michigan counties, ten states and several provinces in Canada, and, from reading his and other officers' reports over the eighteen years of the investigation, had compiled an alphabetical list of 820 names.

"All those tips were hunted down and exhausted," he said. "The standard that I used for the tips was the highest standard I could apply. I'd ask myself one question: If this was someone that I loved, what would I do with this tip? And that was the standard question, and it was easy."

"Did you receive tips from psychics?" Pendergast asked.

"Yes, I did."

"Tips from people who had dreams?"

"Yes."

"Tips from people who in your opinion were mentally unstable?"

"Yes."

"Were those tips investigated nonetheless?"

"To the very best of my ability."

Bronco told how the dental records of Tyll and Ognjan had been checked against all unidentified bodies in the U.S.

in the last eighteen years. That state police dive teams had
been in the ponds, lakes, streams and several branches of the
AuSable River. Aerial searches had been done in Newaygo,
Ogemaw, Iosco, Oscoda, Alcona and Roscommon Counties.
That there had been at least five searches by cadaver teams
over the years in four counties. That Interpol had been contacted early on and the hunters' guns and the Bronco entered
into international databases.

And then Pendergast got to the crux of his testimony, the
crux of this trial. She asked him to recount how he'd come to
hear about Barb Boudro—a tip from David Tyll's sister-in-
law, Margene Tyll—and how he'd come to find her, by
knocking on doors.

"Can you tell the members of the jury how Barbara
Boudro acted when you showed her your identification?"

"She just lost it. She started crying and shaking uncontrollably. Her whole body was shaking."

"What did she say?"

"She said, 'You're going to get me killed.' "

Schwartz objected: hearsay.

The judge ruled that it was an excited utterance, and an
exception to the hearsay rule.

Bronco continued to recount his view of that fateful first
encounter, and then of his take on her testimony years later,
after being subpoenaed by the attorney general.

Schwartz kept objecting. The judge, a bit perturbed and
even a tad rude, kept overruling him.

After another objection of hearsay that was shot down,
Pendergast asked Bronco about the moment when he realized he finally—*finally*—had his eyewitness.

"She [Boudro] said, 'Bronco, you know I know more'—
something to that effect—'you know I know more.' And I
said, 'Yeah, I know you do.' She said, 'You know I can't tell
you what it was.' "

"Your Honor, are we going to allow him to testify to
everything that happened?"

"The objection is . . . ?"

"That it's hearsay, and it's ongoing."

Bergeron overruled him, again. Schwartz was nearly apoplectic.

"At that time, did you remain on the record?" asked Pendergast.

"We went off the record."

"All right. At that point, was she willing to talk, or was she just telling you, 'You know I saw it'?"

"She told me she saw it, but she continued to tell me that she was scared to death, that she—she just couldn't testify."

Schwartz, back to his feet: "Your Honor, I object. It's hearsay."

Bergeron: "That she couldn't testify?"

"He said that she's scared. It's hearsay."

"So you think she wasn't scared?"

"I don't know whether she was scared or not. It's hearsay. It's not his observation of her. It's him quoting what she said."

It was a logical legal argument, and hard to refute.

Bergeron looked at him and said, "Well, if it's offered to prove the truth of the matter asserted, maybe they're hearsay. But if they're not, they are not. Go ahead."

It was clear Bergeron wanted to hear what Bronco had to say, hearsay rules or not. Pendergast fought successfully against breaking into a big smile at Bergeron's double talk in her favor. Schwartz fought his urge to scream. The effect of Bronco's testimony was to reinforce in the jury's mind Boudro's compelling testimony of the week before, and to make palpable, again, her overbearing fear, and concrete, again, the horror of what she had seen.

"Did you in fact go back on the record and take testimony?" asked Pendergast.

"Yes, we did."

"And was that the testimony, basically, that you heard in this courtroom as to what she had seen that night?"

"Yes."

Bronco also recounted an experiment he'd helped conduct at Barb Boudro's home. He'd sat in the house with her while Douglas Gough down the road at the clearing where

the murders had allegedly taken place yelled and hit plastic
milk jugs filled with frozen water.

"You could hear it clearly from inside the home," he said.
Pendergast was done with him.

~

Cross-examination began just before lunch. Schwartz started
right in on the sound test, asking Bronco, "When you ran the
sound test, there was nothing scientific about it, was there?
Well, was it based on the general scientific principles? Did
you bring in any sound engineers or anybody to set it up?"

"No, sir."

"Were you drunk? Had you had at least nine mixed drinks
and a couple of beers before you started to listen?"

"No."

"Did you have *Scarface* turned up loud on the TV?"

"No."

"Was there a barking dog running back and forth?"

"No."

Schwartz tried to impeach the various witnesses by asking if they'd been rewarded financially, or if Bronco had interceded in their behalf in various legal proceedings. The
questions backfired. They made Bronco look all the better.

He hadn't interceded in any of Charles McMullen Jr.'s legal troubles. The state hadn't paid him a dime. Bronco admitted he'd given him money out of his own pocket to pay
for gas from Kentucky to Lansing and bought him dinner
and rented him a motel room so he could sleep the night before driving back to Kentucky.

Money he never put in for reimbursement for.

He said he'd given Connie Sundberg gas money to drive
from West Virginia to Lansing, too.

"I gave them money for food, and they turned around and
drove back. They didn't spend the night. And that's it," said
Bronco.

"Did you get reimbursed?"

"I have not . . . I didn't go through the proper channels. I just did it rather than go through all the red tape."

He wasn't asked and didn't tell another anecdote. Pendergast had also subpoenaed Larry Asher for the trial. He, too, lived in Kentucky. He'd called Bronco on his cell phone the Saturday before the trial, Bronco and his wife on a long-overdue weekend out of town, down for a concert at the Detroit Pistons' home, the Palace of Auburn Hills, near Detroit. Bronco had reserved a hotel room for the night, make something special out of it, his and her reward.

But the cell phone had gone off during the show and Bronco answered it and it was Asher. His truck was broken, he needed $150 to get it fixed, and for gas money. After the show, Bronco apologized to his wife and they drove straight back to Tawas so Bronco could go to the Western Union in the morning and wire Asher the money.

When Asher got to town the next day, he was so sick Bronco had two troopers escort him to the doctor's office. Bronco paid the doctor bill, and for his medicine. But the day the trial began, Asher told Pendergast he'd seen the Duvall family at his motel in Standish and was so scared he wouldn't be able to testify, and got in his repaired truck and drove back to Kentucky. Bronco didn't expense any of that, either.

Schwartz got Bronco to acknowledge that video cameras he'd installed on Boudro's and Sliwinski's houses never recorded any instance of threats or violence by any Duvalls or their friends.

But the detective did say Boudro had called once before the camera was installed to tell him that someone had stopped by her house to threaten her.

"Did she describe the vehicle they were in?"

"She did not."

"Did she say they walked by or they flew by or, you know, rode up on a pink elephant?" asked Schwartz derisively. It wasn't a good tactic, clearly. Bronco had come off as some kind of super cop with a heart of . . . Well, maybe not gold, but a good heart. It wasn't going to win Schwartz any friends on the jury to mock the detective or his star witness.

92

ASKING FOR A DISMISSAL

After a lunch recess the court reconvened at 1:10.

Schwartz and then Williams tried to turn the length of the
exhaustive state police investigation to their advantage. Despite all the work, Bronco had to admit no bodies had been
found, and there was no fingerprint evidence, no hair sam-
ples, no DNA linking the Duvalls to any murders.

By 1:45, they were done with Bronco, too.

With the jury out of the room, Schwartz and Williams
then asked Judge Bergeron to dismiss the case for a lack of
physical evidence. Pendergast hadn't proven the hunters
were dead, much less who'd killed them. Police had searched
exhaustively for the bodies and the Bronco, using divers,
backhoes, cadaver dogs, helicopters, planes and psychics,
and never found a thing. They'd searched every place the
Duvalls had pigs, and in every place a pig could eat and
defecate. If the pigs had eaten bodies, why hadn't they
found any of the undigested human remains? They'd found
a grand total of one piece of bone in all the years, and that
wasn't human.

"There isn't any, as you know, physical evidence of any
nature or description to connect these two defendants or any
other defendants to the death of the missing hunters . . .
There is just rumor and innuendo," said Schwartz. "There's

no evidence that they're dead. The only evidence is that they haven't been around for eighteen years."

Williams argued that, at the very least, the judge ought to dismiss the charges of first-degree murder because no premeditation had been proven, either.

"Certainly I don't think that there's been a sufficient showing to warrant going to jury deliberations or for further deliberations," he said.

Bergeron responded: "We have no physical evidence in this case. We don't have a body, blood, car parts, things like that. But we have lots of circumstantial evidence . . . It's my finding that there's evidence to support each of the elements of the crime of first-degree murder regarding each of the victims against each of the defendants. Therefore, both motions for directed said verdicts are denied."

At 2 p.m., the jury returned. It was time for the defense to present its case.

93

FOR THE DEFENSE

Things got off to a good start for Schwartz.

Genevieve Yaklin, an avid hunter who had at that point participated in forty-nine consecutive deer seasons, told the court she'd seen the two missing hunters on Saturday afternoon, November 23, while out deer hunting with her husband. She remembered it all so vividly—the day and the year—because that was the year she'd gotten a big honking eight-point buck and everything about that hunting season had been frozen in her memory.

Never mind she'd shot twenty-seven deer in those forty-nine seasons, that eight-pointer stood out like it was yesterday. She and her husband had seen the hunters and their black Ford Bronco on a roadside in Roscommon County, the two of them talking to a third man. Her husband got his buck that afternoon, and they'd dragged it to their car and loaded it up about 4 p.m. and were just taking off. A beautiful day it was.

And there was the Bronco and those three guys. One guy, standing in front of the Bronco, wasn't a hunter. Didn't have any hunter's clothes on. Wasn't wearing any hunter's orange. The other two? One was tall and slim. Both had some scraggly few days' growth of beard.

In 1988, she recognized the picture of one of the guys, Joel Hanna, after seeing his photo in the local paper, *The*

Houghton Lake Resorter. Hanna later had been shot and killed in Georgia after trying to attack two cops with a pitchfork. They'd approached him because he was wanted for the shooting and killing of Otsego County Sheriff's Deputy Carl Darling Jr. after Darling had picked him up for hitchhiking. Had shot the deputy, then abducted an old man with a motor home, killed him and buried him in the woods and drove that motor home south.

She saw his photo and said, "Ohmigod!" It was the same guy she'd seen with the hunters. She'd called the police, who sent two officers out to her house, and told it all to them, she said.

The testimony lost its edge when Pendergast reminded her that when the troopers got to her house, she wasn't able to identify photos of either Tyll, Ognjan or Hanna.

"More or less, you're correct," said Yaklin. "But, yet, I know in my mind who I saw. I mean, that's the way it goes."

~

Warren Steven Linker, who'd owned Linker's Lost Creek Lodge, where tensions had allegedly built between the Duvalls and the hunters and set off the tragic series of events, was next. He was an excellent and effective witness, whose memory of the night contrasted sharply with Boudro's.

He said he didn't remember either the Duvalls or Boudro that night. In fact, he didn't remember the Duvalls ever coming into his place in the five years he'd owned it, and while he got to know Boudro later, he didn't think she'd ever been in the place up till then.

But he did have a clear memory of the hunters. There had been "a very minor incident. It was just verbal. I sat with them, talked with them. They were fine. They stayed for a while. They left."

How long had they been there? Less than two hours.

There was no trouble of any kind that night, or the entire weekend. No police were ever called.

Linker agreed upon prodding by Pendergast that it was

possible the Duvalls and Boudro had been there, and he just didn't notice them.

"You're not telling this jury that you knew everything that was going on in your bar that night, are you?"

"Not everything, no."

"It's a rather large bar?"

"Quite large."

94

A RECOVERING AMNESIAC

Daniel Dutton was next on the stand. On the face of it, his testimony was a bombshell.

The Duvalls are innocent, he said.

Friends of his, brothers named Artie, Mickey and Jeff, had killed the hunters in brutal fashion. With an ax. Then they'd stripped them and passed out their clothes to friends. Asked Dutton if he wanted some pants, but they didn't fit. Took the Bronco and sold it for $1,200.

His friends, they told him they'd killed the hunters outside a bar in Grayling. They were mouthy, mouthy with the wrong guys. Had words inside the bar and more words outside and got themselves shot. His friends had taken their clothes, found a car key, then gone up and down the street trying every Ford they came to until a door to one Bronco opened.

What happened was, they shot them, then loaded them up in their car and drove them a short way to the AuSable River. That's where they stripped them and disposed of their bodies.

He'd told all of this to Lesneski some time back, and Bronco, true to his nature, had followed up. He'd done a fly-by over the brothers' property and had visited the spot on the river where Dutton said the bodies had gone in.

He'd told Bronco a lot of other stuff, too, which the jury and those in attendance were about to hear in detail. Schwartz had read Bronco's reports about Dutton. Why he'd let anyone else hear about them—especially those deciding his clients' fate—would soon become something of a mystery. Mystery riddled with humor and outright guffaws.

Those gathered in the Standish court were there because of the tragic disappearance of two young men. Two families had been irreparably damaged and a third was being accused of bloody, evil savagery. If any trial ever called out for comic relief, it was that of J. R. and Coco Duvall, and along the way there had been plenty of it.

You could try to stifle your snickers, try to keep your lips properly pursed, but the fact was, this cast of characters seemed to have wandered in from some Hollywood black-comedy set, their lines too good, too funny, to ever be muttered by real-life north-woods miscreants or ne'er-do-wells. You'd want to laugh, laugh out loud till tears came, if you weren't so concerned about decorum, too aware of what really was at stake.

Or you could just look over at the Duvall brothers and suddenly things didn't seem so funny anymore.

Boudro rapping her fist for good luck, later denying personal involvement with the porcelain god.

Welch, the seven-day-a-week drinker at the bowling alley who'd had a crane fall on him and whose deadpan delivery when telling of the evils of drink seemed almost rehearsed.

Ken Duvall, who could no longer remember what he told the grand jury because of a combination of a stroke, crack-cocaine abuse and Alzheimer's disease, but still was sharp enough to impress a stranger into investing in his thriving auto salvage business.

But it was Dutton, once Pendergast got to him, who made all those before him seem like guest hosts on *Masterpiece Theatre*.

She started her cross-examination: "The first thing you told Sergeant Lesneski, 'I'm an amnesiac, but I'm cured'?"

It was, she would admit later, the first and likely last time she'd ever get to ask that question of a defense witness—they just don't prepare you for that in law school—and she'd savored the moment.

Observers throughout the courtroom chuckled. Some of the jury registered brief smiles. *Free Press* reporter Hugh McDiarmid Jr. tried to keep from laughing, but got up and left the room briefly when he realized he was fighting a losing battle. He should have bitten his lip, and stayed put.

"Yes, I did."

"And, in fact, that's why you didn't report this for some—What? Fifteen, sixteen years?—is because you had amnesia about it?"

"Yes, ma'am."

She recounted for him and the jury details of a written report he'd made for Lesneski that Schwartz and Williams had neglected to mention.

A hatchet blow had ended each of the hunters' lives, he had written. After stripping the bodies, the brothers had set them in the river, prying the victims' mouths open with their fingers and letting the river water fill their lungs till they sank.

It was not a common way to dispose of bodies, Dutton had written. It was ghoulish, but it worked.

Pendergast asked him if he had written " 'Mickey had it down to an art. He's done it thirty times.' "

"Yes, ma'am."

"Is that what you told police, that Mickey's done this ghoulish thing thirty times?"

"Yes, ma'am."

Pendergast, holding up a copy of his report, continued to paraphrase for him: "And you said after a couple of minutes, you couldn't stand it, because your Christian soul wanted to vomit?"

"That's true, ma'am."

"All right, and at the bottom of the page, 'After the hunters were killed I saw Mickey wearing a new green hunting coat. Mickey's a long-haired hippie, and a new coat looks strange on him, but Artie was always the slicky boy with his hair slicked back, and Artie was wearing this light duty black coat.' Is that what you said?"

"Yes, ma'am."

" 'The arms were too short, but it was a souvenir.' Is that what you said?"

"Yes, ma'am."

"And they offered you a pair of jeans that were too big?"

"Yeah."

"Then you said the next time you were over at Mickey and Dawn's, Artie came over wanting Mickey to sink some-one that they had tied up?"

"Yes, ma'am."

"And Artie wanted to tie you up, too, but Dawn stuck up for you?"

"Yes, ma'am."

"You said they've killed thirty-one or so people, twenty-four of them in the Rouge?"

"In the Rouge River, yeah."

"Two bikers by Six Mile Road?"

"Yes, ma'am."

"And two in the stream on their dad's land when they moved into Fowlerville?"

"Yes, ma'am."

"And then the old lady Jeff punched to death for the ruby necklace?"

"I've seen the necklace."

"Did you remember all those things, or did you remem-ber them after you were cured from your amnesia?"

"I saw the ruby necklace. I saw the white gold and ruby necklace. Mostly, most of the stuff I remembered after my amnesia lifted."

"Did you say back at that time Jeff was buying gold for his girlfriend, Michelle, from serial killer Leslie Williams?"

"Yes, ma'am."

"And Leslie Williams is a mass murderer who your buddy Paul Butterbaugh worked for?"

"Yes, ma'am."

"Do you have any idea who prosecuted Leslie Williams?"

"No."

"You're looking at her."

It was true. A rapist and murderer who had been in and out of prison for a variety of offenses over the years, Leslie Allen Williams was put away for life in 1992 after confessing to a string of murders.

Not a funny topic, but the timing drew more courtroom chuckles. McDiarmid managed to stay in the room.

Dutton had heard the brothers kill a fat black man inside a truck in their garage. Up till then they'd just been murdering bikers. The next day he'd seen the guy's brain matter sitting there. And Artie had axed another guy to death right after that.

"I forgot mostly all this and it returned later on."

"And according to your words, Michelle would dispose of the clothes in Dumpsters, but once she threw some bloody clothes off at the Salvation Army at Inkster and Schoolcraft [Roads], and that's where they found pants Mickey used when Mickey Mehay, Billy Shook, Mose and Black Rod robbed the gambling casino?"

"Yes, ma'am."

"And somebody after that gambling casino incident bugged you to go to the Salvation Army, and the lady who worked there went berserk about the bloody clothes?"

"Yes, ma'am."

"All right. Then—are you following along with me on this?" she asked him. Everyone in the room was, raptly. It was the next best thing to having your own opium visions. "Then you put in your document: 'Jeff knew I knew too much, and he got me into his truck, because I had amnesia and forgot he was a killer, and he was just about to punch me to death, and he threatened me and I remembered he was a killer and I realized those bloody clothes at the Salvation Army must be from them, and I told them how stupid they were, and when I saw by the way he acted that I was right, I lied to save myself'?"

"That's exactly true, ma'am."

"Wait a minute!" said Pendergast dramatically, enjoying herself more than you're supposed to at a murder trial. "If I understand this series of events, they forgot you had amnesia?"

Another sentence, as a prosecutor, you just never think you're going to get to ask.

"They weren't exactly sure what the deal was with me."

"How long have you had this amnesia for?"

"Well, I first had the amnesia when I was hit by a truck in 1975. Then it lifted. And then, apparently, in 1990 I got the amnesia again after I'd been over to Leslie Williams' house."

They were only at the bottom of page 6 of his 9-page report, where he'd made a notation for Lesneski: "I'm going to tell you what else they've done at the risk of losing you."

He'd recounted for Bronco, and Pendergast recounted for the courtroom, that Dutton knew about another high-profile Michigan murder case. Deanna Seifert was a 10-year-old girl in the Detroit suburb of Warren who had been abducted and killed in 1992 in a case that provoked headlines for weeks. The guy convicted of it was innocent, Dutton claimed, Artie, Mickey and Jeff had done it.

"You certainly seem to be around a lot of high-publicity cases, aren't you?" asked Pendergast.

"That's why I say 'at the risk of losing you' when I wrote that in there, because it does sound like a lot."

The brothers had done it, he said, but they'd been trained by Leslie Williams to throw police off. A friend named Michael Willis had come up with the idea that they needed to frame someone. They'd asked Dutton for his pubic hairs, but he slammed the door on them. So they decided to get some from poor schmoe Andy Trombley, and sure enough the police fell for it and Trombley got convicted. They framed him because he'd been having sex with Jeff's girlfriend. And what tied it all together was, Michael Willis was Andy Trombley's brother.

That got them to the bottom of page 8. Only one page left to go.

Then there came his recounting of the two sisters Paul had killed on Bentler Street and the little girl Paul had murdered on Wilson's dairy farm for the necklace that Jenny didn't want 'cause it was too small.

"How many murders do you have information about?" Pendergast asked with a straight face.

"I counted over a hundred that I've been told about."

"I see. Nothing further," she said.

What may have been even more astounding than his tale or the fact that Schwartz had put him on the witness stand to begin with was that Schwartz actually tried to salvage Dutton's testimony through a redirect.

When he wasn't witness to murder and mayhem of all descriptions, Dutton told Schwartz, he was a department manager at Wal-Mart. Had been for a year and a half.

"Now you weren't part of any of these murders that you talked about in your reports, were you?" asked the defense attorney.

"No, sir, I wasn't."

"Okay. So this is just information that came to you through the neighborhood, right?"

"I only wrote down what they told me, sir."

Inexplicably Schwartz asked him if he'd ever testified at a trial, and that got Dutton talking about statements he'd given about the Oakland County child murders, an unsolved series of killings in the 1970s that stopped as suddenly as they'd started.

"So, you also have information about the Oakland County child killer?" asked Pendergast, taking another brief crack at him.

"Yeah."

"That's the task force that's been going on for some twenty-five years?"

"Yes, ma'am."

"Nothing further," she said.

It was 4:25 p.m. There was no way to follow Dutton except to break for the day, and that's what the judge did.

Pendergast could only imagine how well her key witness was going to come off in the jury's mind, now, in comparison to Schwartz's. It made for a happy night for the vastly more confident prosecutor.

95

YOGI'S BLACK BLAZER

Randy Duvall started things off at 9 a.m. Tuesday, October 28. It didn't take him long to strain the jury's credibility. Schwartz only asked him a few questions. Duvall said he'd been driving a black Blazer in 1985, not a Bronco. It wasn't his. It was Yogi Bastine's, his father-in-law's. Well, not quite, since Randy wasn't married to his girlfriend, and Yogi wasn't married to his, either.

"I consider him as my father-in-law, but he's my ex-girlfriend's ma's boyfriend," said Randy.

He also said that he hadn't seen his cousin Charles McMullen since 1992; and that he and his brothers had not once, ever, had a conversation about the missing deer hunters.

"You've never had a discussion with either of them about it?" asked Schwartz. It sounded preposterous on the face of it, the kind of question Pendergast might have asked, straining with incredulity. Schwartz asked it with a straight face.

"No. We just all knew we was getting accused of it."

Williams had no questions.

David Yonkin was next. He'd been at O'Shea's Tavern the night the Duvalls had supposedly talked about killing the hunters. He said he hadn't heard any such talk, and he'd been sitting right across from them. He said, too, that over the years he'd known where Charles Jr. lived, and the Duvall brothers had never asked him to tell them. They knew he'd been yapping to the police and they'd never once made an effort to find him.

"Mr. Yonkin," asked Pendergast when it was her turn, "it's been a running theme in your family for eighteen years about some hunters getting cut up and fed to pigs, hasn't it?"

"Yes, it has."

"In fact, for eighteen years, members of the family have talked about it?"

"Yes, they have."

Not exactly a stellar defense witness—hadn't heard any talk that night, but the whole family had heard and shared plenty of talk about the murders over the years, he was saying, eighteen years, in fact.

With defense witnesses like that, who needs a prosecution?

Susan Yonkin was next. She told of being at O'Shea's the night Rocky said he'd heard the boys bragging about murder, but said she'd heard no such thing. Hadn't happened.

She'd known all through the years where her brother Charles Jr. lived, and if Coco or J.R. had asked she'd have gladly told them, but they didn't, and she didn't. So much for their wanting to do him in, and for his fear that they would.

The whole time she's talking, Bronco's sitting there thinking of snakes. Not snakes in the woodpile, snakes in Yonkin's house.

Bronco's a big, tough guy. One thing he's afraid of? Snakes. Hates them. Hates garter snakes, even. Sees a little striped garter snake slithering off a sunny spot on a trail as he comes jogging up and it almost gives him a heart attack.

So there he was on one of his trips to Florida knocking on Susan Yonkin's door, and she lets him in and sitting right freaking there in the corner of the room, on the floor, not in any glass cage, is a snake—looks to him like it's as big around as a soccer ball—curled up on itself in a pyramid, gotta be eighteen or twenty feet long, and that snake is staring at a little baby crawling on the floor, and Bronco's staring at them both.

Finally he says, "That snake's looking at that baby."

"It's okay," says Yonkin. "We fed him a live chicken yesterday."

96

MISUNDERSTOOD COCO

Most defendants don't testify in murder trials. It's their right to remain silent, and the jury isn't supposed to draw inferences about a lack of testimony. It's too easy for a good prosecutor to get a defendant, innocent or not, squirming on the stand.

But J.R. and Coco both testified. After Dutton's performance of the day before, what choice did they have? Leave *that* as the defense's punctuation?

Coco went first, taking his seat at 11:19.

Coco calmly, quietly testified that he couldn't remember after all those years where he'd been that weekend. Ask him what he was doing on Thanksgiving, he'd say, "Probably eating a turkey." Ask him about the weekend before, who knows?

Nothing unusual happened, that was about as specific as he could recall.

Safe to say he drank a lot in 1985?

"All depends on what you say how much is a lot."

"Did you drink every day?"

"Yeah."

"Were you drunk every day?"

"No."

As for Connie, while he was drinking, she was smoking weed.

Any other drugs?

"If she could get her hands on it."

Connie and he started out living in a trailer in Rex's yard, then over on East County Line Road, then Aldridge Road. "We lived in Ed Brody's house for a little while, but I don't know the name of that road."

"Why did you move so frequently?"

"Better places. Improved places, you know?"

He admitted to owning pigs, denied their reputed diet. He got them feed at the feed store, would pick up bags of fruit at the fruit market, sometimes gave them bushel baskets of grass. Never meat. Didn't own any carnivorous pigs.

He'd never boasted to anyone about the killings, hadn't threatened anyone for talking. He wasn't such a tough guy, after all, not the champion brawler he'd been painted out to be.

Proof it was all an exaggeration? He and Connie had duked it out on occasion, and "a couple of times, she won."

One time, they'd been arguing—he'd had a few beers, she'd been smoking weed—and Sundberg got so mad she picked up a gun and "seven or eight times she shot and she missed and I would laugh."

Not a tough guy, a funny guy. Laugh at a thing like that, not take offense.

"Who did you primarily fight with back in the day when you were fighting?"

"Brothers."

"What happened after the fights?"

"Drink."

"Were there ever any fights with other people where, when it was over, you'd sit and drink?"

"Mostly every one."

Duvall told about coon hunting the day they'd ended up at the infamous party at O'Shea's. Wixom was a far western suburb of Detroit, home to a sprawling Ford factory, but just minutes away from cornfields, lakes and woods, much of it bisected with dirt roads.

Coon hunting was a citified way of killing game. You

didn't have to prowl the woods, do any stalking, you just needed a good dog, a car and a rifle.

"A dog, you put her out front and she'll go down the middle of the road, a dirt road, and then you follow her."

"How did you kill the animal?" asked Schwartz.

"A twenty-two."

"Did you have one with you?" Not the smartest question, granted.

"Yes."

"And did your brother, J.R., have a gun?"

"No, you only need one gun."

"What?" Took him by surprise. You don't expect two brothers to be sharing a gun while hunting.

"You only need one gun."

"And who was carrying the gun?"

"You don't carry it. It's locked up in the car. Then you go down the road till the dog strikes on one, then you get out your gun and you go to the tree."

"Judge," said Pendergast, interrupting, "with all due respect, relevance is my objection at this time."

"Well, it's not really relevant, but I started to get curious, Your Honor."

The judge upheld the objection and that jumped them forward to O'Shea's. Everyone had been drinking and dancing, conversation at a minimum.

Had he talked to Rocky?

"No."

"Why didn't you talk to Charles Jr.?"

"Never really cared that much for him, 'cuz he had big rumors of being a snitch. I ain't never talked to him for years."

"Why didn't you talk to Rocky?"

"Heard rumors of what he was. I never did like him."

"Why didn't you like Rocky?"

"Because he was a snitch. Would say rumors or whatever to the cops and then stuff like that."

At the party they might have talked about coon hunting, but nothing about deer hunting, nothing about missing hunters, certainly nothing about killing anyone or feeding them to the pigs.

As for Barb Boudro, he'd never seen her until she stepped forward to claim status as an eyewitness. He'd never been to Linker's Lodge, where he was supposed to have glared at those guys. Didn't even know where it was.

Well, he might have been there, but only "if they played horseshoes in the summer, 'cuz we did go to different bars playing horseshoes."

~

They broke for lunch. At 1:04 p.m., Pendergast began her cross-examination, asking about Georgia, Coco's first wife, "the one whose nose and jaw you broke?"

"Well, do you want to know how it got broke? You're saying I broke it. She was in— she got in between another fight between me and another person at Annie's," said Coco, referring to his favorite bar in Monroe. It wasn't bad intent, it was bad luck. She just happened to catch one. The guy Coco was trying to hit? Her uncle. Keep it in the family.

Coco said folks didn't have reason to fear him, he didn't know why his cousins had said they were afraid.

"Let me show you what's been admitted into evidence as People's Exhibit Number Six, that being the grand jury testimony of your own brother, Frank Duvall. I'm going to ask you to read it," said Pendergast.

She handed it to Duvall, who seemed genuinely surprised. "Who said it? Frankie?"

"You can look on the front cover if you don't trust me."

Duvall started to read aloud in the slow, halting manner of a second-grader just learning.

"Read it to yourself, first," interrupted Pendergast.

"I can't read that good, so I might as well just read it once instead of doing it twice."

"Well, I'll read it to you and ask you if you can explain it. Do you have any explanation as to why your own brother, when asked why he would have lied to the grand jury the first time, would say, 'Just kind of scared over it all, scared for my wife, kids. I don't know what they might do, you know, if they find out that I'm the one giving the information'?

"Can you tell this jury why your own brother, Frank Duvall, would be scared of you to the point that under oath at a grand jury, he would say that he was afraid for his wife and kids?"

"Well, there's two things to that. Probably one, he's a younger brother. The oldest is always the toughest. And that he was screwing the hell out of my girlfriend."

"Because he was, to quote you, excuse my language, screwing the hell out of your girlfriend?"

"Yes."

Pendergast did a countdown of family members or former girlfriends who had come forward—Harmon, Tammy Morris, Frank, Connie. "Charles McMullen—he's your cousin, is that right?"

"Yes."

"We're up to five who got it wrong against you."

"Yep."

"Barb Boudro, she's wrong?"

"Yes."

"That's six."

Ed Lavere's testimony, seven. Eileen Seitz—whose grand jury testimony had been read into the transcript, where she said she'd overheard J.R., Coco and Sherm Heilig agree to never talk about something again, and Coco had said, "I know we're going to get caught"—made it eight.

"There's just a conspiracy of people that got it all wrong about Donald Duvall, don't they?" she asked, somewhat ungrammatically.

"Yes, it is."

"Nothing further."

97

J.R. took the stand at 1:30, a slight 52-year-old who looked 60, looked like someone's grandfather, a night-and-day contrast from the long-haired, bearded biker-looking dude whose twenty-year-old photo had graced many of the newspaper stories. In the papers he'd looked more like Charles Manson with an attitude.

He was Williams' witness, and told him he hadn't met the hunters, had never been to Linker's, might know how to get to it, now, but only from reading about it in the papers. Had never seen or heard of Barb Boudro until "we got arrested and what-have-you."

J.R. said best he could recollect he was at an early Thanksgiving dinner with his ex-girlfriend's family in Cass City the weekend of November 23–24, 1985, when the hunters went missing.

For the most part, J.R. came off as calm and reasoned, a sharp contrast to the image painted of him. He got worked up talking about a pig, though, and about Donna Sundberg's testimony about the snake in the woodpile.

It was all a misunderstanding, he said. Donna didn't exactly put two and two together right. There was a perfect logical explanation, he said, perfect logic having something of an elastic nature to the Duvalls.

"My brother had a pet pig," explained J.R., "and it come in and out, did whatever it wanted to, more or less. And it backed its ass up against a wood stove and it burned a big scab on its pussy." Another line new to the annals of American jurisprudence.

J.R.'d been binge drinking, and when it came time to pass out, it just happened to be in the pigpen next to his house. When he woke up, there was this big female pig standing over him, her private parts just a few inches from his face.

When J.R. woke up and there was that pig there with its scab staring at him, the other partygoers started teasing him about how she'd gotten that scar, must have been from J.R. kissing her.

"They said I kissed the pig's pussy. I didn't," J.R. told the court. One more for the record books.

The snake in the woodpile remark wasn't him referring to someone who had told police about the missing hunters, it was about whoever had repeated the story about him kissing the pig.

As for pigs, he'd owned as many as nine at a time, he said. But none of them ever ate any body parts. If he had warned a former girlfriend he would feed her to pigs if she didn't stop talking, it was just him joking around. Exasperated, maybe, but not serious. You'd have to know her to understand.

"Donna Sundberg, if you asked her what time it is, it's going to take forty-five minutes for her to tell you what time it is. She just likes to babble on, babble on, and whatever. And I just said, 'Shut up,' because we was going to bed. 'Just shut up!' I told her that, hoping she would shut up."

"She was asking you about pigs and things like that?"

"Yes."

"And that's when you told her, 'Shut up or I'll feed you to the pigs'?"

"I don't know the exact words, but it was similar to that."

"Did you consider that a threat to her?"

"No. It was just talk, conversation."

J.R. said he hadn't threatened his son's girlfriend. She had lived at his place, but he said he only knew of her, didn't know her, he'd been living down in Monroe when they were at his place. He didn't kill Brian Ognjan. He didn't kill David Tyll.

"Nothing further," said Williams.

Pendergast didn't ease into it.

"Mr. Duvall, you just lied to this jury, didn't you?"

"No, I didn't."

"You're one of seven Duvall brothers?"

"Yes."

"And you guys stick together, don't you? Family sticks together?"

"Yes."

She asked him what she'd asked Coco. Why would Frank tell a grand jury in 1989 that he had lied to it previously because he was " 'scared for my wife, kids. I don't know what they might do, you know, if they ever find out that I'm the one giving the information.' Can you explain to this jury why your own brother might make a statement like that under oath?"

"He also, he was having an affair with my Eileen at the same time, too."

"Eileen, the one that's dead?"

"Yes."

Pendergast brought up another of J.R.'s pig tales. She said he wasn't worried people were talking about him kissing a pig in odd places, "you were concerned because the police had some information about you eating pig feces for five dollars, is that right?"

"That also was another thing. That was just another thing."

"And after you ate the pig feces for five dollars you passed out near the pig's private parts, for lack of a better term, and it was a joke in the family that you were kissing the pig in that area, correct?"

"Yes."

"And the police knew about this incident and that provoked you to say, 'There's a snake in the woodpile.' You're agreeing to that, right? Gotta find out who it is and get to 'em, right? Recall that part of it?"

"No."

"All right, Donna Sundberg's wrong about that, too: 'It would be Eileen, because she knows what I'd do to her.'"

"I never said that."

As she'd done with Coco, Pendergast got J.R. to deny, one by one, statements made by the various witnesses, and as he did, she kept a running total. When they got to Barb Boudro, she said, "So, we're up to seven?"

"Pardon?"

"We're up to seven people that are wrong?"

"You're counting, right? I'm not."

"A number of people saying things against you and they all got it wrong, but you?"

"Yes."

Testimony was over. At 3:33 p.m. the jurors were sent home for the day. Their work would start in earnest tomorrow.

98

CLOSING ARGUMENTS

> *"There is no understanding of evil, only the recognition of what it is"*
>
> —Donna Pendergast

Pendergast didn't have to wait for closing arguments for drama and excitement on Wednesday, October 29. After trial the day before, one of the friends or family of the Duvalls had told one of the many deputies, "They're going to kill her," referring to Pendergast. Whether he had been making a threat or delivering a warning, no one was sure.

But security was tight the next morning. State police followed closely behind Pendergast's car for the forty-minute drive down to Standish from her motel room in East Tawas.

She was told not to leave the courtroom, even to go to the bathroom, without an armed escort.

A few last red and yellow leaves still clung to the trees outside the courthouse and in the deep woods nearby as Judge Bergeron strode into the courtroom promptly at 9 a.m., as was his habit.

The emergence of bare branches the last two weeks where there had recently been a wall of green—rain showers or gusty winds knock leaves off by the thousands every time they blow through in October—means one thing in northern Michigan: firearms deer season.

It seemed a fitting time of year to conclude a case involving two deer hunters who had been missing for so long, to either finally end the mystery with a guilty verdict, or, in the event of a not guilty, to deepen it with the addition of one more chapter.

"Please be seated," said the judge. "Good morning, ladies and gentlemen. We're going to have our closing argument this morning without further delay. Ms. Pendergast."

For veteran court watchers, closing arguments often epitomize the concept of an anticlimax. The days of testimony have built toward this, for days or weeks, but *this* often ends up as a monotonous, sleep-inducing recitation of facts and dates, with the occasional piece of rhetoric thrown in, a stab at drama that barely stirs the audience.

Donna Pendergast, however, wasn't in the habit of putting jurors to sleep. She hadn't been recruited by the state's attorney general and given this case at the last minute just to start droning now.

She took a breath to settle her nerves and stood up. It had been a defense theme that eighteen years had passed, that memories had faded or blurred or been exaggerated. Anticipating that the defense would use the passage of time to buttress their claim that this was a cold, cold case made all the weaker as it receded into the distant past, Pendergast had decided not to downplay the passage of time, but to use it as a hammering, metronomic device. Like the raven quoting "Nevermore," she built her poetic closing around a phrase she would repeat, and repeat, and repeat: "eighteen years."

"It's been almost eighteen years since David Tyll and Brian Ognjan were horrifically murdered in cold blood, and yet the final chapter to this story has been written in this courtroom in a very few days. It awaits only an ending which will be written by you . . .

"For eighteen long years, Brian and David's screams have been bottled up in boxes, in binders, because of fear and intimidation, while two families sat waiting and wondering, waiting and wondering for eighteen years."

She shifted her eyes from the jury to the Duvalls. "Don't reward the defendants for eighteen years of lies and intimidation. Don't reward the defendants for being clever enough to cover up their tracks and dispose of the evidence of their crimes, because the truth is that the defendants have been rewarded enough, already. They have gotten away with this for eighteen years, while a father died never knowing what happened to his son. They have gotten away with this for eighteen years, while their surviving parents grew old without their child. For eighteen years, witnesses have led frightened, quiet lives, always looking over their shoulders, for the fear of the Duvalls."

She turned back to face the jury, again.

"And now it's time. Time for you, the jury, to do justice. Time to say: enough. Enough of the lies. Enough of the cover-up. Enough of the intimidation. Too many people have lived in too much fear for way too long."

Staring at the jury, locking those startling eyes onto various members' eyes in turn, Pendergast made a dramatic linguistic shift. And a shift in focus, as she turned her stare back to the Duvalls. Instead of talking to "you, the juror," she began talking of "we." A prosecutor who hasn't connected with a jury might risk alienating them by suggesting they were a common entity. Having looked into their eyes, she knew she had them.

"She was captivating," said Bronco later.

"We, the jury, understand a terrible crime was committed here. We don't understand how you could do what you did, but we know that you did it. And, the truth is that there is no understanding of the why of Brian and David's death—only the hows—alone with their murderers, begging for their lives in a dark field and in an agonizing manner . . .

"There is no understanding of the whys of Brian and David's death, because it's pure evil, and there is no understanding of pure evil, only recognition of what it is." She stared at the Duvalls, hoping for eye contact, hoping to show them that her animus for them was pure and palpable, that this had become personal.

"Surely, when you're twenty-seven years old, your world doesn't end like this, on a cold, snowy fall night in a dark scary field at the hands of a bunch of individuals—savages, really—who are ruthless enough to laugh and say, 'Did you see that?' when a man's head explodes 'like a melon,' to use their words. But for Brian and David, it did. Their life did end like that. It did.

"You know," she continued, turning again to the jury, "it goes without saying that over the course of this trial, the two defendants have become real to you. You can see them. They're real to you . . . They may be real to you, but don't let their faces mistake what they are, because as you heard from Barb Boudro, based on what she saw in the field that night, their human faces are nothing more than masks for monsters.

"David and Brian are not real to you. You've heard their names [but] the truth is you don't know anything about Brian and David except for how they died. You don't know what their favorite colors were, their favorite food, favorite TV show. You don't know what their future dreams were or their past regrets. You don't know anything about them besides how they died. But they were real and they were alive and without question their lives were taken by an act of brutality, an animal-like act of brutality."

And so ended Pendergast's prologue. For the next twenty minutes she summed up the case. That it was absurd to think that two gainfully employed men, one married, the other with a girlfriend, would just run off. That they could still be alive, but would never have used their credit cards since they went missing, never accessed their bank accounts, never dropped a line or made a call.

"Mr. Williams suggested to you in his opening statement, well, maybe they ran away to— I don't recall if it was Alaska or Hawaii. I think you all know it's ludicrous."

She recounted the chain of events—the eyewitnesses who could place the missing hunters in the Luzerne–Mio area.

Who had seen them in one bar or another, who had given them directions, who had told them where they could meet women.

Pendergast acknowledged they had come into Linker's already intoxicated and acting "like idiots." Pinching waitresses on the rear, rubbing up against them, in general acting like stereotypes of drunken deer hunters from the big city coming up to spend their money and act the fool and enrich the local folks while pissing them off no end. Pissing them off enough that one of the women they'd come to the bar to impress admitted saying, "Those guys need to get their asses kicked."

And that same woman, Barb Boudro, later climbing out a back window, walking with her friend through the woods and, "in that clearing she saw a horrific sight that she will never forget—has never forgotten to this day, and I'm sure will never forget. Lights in the clearing, the Bronco pulled over. In the headlights, David Tyll: 'Please, God, somebody help us!' Coco Duvall, a bat or metal pipe in his hand, making those pinging noises that she earlier described.

"J.R. Duvall, kicking and hitting David Tyll. Coco Duvall hitting David Tyll with that metal item that appeared to be a bat, to the point where his head, according to Barb, like, exploded, and then these two savages saying, 'Did you see that?'

"Can you imagine that? That's the Duvall brothers. Make no mistake about it. Can you imagine that? Seeing a man's head explode—which is everybody's version of it, even their own—like a melon, and saying, 'Did you see that?'

"In that same clearing, Brian Ognjan, being held back, held down, knowing what was in store for him, because, you see, he knew that they couldn't leave a witness. He saw what was happening and he knew what his fate was, and he made a desperate break to try and get away, and he was dragged back into that circle of savagery, where he collapsed, and they began to beat at him as well. But not until after they had laughed at him because he had peed his pants.

"You bet he peed his pants. Can you imagine that? A man's begging for his life, terrified, trembling, and they're laughing at him for peeing his pants. That's the Duvall brothers. Make no mistake about it. So, Brian was kicked and hit by the Duvall brothers until he stopped moving. Barb had seen enough. She headed back up the path towards the house.

"And from that point on, the cover-up would begin. A cover-up that was engineered even before the bodies were even cold because, as you remember, shortly after this incident, Coco Duvall came to Barb's door, J.R. standing behind him. She said she opened the door a little bit, saw the bushy hair. 'Pigs have to eat, too.' "

The pigs. Whether or not David and Brian had been fed to pigs was irrelevant to the murder charges. But it was such a ghastly image, so powerful a way of continuing to paint a picture of the Duvalls.

"You know, I'm not going to stand here and unequivocally tell you that these guys were fed to pigs. I don't know. I am going to tell you that's one of the versions [the Duvalls] have put out there and they've put it out there consistently, not only in terms of what happened, but in terms of a threat, like what could happen to others as well."

She reminded the jury, and audience, about the Duvalls' pigs and their nasty reputation for eating animal parts. And about the testimony from various witnesses about what they'd heard about pigs and wood chippers over the years.

Having planted the images of bodies being fed into a chipper, and the remains being fed to pigs, Pendergast then, brilliantly, anticipated the defense counsel's upcoming response.

"The individuals were cut up and fed to pigs—is that true? I don't know, but don't be fooled into thinking I have to prove it, because the judge will give you the elements of the crime and that's not it."

Pendergast singled out Sergeant Lesneski for praise, quoting him as saying: 'I continued to follow leads—even crazy ones—on this case beause I ask myself one question: "What would I do if it were my family member?" '

"Luckily, these dedicated policemen have brought us to this courtroom today, not just the Michigan State Police, but all the agencies that have worked on this case over the years. Luckily they never gave up, and they have finally found the one person who was finally willing to speak out, who was finally willing, after a little coercing, to say, 'Enough, enough, enough of the lies. Enough of the cover-up. Enough of the intimidation. Yes, I am afraid of you. However, I am going to tell the truth.'

"Ladies and gentlemen of the jury, what happened to David Tyll and Brian Ognjan on that horrific weekend was savage and barbaric and completely unjustified by any circumstance imaginable, and even those words don't do this justice in this matter. And you know what? Even you, the jury, will never be able to do justice in this matter. How could there be enough justice for the ruthless obliteration of two human lives?

"How could there be enough justice for the act of savagery that we now know took place? How could there ever be enough justice for the terror, panic and pain suffered by David and Brian in the last moments of life? The truth is that two human lives have been ruthlessly obliterated and there will never be enough justice for that. Never."

The court recessed at 10:13 a.m.

Pendergast and Lesneski left the courtroom and joined the Tylls in an adjacent room.

"How did I do?" asked Pendergast.

"You were magnificent," said Mrs. Tyll, her eyes tearing up as they hugged.

Bronco looked at her and said, "Ohmigod."

Later, he said, "I can tell you that I'll probably never again, the rest of my career, be so blessed to sit second chair next to a prosecutor as talented as Donna."

99
FOR THE DEFENSE

There'd been a lot of testimony, recountings of rumors and overheard conversations, hearsay and innuendo. One thing was clear to everyone: If the jury didn't believe Barb Boudro, the rest of it was meaningless. Like trying to hang tinsel before you had the tree. She was the tree Pendergast was hanging everything else on.

But even if the jury believed the essence of her testimony—there had been a fight in a clearing down from her house, she had witnessed unspeakable brutality and hadn't spoken about it for many years—they could still have enough reasonable doubt to come back with a not guilty.

It was dark, she was drunk, there were guys with beards and long hair at a time when a lot of north-woods guys wore their hair long and didn't shave. Sure, she might have witnessed two murders, but that didn't mean she was right about the killers being the Duvalls.

There had been a lot of damning testimony against J.R. and Coco, but there had been a lot of contradictory testimony, too, that Schwartz and Williams could, and would, point to. And a lot of it came from people who had been arrested and were hoping to catch a break for their crime by talking about someone else's. Boudro was hardly the only impeachable witness.

The prosecution made a big deal about the hunters being eaten by the Duvalls' pigs, but it had also made a big deal out of Coco saying that if they found one hunter, they'd find the other underneath him. Well, which was it? Had they been eaten, or dumped in a single shallow grave?

The prosecution made a big deal of an altercation at Linker's. But there had been testimony about several vastly different kinds of arguments. The hunters had stolen the Duvalls' deer, and when they ran into them that night, the brothers had exacted revenge. The hunters in a pack of five had beaten up J.R., but later that night he and his cohorts had caught them, alone. Or they were strangers intersecting in a bar with bad results.

There was contradictory testimony about what had happened when. Barb first told police that it had to be on Saturday night, because she didn't go out partying on Sundays because of work Monday, and Saturday was the day her buddy had gotten his first legal buck. Moreover, she remembered she'd worked that day, and she didn't work Sundays. But too many other people had seen the hunters in various places Saturday night to allow them to be at Linker's, too, so if they'd gotten into a scrap with the Duvalls, it had to have been on Sunday.

But what were they doing still up north on Sunday night, partying the night away? There had been testimony from former girlfriends and wives and relatives that neither was the irresponsible type. They might go to the wrong place to hunt deer and good times, but they weren't the kind to not come home at all, and they'd both been expected home early Sunday evening at the latest.

They certainly weren't the type to miss work, and it was hard to imagine how they'd be up north at midnight Sunday and get to work on time Monday.

Would there be enough of those kinds of contradictions and uncertainties to rise to the level of reasonable doubt? With a jury, one never knows. Schwartz and Williams weren't holding full houses or flushes, but, with no bodies and no physical evidence, neither was Pendergast.

At 10:26 the jury reentered the courtroom. Schwartz got first crack. It was, of course, at Boudro.

"This will be the last time I have an opportunity to say anything to you about what the evidence was, or in this case the incredible lack of evidence, and what the witnesses said, particularly Barb Boudro, neighborhood party girl and drunk, the linchpin, the linchpin of the whole thing."

The trouble was, he said, that no one else saw what Boudro claims to have seen. He reminded the jury that Cindy Socia, the waitress, remembered the hunters, sure enough, but not the Duvalls. Steve Linker, the owner, didn't remember ever seeing the brothers, that night or any other.

"The famous Barbara Boudro who saw trouble brewing, trouble brewing. Nobody else saw it, but Barbara Boudro saw it. Who knows what else she saw? Pink elephants? The drunken Barbara Boudro, who drove home, she says, with her case of beer on her shoulder, or wherever, you know, however she carried it out, with her two buddies . . .

"Barbara Boudro, the drunk who didn't quit drinking until she got her last ticket in '94, the last drunk driving ticket in '94. Then she found out she was depressed, so now she's on medication for that. Barbara Boudro, whose only problems were self-inflicted: drunk driving, her drinking, her drug abuse, her— whatever else she did. Who knows what she did? That's Barb Boudro. That's the person they want you to believe, and they want you to find them guilty beyond a reasonable doubt because drunken Barbara Boudro says she saw it."

Schwartz then lit into Rocky Harmon, "the snitch, who says he wasn't a snitch."

"Charles 'Stinky' McMullen Jr. claims that out of nowhere Coco comes up behind him and says, 'Head burst like a melon.' The detective didn't get to him, he got to the detective. He's being held for a felony involving theft. Of course he's got a statement, a real thick statement of all sorts of allegations, all sorts of good stuff, and he's sitting here with the prosecutor and his defense attorney. He's there with his defense attorney. Yeah, that's who he's there with. Figure out why he gave that statement."

Schwartz mockingly recounted McMullen testifying about how afraid he was of the Duvalls, how tough they were. "Never heard anything like that since Jesse James and his gang rode," said the defense attorney. "These guys are the most dangerous guys in town. You know what? They knew where he was all the time. They always knew where he was. And they'd known all along that Stinky McMullen was going to make up, had made up, some stories about them. They knew it, that he'd taken that stuff and he'd gone to the police and traded it."

Schwartz told the jury they ought to keep in mind that in eighteen years of investigation, the Duvalls had never fled, never tried to hide. "How their names came into it is beyond comprehension, but once they came into it, they still didn't run. They were told in '89 and '90, 'You're the focus of the investigation. You're the focus.' They didn't leave."

He mocked Kenny Duvall as a crackhead. He mocked Frank Duvall. "Frankie, who says he's scared of his family, scared of his brothers. Frankie, who's lived in Monroe all his life. Who says he's scared for his family, for his children, whatever he's scared of . . . Frankie, poor Frankie, probably just scared, scared of a grand jury, whatever. Poor Frankie."

He seemed to be overdoing the ad hominem bit, laying it on just a bit, or more than a bit, thick.

"Then they have the lovely Connie Sundberg. Another incredible story from a woman who smoked weed all day, every day, all day."

Then Schwartz hit on the most vulnerable part of the prosecution case, other than Boudro's credibility: the time-line. David Welch and Beverly Pasternak were unshakably sure they'd spent Saturday night in Walker's with the hunters. They were supposed to be home Sunday afternoon or early evening. That meant they had to have been in Linker's Sunday night, but Steve Linker was sure the Duvalls hadn't been in that evening, or any other, for that matter.

"He's been shown all kinds of pictures of them. Long hair, short hair, whatever kind of hair. He's never seen them there. It's a huge problem. It's a huge problem. They hadn't been there."

And Schwartz reminded the jury of another possibly crucial bit of contradiction. Eileen Seitz's grand jury testimony had been read into the record. Seitz had told the grand jury that on Sunday, the 24th of November, J.R. had been in Cass City, two hours away in Michigan's Thumb, having Thanksgiving dinner with her family. And the reason she was so clear on the date was that her family's tradition was to eat Thanksgiving dinner the Sunday before Thanksgiving, so they'd all be free on the actual holiday to eat at their various in-laws'.

"It's a great idea," said Schwartz. "I'm thinking of doing it myself."

The attorney started to wrap it up.

"It's a tragedy. It really is. Everyone feels bad and no one wants to diminish their loss, whatever that loss is, death or disappearance," he said, attempting to minimize it. "Whatever it is, no one wants to minimize it, but nobody wants to convict the wrong person, either."

He acknowledged that the Duvalls were brawlers and had had fights with their wives and their girlfriends. "Nobody's condoning that, but that doesn't make them stone-cold killers as brutal and as sadistic and as savage as they were held out to be."

He told the panel that there was no evidence. "None, zero, nothing. No body, no car, no blood, no body parts, no fingernails, nothing. They've dug up every house back yard where these guys lived and were supposed to have pigs, and all they found was a deer bone. That's it. No nothing.

"What I'm asking you, after reviewing the evidence, considering everything you've seen and everything you've heard, what I'm asking you is to find Coco Duvall not guilty, and the reason we're asking is because he didn't do it, but more importantly, we're asking you because there's such a tremendous lack of evidence and such an incredible disparity in what you've been told, that he isn't guilty. The people have not met their burden of proof and found him guilty beyond a reasonable doubt. For that reason we are asking you to find him not guilty. Thank you."

~

It was 11:28, and Williams' turn. He was J.R.'s attorney of record, but each of the attorneys was clearly arguing for both defendants. One wasn't going to be found guilty and the other not guilty.

He, too, told the jury that neither Cindy Socia nor Steve Linker had seen the Duvalls the weekend the hunters had gone missing. He hammered away, too, at Boudro: "Every time she has told her story, she has told it differently."

He hit at the inconsistencies of time, of Boudro, in various statements over the years, being positive the beatings were on Saturday when Saturday was ruled out by other evidence. "If Barb Boudro saw this fight on Saturday night, how did Beverly Pasternak see them on Sunday, the twenty-fourth? And if you believe Ms. Boudro is mistaken as to the day, why would the hunters be sitting at a bar on a Sunday night when they are supposed to be home, on their way home to go to work the next morning?"

He hammered away at Rocky and at Charles McMullen. He hammered away at Katherine Sliwinski, Tommy Duvall's ex-girlfriend, who was in a bitter custody dispute with J.R.'s son.

"Like I told you on day one, this case is like an urban legend, with parts being added and added, growing bigger and bigger, as the rumors and gossip are repeated over and over," he said. "Ask yourself: What's missing from the prosecutor's case? I think the answer is clear. Proof, proof beyond mere rumors, beyond gossip, beyond testimony of an admitted alcoholic on her fourth or fifth version of her story. Proof beyond a reasonable doubt, that's what is missing."

Like Schwartz, he reminded the jury of the evidence, and its lack. "Evidence has shown no bodies, no vehicle, no vehicle parts, no body parts, no bones, no teeth, no guns, no alleged murder weapon, no gear, no clothing, no DNA, no fingerprints, no blood, no hairs. None of it has ever been located. They tried. Trust me, they tried. They searched all the rivers, the lakes, the ponds, the pigpens, everything. They talked to psychics. Nothing's been located.

"People testifying about rumors and gossip does not equate to proof beyond a reasonable doubt . . . After eighteen years, it may be a very good assumption that they are dead. But it's possible in five years from now, two sets of remains will be found somewhere, maybe in the Upper Peninsula, maybe in the White Cloud area. It's possible.

"There are countless possibilities. Without anything scientific to rely upon, we can only guess as to what happened. That's the point. A guess is not proof beyond a reasonable doubt. Without proof beyond a reasonable doubt, you've got to find the defendants not guilty. Thank you."

It was 12:31. The judge broke for lunch. Schwartz and Williams had hit hard and effectively at the weak spots in the prosecution's case.

Because the burden for the prosecution is to prove a case beyond a reasonable doubt, it gets to have both the first and last say at closing. Pendergast would get to finish the trial with a rebuttal of the defense's closing arguments. Her performance in the trial thus far had attested to her ability to think on her feet, to always seem to be one step ahead, a little bit quicker, than either of her opponents. At every objection she'd had the proper citation at the tip of her tongue, deftly and effortlessly countering Schwartz's and Williams' arguments. Her objections were sustained, theirs overruled, nearly without exception.

She wouldn't have to be fast, now. The judge had ordered everyone back at 1:35 p.m. She'd have sixty-three minutes to prepare her final attack. It hardly seemed fair.

100

FINAL VOICE FOR THE PEOPLE

At 1:35 court promptly reconvened.

"Mr. Williams left you with a number of possibilities, including that maybe the hunters would show up in five years," she said, facing the jury. "Well, you know, it's possible that the moon will turn purple tomorrow. It's possible that we'll have a ninety-five-degree day in February. It's possible that the sun will explode next week. But what we're dealing with here is what the evidence shows, and all of those possibilities are as likely as the hunters showing up in five years—and they know it."

She briefly reminded the jury of similar threats over the years by the Duvalls—to Ed Lavere in Monroe, to Katherine Sliwinski up north, to others—to do to them what they'd done to the hunters.

She told them Williams had been disingenuous when he'd said in his closing arguments that police have " 'the technology now. They have DNA.' They have this, they have that. Yeah, they do. But you know what? You have to find something, first. You can't do DNA technology on a car that's been parted out somewhere. You can't do DNA technology when a body's been fed through a tree shredder or whatever they did to it. So, to suggest to you that there's technologies available today and they didn't use it is really, I guess, for lack of a better term, a red herring.

"Talk about red herrings. Well, Denise Tyll, Denise Dudley, now, she got married within a year," said Pendergast, a point brought up and stressed by the defense. "What is that all about? Are they faulting this woman who told you from the witness stand that she knew her husband was dead the first week because he just wouldn't have done this? Are they faulting her for getting on with her life and getting married? Lucky she found someone. I mean, what is that all about?"

Pendergast acknowledged there were questions about the time-line. It was eighteen years ago, and who can remember with certainty if something happened on a particular Friday, or Saturday? And if witnesses differed on what day they thought something had happened, so what? "I think you can all use your common sense and figure out, you know, 'Two weeks ago, jeez, what was I doing on Thursday?' It doesn't matter. I don't have to prove the day. And if, in fact, David and Brian were still in Linker's bar on Sunday night, which, if Mr. Welch and Ms. Pasternak are correct, would be the case. We don't know whether or not they were going to leave late, go to work hungover the next morning, we don't know."

Pendergast pointed out that Eileen Seitz's so-called alibi for J.R. on Sunday really wasn't. She had told the grand jury J.R. was in Cass City at 5 p.m. Cass City is two hours from Linker's. J.R. could easily have had an afternoon dinner in Cass City and been drinking in Linker's by 9 or 10.

As for Linker, "You've heard Mr. Schwartz's testimony about Steve Linker, and in his opening argument he made it sound like Steve Linker was going to be this bombshell. Steve Linker was going to come into the courtroom and blow this trial wide open. Well, I would suggest to you that it was anything but that. Does he sound like a man who doesn't believe Barb's telling the truth, even though he came in as a defense witness?

"On cross-examination: 'Tell the members of the jury about the last conversation you had with Barb Boudro.' 'Oh, well, oh, I saw her at her brother's shop a month ago.' 'What did you say to her?' 'I said to her, "Barb, please tell me this didn't happen in my parking lot."' Does that sound like a man who doesn't believe Barb Boudro?"

Of course the logic of the sentence was that he was perfectly willing to believe Boudro, but was hoping it wasn't bad news. Pendergast brilliantly segued to someone who had good reason to inspire disbelief.

"Both Mr. Williams and Mr. Schwartz have talked about Mr. Dutton. 'Well, you know, how do we know Dutton's not telling the truth?' You know what? I'm not going to waste my breath on that one. Dutton? Like I said, I'll leave that up to you, the jury. Once again, not worth the nine-page, incoherent—frankly, I think crazy—statement that I went through with him.

"You know, I could stand here a long time—and I know you guys are tired—I would have to stand here another two hours, because they both spoke over an hour, to refute point by point what they said. I'm going to rely on your collective memories, the twelve of you that go into the jury room. Because obviously you were in the same courtroom that I was, and they were in the same courtroom that I was, and many of the things that came out of their mouths I don't think matched the testimony.

"Mr. Schwartz has termed this case a tragedy. Well, you know, when a small child dies of cancer, that's a tragedy. When thousands of people are lost in a typhoon, that's a tragedy. But when two men beat two human beings to the point where one of their heads explodes, that's not a tragedy, that's a crime. And the crime is called murder.

"Ladies and gentlemen of the jury, the defendants sit before you—and may I suggest to you that they knew what they were doing when they came into Linker's bar that night. They knew what they were doing when they followed David and Brian out of Linker's bar that night. They knew what they were doing when they threatened many, many witnesses and as they sit here today, they know what they did. They know and now you do, too. The snake in the woodpile has spoken. Now, it's time for you, the jury, to do the same."

The judge gave the jurors their instructions, defining reasonable doubt and detailing the charges and what was needed
to prove them. They were given the option of second-degree
murder if they believed the defendants had killed the hunters
but did it on the spur of the moment, without planning or
without reasonably expecting that their actions could lead to
death.

The clerk drew two juror numbers at random, juror C-11,
Richard Danjin, and juror B-36, William Morgan. "You may
be excused. Thank you for your service, your inconvenience,"
said the judge.

At 2:54, the jurors began their deliberations.

101

A VERDICT

Just before 5 p.m., word swept through the courthouse that the jury of six men and six women had reached a decision. At 4:59, court was reconvened. "Please be seated," said Bergeron. "Counsel, I have a note. The jury has reached a verdict. Please bring the jury in."

Bergeron asked foreman Timothy Ball to stand. J.R. put his hand to his head. Coco showed little emotion.

"Has the jury reached a verdict?" asked the judge.

"Yes, it has."

"Are the verdicts unanimous?"

"Yes, they are."

"All right. Well, regarding Mr. Donald Dean Duvall, also known as Coco Duvall, file number 03-772-FC, could you indicate the jury's verdict to count one?"

"The jury's verdict of count one is guilty of first-degree premeditated murder."

There was an exhalation from the audience, trying to do as it had been told and refrain from reaction, trying at the same time to express all the emotions that had built up for eighteen years and had less than a second to come out. It was a sound hard to describe, but clear, a sound of relief, of satisfaction, of *finally . . .*

All that followed was anticlimax. Coco was guilty on count two, as well. J.R. was guilty on both counts.

Schwartz asked that the jury be polled. "Yes, sir," each of them said in turn when asked by Bergeron: "Are those your verdicts?"

The judge thanked them for their time, told them where to go down the hall to be paid their nominal per diem for the seven-day trial, asked if the attorneys had anything further to say to the jury and at 5:03 p.m. said, "You may be excused. Thank you, again."

Bergeron said sentencing would be held as soon as possible following pre-sentence reports by the Michigan Department of Corrections. All of it was moot—the sentence by law would be life in prison without parole. He asked the lawyers, again, if they had anything to say.

At 5:04, he said, "That concludes the hearing."

The audience rose. Helen Ognjan and Cathy Tyll stood, turned to each other and embraced as a photographer shot a picture of them that would run in the next day's *Bay City Times*.

The Duvalls' family and friends hurried out. The rest remained. "God answered my prayers," said Helen.

"It's been a long eighteen years," said Anthony Ognjan, Brian's cousin. "My family can't express its gratitude for the people who worked on this case. It was just a long, hard road."

"It won't bring my son back, but it will help," said Arthur Tyll. "It's about time somebody paid for it. It's kind of justice, but they owe me eighteen years and a son, and they can't give me that. I was glad to see them cuffed, and I can't wait to see them in chains."

Bronco came up to the Tylls. He had tears in his eyes. He spoke with a hitch in his voice. "I just wish I could have brought them back."

Cathy Tyll held out her hand to Donna. She was holding a charm, a small angel. "You're my angel," she said. Pendergast misted up, too, one or two tears sliding down her cheek. They hugged.

Outside the courtroom, Schwartz told members of the media he was going to appeal. Defense attorneys always say that, and it always has a certain dramatic ring to it. *This is such an injustice, we are going to appeal.* In fact, in Michigan an appeal in first-degree murder cases is automatic, written into the law. It's paid for by the state. You can't *not* appeal.

Nonetheless, Schwartz sounded like he might even believe it when he said the state had not met its burden of proof, that the case depended overwhelmingly on the testimony of an admitted drunkard whose story made little sense.

"We don't know what happened, but we do know they didn't do it," he said.

Paradoxically, he also said, "I'm drained. I'm not sure what else I could do. The testimony was brutal."

The Duvall family refused to talk to reporters.

Ball told reporters, "Personally, I don't think there was any one thing that swayed me. It was a collaboration of all the evidence. And when you put it all together, it was pretty convincing."

Later, he told Bronco and Pendergast that the jury had decided in the first ten minutes on its verdict, but worried for decorum's sake how that would look. So Ball, playing devil's advocate, had run all the defense arguments past them, to no avail.

On Thursday, November 13, nine days short of the eighteenth anniversary of their disappearance, the killers of David Tyll and Brian Ognjan were brought into the courtroom for sentencing. Though the trial had been held in Standish, the sentence, fittingly enough, was pronounced in Mio, near where the killings had occurred.

Before Bergeron made his pronouncement, family members were allowed, under Michigan law, to make victims' impact statements, and address the two Duvalls.

"We hope in the years to follow that they will find sadness and remorse for the vicious murders of our two sons," said Cathy Tyll.

"When you wake up in the morning, you will hear Dave's screams," said Shawn Tyll, David's brother. "All we have left are memories. You guys are still alive."

Helen, 84 now, and frail, in the early stages of Alzheimer's, stood as a relative read her statement for her: "Many good memories of Brian remain with me. You deprived me of having grandchildren. May God have mercy on your souls."

The Duvalls were given a chance to speak. J.R. stood, looked at the Ognjans and Tylls and said, "I really feel bad for you," he said. "But it's hard to find remorse when you didn't do it.

"In this lifetime, you might not find out what happened," said J.R. "But in your next lifetime, I guarantee you will find out what happened. That we did not have nothing to do with this or know nothing about it."

He was just a little old man, now, hard to imagine him as a fearsome creature who'd terrorized a region for years. A lying little old man, thought those family members who stared at him with all the disgust and hatred they could muster.

His attorney, Scott Williams, formally asked the judge to reduce the charge against J.R. to second-degree murder.

Bergeron refused. Then he sentenced both J.R. and Coco to jail for life, without parole.

Cathy Tyll told the members of the press, "We have heard of evil, cruel people here, but we have also heard of caring, loving people. We got our answer. We got our bittersweet justice."

Bronco had a warning for some of those who thought the trial was the end of the mystery. There were others who had taken part in the beatings, he said. He wasn't done. He'd be after them, too. "This investigation remains open and we have some additional irons in the fire," he said.

PART 5
AFTERWARD

102

TWO SERIAL KILLINGS

So far, the irons haven't heated up much, but Bronco considers the investigation still open. Over the years, there were hundreds of leads that went nowhere. Many potential suspects were investigated and ruled out. Many pieces never quite fit into the puzzle. Even though several witnesses told police that others might have been present that night in 1985 when the two hunters lost their lives, only J.R. and Coco were arrested, tried, and convicted for the crime. And, while the statute of limitations never runs out on murder, as of now, there is no hint from the authorities that other arrests are likely. If others helped beat the hunters Bronco hopes to sit second chair one day while Pendergast or someone else prosecutes them. On the other hand, even if they could mount a case against Rex Duvall as an accessory after the fact, the statute of limitations had run out on that offense.

But Bronco wasn't without other irons. The month after the Duvall trial, he inherited another cold case, involving, implausibly enough, the murder of another deer hunter. Charles Murray, 33, of Chesterfield Township near Detroit had been shot, apparently without motive, as he sat in a tree on October 11, 1993, in the Huron National Forest in Iosco County while bow-hunting.

His body was found at the base of the tree the next day,

and it was thought at first that his death was accidental, that he had perhaps been killed by someone target shooting nearby or hunting small game.

But police soon noticed the strap to the harness that hunters wear while up in trees to keep them from falling if they slip or a branch snaps. It hadn't been broken, it had been cut. And they quickly found at least one other bullet wound. Murray—an avid guitar player and a big Detroit Red Wings fan who had just started a new job—had been shot in cold blood, then cut out of his harness and left at the base of the tree.

A regular firearms deer hunter, it was the first time he'd ever gone bow hunting. He'd told his mother, Sandy Murray, that since the weather was mild, he was just going to sleep in his car. His first night up north, though, was spent at the base of the tree, dead.

The next assumption was robbery, since his wallet and other personal possessions were missing. There was little evidence, no leads and the case went cold.

Lesneski reopened the case, thinking there might be something that might have been overlooked at the time. A little later two Iosco County sheriff's deputies told Bronco they suspected a guy named Ronald Brown, 45, who was already serving a life sentence for murder in the nearby maximum-security prison in Standish.

What made Brown an unlikely suspect was that he was in prison for murdering someone during a home invasion and robbery in Eaton County, several hours southwest of Iosco County, the same day that the hunter was shot. But if anyone was capable of two unrelated homicides in one day, Bronco thought it might be Brown.

He'd been convicted of second-degree murder in 1977 and served 8 years in prison before an early release. He later was convicted of armed robbery, and in September of 1993 was once again given early release.

Bronco interviewed Brown, a cocky smart-ass, and got nowhere the first time. Captain Dan Miller, Bronco's supervisor on the other hunter case, suggested they profile Brown, a rare move. They normally work up profiles from crime scenes, trying to get a feel for their unknown suspect. This time, though, Miller thought they ought to let the psychologists at the state police's Behavioral Science Section examine Miller, find out some clues about what might make him tick.

Bronco was reluctant, but Miller pushed it. The psychologists did a work-up, told him what they thought the guy's triggers were. They told Bronco to get in touch with his feminine side, to come at Brown in a such way that he'd see Bronco—though highly unlikely, to look at him—as a substitute mother figure.

"Bronco played him like a trout," said Miller. During their last prison interview, Brown got so distraught that the guards thought he was about to attack Lesneski. Suddenly, he demanded to confess.

"I was driving around looking for someone to shoot," he said. His crime of motive earlier in the day had unleashed a craving for one without motive. He saw a car parked at the side of the road, thought it likely belonged to a hunter and went hunting, himself.

"He was there and I shot him."

And he told Bronco there were others he'd killed, too, but offered up no details.

Brown was charged in August of 2004 and a trial date was set, but to spare the state the expense, Brown was allowed to plead guilty to second-degree murder. It was moot, since he was in jail for life, but the plea enraged Bronco. He wanted him convicted of first-degree murder and he wanted the family there to see it.

Typical of Bronco, he'd gotten to feel close to Murray's mother. The first thing he'd done when taking on the case had been to call the family. "They probably thought, 'Who is this joker?' I was probably the fourth detective who'd been on the case and they were gonna have to start all over again." And then he'd promptly made the long drive down to the Detroit area to meet the Murray family in person, to show them his call hadn't just been lip service. After that, he followed up with monthly phone calls. Even if nothing had happened, he wanted them to know he was thinking of them. "You build a relationship with the victim's family. You form a bond. A trust," says Lesneski.

Bronco called them again after hearing about the plea-bargain. The prosecutor hadn't called them to let them know there would be no trial. "I felt so bad because I knew they trusted me," he said.

~

In 2005, Bronco was temporarily assigned to Saginaw, a down-on-its-luck factory town an hour and a half south of Tawas, whose factories were closing, whose downtown store-fronts were shuttered, whose teen gangs were killing each other. Miller wanted him to work another cold-case serial killing.

This was as cold as they come, a pair of murders of teen-age boys in 1972. Norbert Peck was an 18-year-old Polish immigrant, adopted by a woman who had survived intern-ment by the Nazis. He was working with his mother at the time picking vegetables in the rich farmlands surrounding the Saginaw River.

He disappeared on May 1, and his body was found in a drainage ditch eight days later. He had been strangled and most likely left for dead in the ditch. But there was water in his lungs, meaning he'd died from drowning. There was a six-foot piece of rope nearby.

On September 25, Oscar Garcia, 14, was found in a cul-vert, strangled, a six-foot piece of rope near him, too.

Police had saved bits of skin they'd found under the vic-tims' fingernails. It gave Bronco, with all the new technology available, something to work with, if he ever came up with a suspect.

Bronco started ringing doorbells, asking people what they knew, hoping to hear something that would cause him to stick his foot in a door once more as it was slamming shut.

He re-read all the old reports, cross-referencing names of suspects with databases. He got a hit. A man named Todd Warzecha, at the time a resident of nearby Bay City who had been a suspect in the Saginaw murders but never charged, was sentenced in 1974 to 2–10 years for criminal sexual misconduct with a young male.

Warzecha had also been a suspect in the still-unsolved Oakland County child murders of the 1970s. He'd been cleared in the Oakland County case, but not of the Saginaw murders.

Moreover, startlingly, in one of his interviews with police in Oakland County, Warzecha had made reference to trouble he might be in because of something he'd done in the Saginaw area.

"But no one had connected the dots," said Bronco.

Bronco found that Warzecha, now 53, had moved to Austin, Texas, and had stayed out of trouble since being released from jail in Michigan. He seemed to be living, or at least involved, with a well-to-do male physician.

Bronco flew to Texas in June of 2005, rented a car and tracked Warzecha down while awaiting approval for a warrant, which took a few days to process—"I figured it would be a snap, being in Texas, but it turns out Austin is the one liberal corner of the state, and I had to fill out all kinds of paperwork and wait for the judge to approve it," said Bronco.

Part of the paperwork required him to know where Warzecha was living. Bronco had three addresses for him: two houses, one of them the doctor's, and a self-storage center.

Bronco staked out the one that he thought was Warzecha's house. Hours later, Warzecha emerged.

Bronco got his warrant signed and came back and waited some more to serve it. Finally, just to give himself something to do, he drove over to the self-storage center, thinking he might find Warzecha there.

When he got there, there were cop cars with their flashers on and police tape blocking the driveway. Bronco got out of his car and walked up.

"What do you want?" asked a cop.

"Michigan State Police," said Bronco, pulling out his badge. "I'm looking for a guy that rents here."

"That explains it," said the cop. "Come here."

He led Bronco to a storage unit. The door was open. Warzecha was hanging there. A relative back in Michigan who'd been interviewed by Bronco had called to tell him the police were looking for him on a couple of old murders.

Sitting on a shelf near Bronco's desk is a new framed photo, Bronco with a big smile on his face sitting between two women, wearing equally big smiles. One is Garcia's mother. The other is Peck's.

In March of 2006, Bronco was promoted to first lieutenant and post commander of the East Tawas Post, a desk job. "I've got to live vicariously through other people, now," he said with a laugh.

103

SERIAL KILLER OF HER OWN

Following her prosecution of the Duvalls, Donna Pendergast got another headliner, Coral Eugene Watts, in 2004. He'd slashed twelve women to death in Texas from 1981–1992. Rather than prosecute what they feared were weak cases, authorities let him plea-bargain to aggravated burglary charges and thought they'd put him away for life when he was sentenced to 60 years.

The aggravated part of the charge came because he'd attempted to drown a Houston coed, Lori Lister, in scalding water. But the Texas Court of Appeals ruled that he could only be sentenced on a burglary charge because he hadn't been told at the time of his confession that his felony would be considered aggravated because of the hot water.

Suddenly he was eligible for parole in 2006, despite having told anyone who'd listen that he'd start killing again once he got free.

Watts was truly a scary guy, if one serial killer can be scarier than another. He'd bragged to Texas Rangers, who were able to corroborate the tale, that he kept a tank of black-widow spiders and would take some of them out to play with, and to terrorize women he was having sex with.

Michigan authorities had long suspected him of several murders there, and, eager to keep him behind bars, they extradited him in 2004 for the 1979 death of Helen Dutcher, 37, who was stabbed twelve times in the face, neck and chest in the Detroit suburb of Ferndale.

Pendergast got the case, and Watts was convicted and sentenced to life without parole. At his sentencing Watts said the killing of Dutcher "is the one murder I did not do," but that if the victim's family wanted to hate him, "that is fine with me."

Ironically Watts also was suspected to have been the killer who had been dubbed the Sunday Morning Slasher, a psychopath who had attacked and slashed several coeds in Ann Arbor in the late 1970s, and had the campus so fearful that women, including Pendergast, who was going to the University of Michigan at the time, were required by the dorm RAs to go in pairs when they went out at night.

In 2005, Pendergast prepared for the prosecution of a guy named Ronnie Bullock, 45, who thought he'd gotten away with the rape and murder of a 69-year-old Flint woman named Vadah Warner in 1979. When Jeff Gorton was convicted of the murder of two Michigan women in 2002 (*Blood Justice*, St. Martin's Press), police started looking at old, cold-case murders in the area to see if they could link any of them to him.

At the time of the Warner murder, police found two bloody fingerprints, but couldn't match them to a suspect given the technology of the day. Coincidentally, one of Gorton's brothers had been questioned but he was eliminated as a possible suspect. When State Police ran the prints through the Automated Fingerprint Identification System in 2004, they got a hit, all right, but not to Gorton. They matched prints taken from Bullock during a drunk-driving arrest in 2001.

With trial about to begin, Bullock pleaded guilty on November 23, 2005, and was sentenced to 20–30 years.

104

ACKNOWLEDGMENTS AND POSTSCRIPT

The hunt for the killers of David Tyll and Brian Ognjan was one of relentless determination. A series of State Police took this case seriously, none more so than Bronco Lesneski.

What brought the investigation to life, and what brought to life the dogged determination of police over an eighteen-year period, was reading all of the police reports filed over the years and compiled by Bronco.

You can see the loose ends and the dead ends and the seemingly dead ends that managed to intersect with other leads.

Donna Pendergast was able to make sense of the history of this case, and to pull its bits and pieces into a prosecutable whole, by studying those three thick binders of reports. I was able to fashion most of this book from them, as well, so all credit is due to Bronco and his predecessors with the state police, Norman Maxwell, Doug Halleck, Curtis Schram and Alison King, as well as to investigators with the St. Clair Shores and Troy police before they handed their cases off to the state.

The Tylls have seen more than their share of misfortune over the years. Two sons died young during epileptic seizures in their sleep, Larry at 37, Archie at 34. Another son, Steve, began an odyssey into drug abuse at 15 that ended with his death at 25.

But they welcomed me into their home in the northern Detroit suburb of Utica, just off a major highway whose noise is muffled by the tall shade trees of an old forest that has managed to survive exurbia's relentless encroachment.

When I came calling in the summer of 2005, I found an inviting house, literally, welcome signs on the door, a post and the mailbox.

Inside, what was designed as the front room served as a formal dining room. A small engraved piece of wood on the table read: "Around this table, may peace and love prevail."

Scattered around the room and lining the front window were toy fire trucks and mementos and a figure of a bearded fireman who looked like Santa Claus, all reminders that Art Tyll was a 26-year veteran of the Detroit Fire Department.

You'd never guess the tragedy that has visited Cathy from the sparkle in her eye, her cheerfulness of spirit, her eagerness to put an interloper at ease, and her graciousness in the face of questions that forced her to relive the tragedy that changed her family forever.

~

Donna Pendergast was a delight. Irreverent and quick-witted off the job, passionate and ferocious on it, she was glad to help cut the red tape that threatened to ensnarl this project. Glad, too, to give me encouraging words when one of her boss's minions started throwing roadblocks up on this project. It was an election year and my guess was that the boss didn't want her getting more publicity than him.

Bronco let me read his reports, Donna let me read her trial transcripts and take notes, a not-insignificant cost savings, as those who have ever had to buy a trial transcript can attest.

Her boss, Michigan Attorney General Mike Cox, more politician than prosecutor, the kind who begins running for re-election the morning after winning one, found out the hard way about being careful what you wish for.

Cox was a lover of press conferences and a hoarder of the limelight. In 2004, he'd asked Oakland County Sheriff

Michael Bouchard for help on an investigation into corruption involving local school officials. Bouchard's department put hundreds of man hours into it. When Cox was ready to announce indictments, he called a press conference, but neglected to tell Bouchard until nearly the last minute.

When Bouchard finally got word and showed up with seconds to spare, Cox's staff wouldn't let him anywhere within camera or microphone range.

On November 9, 2005, Cox found himself, unhappily for once, in the glare of TV spotlights in as bizarre a turn of events as longtime watchers of Michigan politics could remember.

Cox was running for re-election in the fall of 2006—some said he was already running for governor in 2010—and had been campaigning hard for a long time. In Michigan, an attorney general's interpretation of law *is* law until a court rules differently or the legislature overrules him by enacting a new law.

Cox was a Republican. His boss, Governor Jennifer Granholm, for whom he had little love, was a Democrat. In November of 2004, state voters passed a ballot initiative against same-sex marriage. Cox then ordered state universities to stop offering health care to same-sex partners of employees. That and other policies inflamed high-profile liberal attorney Geoffrey Fieger, who had gained national fame by successfully defending Jack "Dr. Death" Kevorkian at his trials for actively helping people commit suicide. (Fieger had a falling out with Kevorkian and wasn't part of the defense team in the case that put Kevorkian in prison, growing out of an appearance on CBS' *60 Minutes* where he was shown not just supplying the suicide machine, but working its controls.)

Early in 2005, Fieger called a press conference, verbally ripped into Cox and announced he would seek the Democratic nomination to run against him in 2006.

Fast forward to November 9, 2005. The word went out via phone call, e-mail and fax that Cox was going to hold a press conference. Nothing new there, but the media arrived nonetheless. Cox's wife, Laura, was in his office in Lansing, too.

Cox stunned everyone by announcing he'd had an affair: "A number of years ago, I was unfaithful to my wife," he said. "What I did was inexcusable and it was entirely my fault." He said he'd told his wife about it in 2003, three months after taking office.

And then he dropped the bombshell: He was going public, he said, because he was being blackmailed by Fieger. The attorney general's office had been investigating Fieger's role in a $450,000 TV ad campaign against Michigan Supreme Court Justice Stephen Markman during his run for office in 2004. Cox said Fieger warned him through an intermediary to drop the investigation or he'd tell the world about his affair.

"I will not let a bully prevent me from doing the job the people of Michigan elected me to do," said Cox.

Ironically, it was Bouchard Cox turned to, asking for a criminal extortion investigation of Fieger.

The strange got stranger two days later, when it was revealed that Cox's own political action committee was the biggest contributor to Markman's successful campaign, kicking in $34,000.

Headlines continued for a week. The culmination came on November 17, when the *Detroit Free Press* ran this headline across the top of page one, in large bold type:

TAPES DEEPEN SEX SCANDAL

The first paragraph was one that reporters wait their whole careers to write:

> *Sex in a courtroom stairwell, threesomes, adultery and political espionage—that was the stuff of secretly taped conversations at the heart of the investigation into allegations that Southfield attorney Geoffrey Fieger attempted to blackmail state Attorney General Mike Cox.*

Ultimately, Oakland County Prosecutor David Gorcyca decided there wasn't enough evidence to charge Fieger. Cox's career seemed in a shambles, not so much for the affair, but for announcing a press conference in the middle of a criminal investigation, a move that had alerted the target and in effect brought things to a halt.

~

So, thanks to Bronco Lesneski, a guy so true blue he could have been one of the cowboy sheriffs from the old movies of my childhood. And, to Donna Pendergast, the daughter of a cop who puts killers away. Without both of them, this book wouldn't have gotten started, much less finished.

And to technology. Working a cold case for a cop means one set of procedures. Working it as a reporter means another. The first step is gathering up all the old newspaper clips you can find. Thank God for the Internet and Google. They save the vast hours—and the eyesight—that used to go into working microfiches in public libraries and squinting at blurry black-and-white computer-screen images.

Kudos to Hugh McDiarmid Jr. His dad was a legend at the *Detroit Free Press*, and if his reporting on the Duvalls' capture and trial is any indication, Hugh Jr. will be, too. The *Detroit News*' publisher at the time didn't believe crime sold newspapers—hard to imagine in a city like Detroit, which might explain the *News*' decline in sales and the publisher's forced departure—and McDiarmid and the *Freep* showed that not only was he wrong, but that crime reporting can be chilling, and poetic, as well, when done right.